THE SNAP REVOLUTION

James Fenton

D0370009

18

$6.95 97

Editor: Bill Buford
Assistant Editor: Graham Coster
Associate Editor: Piers Spence
Advertising and Promotion: Monica McStay, Tracy Shaw
Executive Editor: Pete de Bolla
Design: Chris Hyde
Office Manager: Carolyn Harlock
Subscriptions: Claire Craig
Research: Margaret Costa
Editorial Assistants: Michael Comeau, Vicky Ross
Photo Research: Tracy Shaw
Contributing Editor: Todd McEwen
Photo Editor: Harry Mattison
Editorial Board: Malcolm Bradbury, Elaine Feinstein, Ian Hamilton, Leonard Michaels
US Editor: Jonathan Levi, Granta, 13 White Street, New York, New York 10013.

Editorial and Subscription Correspondence in the United States and Canada: Granta, 13 White Street, New York, New York 10013. (212–864–5644).
All manuscripts are welcome but must be accompanied by a stamped, self-addressed envelope or they cannot be returned.

Granta, ISSN 0017–3231, is published quarterly for $22 by Granta Publications Ltd, 44a Hobson Street, Cambridge, England. 2nd Class postage pending at New York, NY. Postmaster: send address changes to GRANTA, 13 White Street, New York, NY 10013.

Back Issues: $7.50 each. *Granta* 1,2,3,4 and 9 are no longer available.

Granta is photoset by Lindonprint Typesetters, Hobson Street Studio Ltd and Goodfellow and Egan, Cambridge, and is printed by Hazell Watson and Viney Ltd, Aylesbury, Bucks.

Granta is published by Granta Publications Ltd and distributed by Penguin Books Ltd, Harmondsworth, Middlesex, England; Viking Penguin Inc., 40 West 23rd St, New York, New York, USA; Penguin Books Australia Ltd, Ringwood, Victoria, Australia; Penguin Books Canada Ltd, 2801 John Street, Markham, Ontario, Canada L3R 1B4; Penguin Books (NZ) Ltd, 182–90 Wairau Road, Auckland 10, New Zealand. This selection copyright © 1986 by Granta Publications Ltd.

Cover by Chris Hyde

ISBN 014–00–8595.9

Contents

The Georgia Review

Celebrates its **40**th

Anniversary

with two retrospectives

Spring 1986 ~ Fiction

&

Forthcoming: Fall 1986 ~ Poetry

(The Summer & Winter will feature our usual blend of essays,
poems, fiction, reviews, & graphics.)

To subscribe, please send
$9 for 1 year or $15 for 2 years
(outside U.S. add $3/yr—U.S. funds only)
The Georgia Review, University of Georgia, Athens, GA 30602

THE SPORTSWRITER
by Richard Ford

"A book of life, full of life, and a grand achievement."
—Frederick Exley

"A beautiful book."—Lorrie Moore

"A wonderful novel for our times... Page after page,
Ford writes about great swatches of contemporary
America with clear-eyed, racy eloquence."
—Howard Frank Mosher

"His finest book to date... can stand alongside
Walker Percy's *The Moviegoer* and Richard Yates's
Revolutionary Road."—*New York Times*

"Richard Ford is a masterful writer," writes
Raymond Carver, and this new novel, his third,
clearly fulfills *Newsweek's* prediction that his is
"a career that could turn out to be extraordinary."

A VINTAGE CONTEMPORARIES ORIGINAL

VINTAGE
CONTEMPORARIES
Now at your bookstore from Vintage Books,
a division of Random House.

Rilke: Between Roots

Selected Poems Rendered from the German

by *Rika Lesser*

With a note by *Richard Howard*
and a preface by *Rika Lesser*

Rainer Maria Rilke (1875–1926) is acknowledged as one of the finest poets of the German language and one of the few great lyricists of our century. Moreover, his spiritual earnestness and peripatetic, romantic life, with his celebrated and stormy association with Rodin, travels in Russia, and eventual retreat to the Swiss Château of Muzot—all have combined with Rilke's genius to sustain the popularity of his work in an era when poetry is more frequently discussed than read.

From *Orpheus. Eurydice. Hermes.*

It was the souls' strange mine:
like silver ore they went, silent
as veins through its darkness. Between roots
sprang the blood that goes on to humans,
and heavy as porphyry it looked in the dark.
There was no other redness.

There were rocks
and spectral forests. Bridges over emptiness
and that great, gray, unreflecting pool
that hung over its distant bed
like rainclouds over a landscape.
And between meadows, soft and long-suffering,
showed the one pale path,
like a long strip of linen, bleaching.

An on this one path they came.

Lockert Library of Poetry in Translation

P: $9.95. C: $21.00

At your bookstore or
41 William Street **Princeton University Press** Princeton, NJ 08540

TRAVELS IN HYPERREALITY

Essays ———

UMBERTO ECO

UMBERTO ECO TRAVELS IN HYPER REALITY

BY THE AUTHOR OF *THE NAME OF THE ROSE*

In these sparkling essays on the art and society of our time, Umberto Eco displays the same wit and lively intelligence that delighted readers of **The Name of the Rose**. Eco's range is wide—from pop culture to philosophy, from the People's Temple to Thomas Aquinas, from *Casablanca* to Roland Barthes. His insights are acute, frequently ironic, and often downright funny; Eco wears his erudition with grace and unfailing good humor. *$15.95*

Harcourt **HBJ**
Brace
Jovanovich,
Publishers

1250 Sixth Avenue
San Diego, California   92101

Photo: Jerry Bauer

Get the Big Picture.

Subscribe
to

AFRICA REPORT

Six times a year, *Africa Report* brings you authoritative in-depth features on political and economic developments in Africa and on American policy toward the continent by on-the-scene correspondents and by the newsmakers themselves—Jesse Jackson, Desmond Tutu, Edward Kennedy, Julius Nyerere, Harry Belafonte, Oliver Tambo, to name just a few. *Africa Report* goes beyond the coverage you get from the evening news and daily papers to give you the BIG PICTURE—analyses, opinions, and predictions on events in an ever-changing continent.

Don't miss the big picture in 1986. Subscribe today and receive a special bonus issue.

AFRICA REPORT, America's Leading Magazine on Africa

Please check the appropriate box below.
Please enter my subscription as indicated (six issues per year)

INDIVIDUAL

☐ $21/1 year —Regular Mail to Canada/Overseas
          Add $6 per year.
☐ $39/2 years —Air Rate Overseas: Add $24 per year.
☐ $56/3 years —First-class within USA: Add $7 per year.

☐ **INSTITUTION** —Add $7 per year.

Bonus issue:

☐ Focus on West Africa (July-Aug. 1985)
☐ Focus on Women (Mar.-Apr. 1985)
☐ Africa in the U.S. (May-June 1985)

Name _____

Address _____

City _____ State _____ Zip _____

Country _____

Total amount of my order is $ _____

☐ My check is enclosed.

Make check payable to:
AFRICAN-AMERICAN INSTITUTE and send to
AFRICA REPORT, Dept. 6
833 United Nations Plaza, New York, NY 10017

"Literary history as it should be written."
–James Breslin

Stealing the Language
The Emergence of Women's Poetry in America
Alicia Suskin Ostriker

"In the past twenty years poetry by women has entered a new phase—lavish, daring, down to earth, full of surprises, fiercely committed to breaking through the barriers of race and class and gender and imagining new ways of life and poetry."—Lawrence Lipking

"This vivid marvel of a book is the most complete and perceptive history yet written of that courageous conjunction: American, women, poetry."

–Catharine R. Stimpson
$19.95

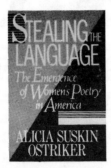

My Soul and I
The Inner Life of Walt Whitman
David Cavitch

"Cavitch analyzes in greater depth than previous commentators certain of Whitman's many thorny relationships as they bear on the major poems...offers...fresh connections between Whitman's troubled private life and his poetic persona."

–*New York Times Book Review*
$18.95

Feminist Aesthetics

Feminist Aesthetics
ed. by Gisela Ecker
translated from the German

Fascinating essays on music, literature, painting and cinema look at women's contributions to the arts and provide new theoretical frameworks for discussions of the relation between feminism and artistic endeavor.

$9.95 paper

Beacon
PRESS

25 Beacon Street, Boston, MA 02108
(617) 742-2110 Visa and Mastercard accepted

MAY WE SEND YOU A FREE COPY OF
LETTERS FROM AFRICA BY ISAK DINESEN?

As a special offer to first-time subscribers, we'll send
a complimentary copy of *Letters From Africa,* by Isak Dinesen.
Subscribe now to *Raritan* and get your free copy.

RARITAN
WHERE STRONG THINKING
FINDS ITS VOICE

...Frank Kermode on being an enemy of humanity...
Eve Sedgwick: Homophobia, Misogyny, and Capital...Douglas Noble
on the craze for computer literacy...Stanley Cavell: What
Photography Calls Thinking...Elaine Showalter on
male feminism...John Hollander on originality...Denis Donoghue
on Christopher Ricks's critical misdirections...Michel Foucault:
A Last Interview...Lincoln Kirstein, an autobiography...
Vicki Hearne on animals and language...Clifford Geertz: African
Transparencies...Leo Bersani: Theory and Violence...
Edward Said on historical conditions of theory
...Harold Bloom on Facticity...

A Quarterly Review edited by Richard Poirier

Please enter my subscription to *Raritan* starting with the current issue, and send my free copy of *Letters
From Africa.*
        ☐ $12 (four issues)   ☐ $21 (eight issues)
Enclosed is my check (payable to *Raritan*). *Sorry, we cannot bill.*
Mail to: RARITAN, 165 College Avenue, New Brunswick, NJ 08903

Name

Address

City/State/Zip

Phoenix Fiction

For the First Time in Paperback

Three Novels by

THOMAS BERNHARD

"Thomas Bernhard is one of the masters of contemporary European fiction."
—*George Steiner*

CONCRETE

"Overwhelming. One wants to read it again, immediately, to re-experience its intricate innovations, not to let go of this masterful work."—John Rechy, *Los Angeles Times*
$5.95   156 pages

THE LIME WORKS

"The book is a jungle of meaning, the opposite of simplistic allegory, and a major achievement."—William Kennedy, *The New Republic*
$7.95   248 pages

GARGOYLES

"[Bernhard's] daring is remarkable, and the chances he takes pay off."
—Robert Maurer, *The Saturday Review*
$6.95   214 pages

also available in the Phoenix Fiction series ————

PICTURES FROM AN INSTITUTION
Randall Jarrell

"One of the wittiest books of modern times."—*New York Times*
  "A searching novel about a mean lady novelist writing a mean novel about a college where she is spending a year teaching creative writing. . . . hilarious and deadly."—Francis Steegmuller, *New York Times Book Review*
$7.95   286 pages

THE UNIVERSITY OF CHICAGO PRESS
5801 South Ellis Avenue, Chicago, IL 60637

THE WHITE HOUSE SENDS FOR US EVERY WEEK. SHOULDN'T YOU?

Every week the White House sends a messenger to pick up 20 newly minted copies of *The New Republic*. They can't afford to be without its up-to-the-minute coverage of the week's top issues, nor can they resist its lively journalistic style and challenging point of view – the kind of award-winning writing that prompted *The Wall Street Journal* to describe the magazine as "the envy of publishers elsewhere for its dedicated and influential readership."

You'll see the vitality in *The New Republic's* thirst for original thinking from every part of the political spectrum. Each and every week you are on the cutting edge of what's going on – not only in politics, but in international events, vital social issues, the press, film and the arts.

Wouldn't you like to know, every week, what the White House knows?

Return the coupon now.

☐ **Yes, I'd like to know what the White House knows.** Please enter my subscription for:

☐ **48 ISSUES AT $36** ☐ **OR 32 AT $24**

Name_____

Address_____ Apt. No._____

City_____State_____Zip_____

Payment enclosed ☐ Bill me ☐

Please charge my VISA ☐ American Express ☐

MasterCard ☐ Credit Card No._____

Exp. Date_____Signature_____

The New Republic, P.O. Box 955, Farmingdale, NY 11735 Phone toll free 1-800-841-8000 Ext. 41.

Allow 3 to 5 weeks for delivery of your first issue. All foreign orders must be pre-paid at $25 per year for foreign delivery, $12 in Canada. Payable in U.S. currency.

THE NEW REPUBLIC

OBSERVATIONS

Thoughts of a Storyteller on a Happy Ending
Gianni Celati

The son of a chemist had gone abroad to study. On his father's death, the son returned home to look after the pharmacy, and took over the business in a small village on the outskirts of Viadana in the province of Mantua.

Word of his great learning had spread to the surrounding countryside: people spoke of his huge library, his prodigious remedy for earache, his entirely new method for irrigating the fields, and his mastery of twelve languages. Among other things, so the rumour went, he was translating the *Divine Comedy* into German.

The owner of a cheese factory in the region made up his mind to employ the scholar, by now a grown man, as private tutor to his daughter. She was doing rather badly at school. Although she excelled in sports, she hated books, Latin and good Italian prose. The chemist accepted the post, more out of a passion for learning than any need for money, and so for a whole summer he went to the young athlete's house every day to give her lessons. One day the young athlete happened to fall in love with him—so much so that she abandoned all her sporting activities, and began writing poetry, Latin verse and, of course, long letters. Even today people still speak of the trips they took far into the countryside, and of the car he bought specially for these occasions, and even of their nightly trysts in a barn.

In any case, evidence of their amorous relationship in those last, fleeting days of summer only came to light the following winter, when a box of the girl's letters was confiscated by the nuns at her college and duly handed over to her parents. The content of those letters so disgusted the owner of the cheese factory that he decided to ruin the chemist and drive him from the village for ever.

*T*he girl's brothers, who at that time belonged to one of the fascist squads, wrecked the pharmacy in the village square a number of times and on one occasion gave its owner a severe beating.

Still, none of this seemed to have worried the chemist much. For a time he continued to receive customers in the ruined shop, among the shattered window-panes, the demolished shelves and the broken bottles. Then one fine day he shut up shop and retired to his library. From then on he hardly left the house.

Everyone in the village knew he was immersed in his studies. Now and again he was seen walking across the square, smiling, in the direction of the post office to pick up some new books which had arrived for him.

Some time later he was admitted to hospital, and from there transferred to a convalescent home. He stayed there for many years, and no one knew what had become of him.

On his return from the convalescent home the old scholar was thin as a rake. An elderly housemaid who had come back to look after him complained to everyone that he was refusing to eat: eating didn't agree with him, he said, and he spent all day shut up with his books.

*T*he man got thinner and thinner and went out less and less; when he did, it was clear that he no longer recognized anyone in the village, not even the daughter of the cheese factory owner (by now deceased) when he met her a few times in the square. But he smiled at everyone, and they say that he even greeted the dogs in the street, raising his hat to them as he passed by.

When his elderly housemaid died, he stopped eating altogether and would fast for weeks on end, so that when one day he was found dead in his library (by a plumber) he looked just like a skeleton: all that was left of him was wrinkled skin and bones. He was bent over the last page of a book, on to which he was sticking a strip of paper.

Years later his huge library was inherited by a nephew who, on rummaging through his books, believed he had discovered how the old scholar had spent the last part of his life.

For this man every story, novel and epic poem had to end happily. Evidently he couldn't tolerate tragic, melancholy or depressing endings to any story. So over the years he had devoted himself to rewriting the closing sections of a hundred or so books in every language. By inserting pages or just strips of paper at the points which needed changing he transformed their conclusion, to bring them always to a happy ending.

Much of the last stage of his life must have been dedicated to the rewriting of the eighth chapter of the third part of *Madame Bovary,* the one in which Emma dies. In the new version, Emma gets better and goes back to her husband. His very last piece of work, however, was on that strip of paper which he had in his hand and which, already half-dead with hunger, he was pasting over the last line of a Russian novel in French translation. This was also perhaps his most accomplished work. In changing only three words he transformed a tragedy into a life resolved to the good.

Translated from the Italian by Piers Spence

Tadpoles
Primo Levi

Our summer holiday lasted the whole length of the school vacation: about three months. Preparations began early, usually on St Joseph's Day (the nineteenth of March): since we weren't rich enough to afford a hotel, my parents would tour the still snow-clad valleys of Piedmont looking for lodgings to rent—preferably somewhere served by the railway and not too far from Turin. We didn't have a car (this was the early thirties, and almost no one did) and for my father, who hated the sultriness of summer anyway, time off was restricted to three days around the August bank holiday. So, just to sleep with the family and in the cool, he would subject himself to the drudgery of a twice-daily train journey out to Torre Pellice or Meana, or any of the other modest villages within a hundred or so kilometres of the city. For our part we went every evening to the station to wait for him. At daybreak he set out again, even on Saturdays, to be in the office by eight.

My mother began the packing around the middle of June. Apart from bags and suitcases, the main load consisted of three wicker trunks, which when full must each have weighed at least two hundredweight; the removal men came and hoisted them miraculously onto their backs and carried them downstairs sweating and cursing. The trunks contained everything: bedclothes, pots and pans, toys, books, provisions, winter and summer clothing, shoes, medicines, utensils—as if we were departing for the Antipodes. Usually we arranged our destination together with other families—relations or friends; it was less lonely like that. In this way we took a part of our city along with us.

*T*he three months went by slowly, and quietly, and dully, and punctuated by the abominable sadism of Holiday Homework: a contradiction in terms! My father spent only Sundays with us, and those in his own fashion. He was a thorough-going urbanite: the countryside did not agree with him. He disliked the emptiness of the fields, the steepness of the paths, the silence, the flies, the discomforts. The mornings he would spend reading, taciturn and cross; in the afternoon he dragged us off for an ice-cream at the only café in the village, and then he would retire to play the tarot with the miller and his wife. But for my sister and me the months in the country meant a regularly-renewed union with nature: humble plants and flowers whose names it was fun to learn in Italian and dialect; the birds, each with their own song; insects; spiders. On one occasion in the wash-basin, a leech, no less, graceful in its swimming, undulating as if in a dance. Another time, a bat that zigzagged dementedly about the bedroom, or a stone-marten glimpsed in the twilight, or a mole-cricket, a monstrous, obese little insect, neither mole nor cricket, repugnant and menacing. In the courtyard garden well-disciplined tribes of ants rushed about their business, and it was enthralling to observe their cunning and their stubborn stupidity. They were held up as an example in our schoolbooks: 'Go to the ant, thou sluggard; consider her ways, and be wise' (Proverbs, 6:6). They never took summer holidays. Yes, they may have been virtuous little creatures, but it was the obligatory virtue of prisoners.

The stream was the most interesting place of all. My mother took us down every morning to sunbathe and to paddle in the clear, clean water, while she got on with her knitting in the shade of a willow. You could wade the stream safely from bank to bank, and it was a haven to creatures the like of which we had never seen. On the river-bed black insects staggered along resembling huge ants, each one dragging behind it a cylindrical case made of tiny pebbles or little pieces of vegetation, into which it had threaded its abdomen; only its head and claws poked out. When disturbed, the creatures recoiled like a shot into their little mobile homes.

In mid-air hovered wondrous dragonflies, frozen in flight, iridescent in metallic turquoise; even their buzzing was metallic, mechanical, bellicose. They were miniature war machines, dropping in one stroke, dart-like, on some invisible prey. On the dry, sandy banks green beetles ran nimbly to and fro; the conical traps of the ant-lion sprang open. Such ambushes we witnessed with a secret sense of complicity, and hence of guilt, to the extent that my sister, overwhelmed every so often with pity, would use a twig to divert some poor ant on the point of a sudden and cruel death.

Alongside the left bank the water teemed with tadpoles in their thousands. Why only on the left? After much fruitless discussion about sun and shade we noticed that along that side ran a footpath much used by anglers; the trout were wise to this, and kept to the safety of the right bank. Accordingly, to avoid the trout, the tadpoles had established themselves on the left. They aroused conflicting feelings: laughter and tenderness—like puppies, new-born babies and all creatures whose heads seem too big for their bodies—and indignation, because every so often they ate each other. They were chimaeras, impossible creations, yet they sailed along swiftly and surely, propelling themselves with elegant flicks of the tail. Between head and tail they had no body, and this was what seemed incomprehensible and monstrous; all the same, the head had eyes and a mouth—a voracious mouth curiously down-turned as if sulking—ever in search of food. We brought a dozen back home and put them, to my mother's disapproval, in the portable 'camping' bidet, slung on its trestle—we had covered the bottom with sand from the bed of the stream. The tadpoles seemed at home there, and sure enough after a few days they began their metamorphosis. This was a novel spectacle, as full of mystery as a birth or a death—enough to make us forget our holiday homework, and for the days to seem fleeting and the nights interminable.

Every morning, indeed, had a surprise in store. The tail of one tadpole began to thicken, close to its root, into a small knot. The knot enlarged, and in two or three days out pushed a pair of webbed feet—but the little creature made no use of them: it let them hang limp, and carried on waggling its tail. A few more days, and a pustule formed on one side of its head; this swelled up, then burst like an abscess, and out came a fore-limb already perfectly formed, minute, transparent—a tiny glass hand, already treading water. A little later, and the same happened to the other side, while the tail was already starting to shrink.

*T*his was a dramatic time: one could see that at a glance. It was a harsh and brutal puberty: the tiny creatures began to fret, as if an inner sense had forewarned them of the torment in store for those who change their shape, and they were confounded in mind and body: perhaps they no longer knew who they were. Their swimming was frantic and bewildered, their tails growing ever shorter and their four legs still too weak to use. They circled around in search of something—air for their new lungs, perhaps, or maybe a landing-place from which to set forth into the world. I realized that the sides of the bidet were too steep for the tadpoles to climb out, as was clearly their wish, and so I positioned in the water two or three small wooden ramps.

It was the right idea, and some of the tadpoles took advantage of it—but could you still call them tadpoles? Not any more: the larvae had gone; now there were brown frogs as big as beans—but frogs with two arms and two legs, folk like us, who swam breast-stroke with difficulty but in the correct style. And they no longer ate each other, so we felt differently towards them, like a mother and father: in some way they were our children, even if our part in their metamorphosis had been more of a hindrance than a help. I sat one in the palm of my hand: it had an ugly mug, but a face nevertheless; it looked at me, winked, and its mouth gaped open. Was it gasping for air, or was it trying to tell me something? Another time it set off determinedly along my finger, as if along a springboard. The next instant it was gone, with one senseless hop into the void.

*B*ringing up tadpoles, then, was not so easy. Only a few of them cottoned on to our little safety-ramps and got out onto dry land. The rest, already deprived of the gills provided for their aquatic infancy, we would find in the morning, drowned, worn out by too much swimming, just like a human swimmer trapped inside a lock. And even those who had understood the purpose of the landing-stage, the more intelligent ones, did not always live long. The tadpoles responded to a perfectly natural instinct—the same instinct that has driven us to the moon, that is epitomized in the commandment, 'Multiply and replenish the earth'—which spurred them to forsake the stretch of water where they had completed their metamorphosis. It did not matter whither—anywhere else but there. In the wild, for every likely pool, for every bend in the stream, there will be another not far away, or perhaps a damp meadow or a marsh. Thus some do survive, by migrating and colonizing new surroundings. Still, even in the most favourable conditions a large proportion of these neo-frogs are bound to die. And it is for this reason that the mother frog exhausts herself laying interminable strings of eggs: she 'knows' that the infant mortality rate will be breathtakingly high, and she allows for this as our country forebears did.

Our surviving tadpoles dispersed around the courtyard garden in search of water that wasn't there. We tried to keep track of them through the grass and the gravel. The boldest, labouring to cross the granite pavement in clumsy hops, was spotted by a robin, who made a quick meal of him. And that very instant the white kitten, our gentle little playmate, who had watched all this transfixed, took a prodigious leap and pounced on the bird, whose mind was still on its lucky catch. She half-killed it, as cats do, and took it off into a corner to toy with its agony.

Translated from the Italian by Simon Rees

Desert Island Discs
George Steiner

*H*is requests did stretch the resources, almost all-encompassing, of the sound-archive. But that is part of the game.

First he asked to hear Fortinbras's belch. The one at the end of the interminable coronation carouse. There was no use denying it: despite tireless scrubbing, new rushes on the floor of the hall, the aromatic salts expended on the long tables and logs in the chimney, the death smells persisted. They hung sweet and rancid in the corners and by the tower stairs. There had been too many corpses. Was it six, was it seven? Fortinbras the King found it hard to remember. A woman's carrion among them, bloated and waxen, with the scent of burnt almonds on her twisted lips. The surviving folk, royal cousins and courtiers, had been pleasant enough. Caps lifted, knees bent to the new monarch. General sentiments of relief. And now the King's chambers were being thoroughly aired, the arras taken down and replaced by more cheerful hangings. Still, the feast had not been unblemished. There was the thin, faintly hysterical child on the balcony, troubling the military fanfare—plain lads out of Norway, not those Danish luteners and players on elaborate pipes, most of whom had, anyway, taken to their heels at the first cannon shot. Flitting among them in her pale, nearly transparent gown. A younger sister, or so the King had been informed, of one Ophelia, drowned. And there was the good Horatio, solemn as a blind horse. Assuring the new sovereign of his insightful fidelity, of his imminent retirement, telling him that the great and dread events of which he, Horatio, had been humble witness, must be memorably noted. Horatio to Fortinbras, in a hushed, dulcet tone; the King having to strain his battle-deafened ears to catch the man's desolate, incessant drift.

The wines had been heavy, and the herring. Dawn could not be far off. Even through the thick walls and battlements, Fortinbras the son of Norway could sense the changing rasp of the sea when dawn approaches. He was bone-tired. Almost envious of the dead prince, who had always seemed to him like a master of sleep, and of the secrets which sleep breeds. Fortinbras belched. It was a loud, cavernous belch. From the inmost of his drowsing, armoured flesh. It was a sound the courtiers would not forget. Thunderous and replete with the promise of a simpler tomorrow.

*T*he second recording he asked for was that of the neighing of the little horse, of the dappled grey with the cropped right ear, after it had cantered into the surrounding hills.

The journey had been hot and dust-choked. The ticks and the blue flies hammered like mad that long day. They had left the high gates and the cobbles of the town well before sunrise. But even at that hour, the air had been listless and the heat trapped underfoot. And there had been a strange unrest in the courtyard. The old woman with the pale eyes and heavy brooch had exuded a kind of quivering. The dappled had felt it in his wet nostrils: night-sweat and spilled seed. Not that the actual trip was of any danger or difficulty. They had made it often. Past the spring with its loud bucket, through the olive groves and into the baking plain. Then onward to where gaps in the burnt hills flashed with the sheen of the gulf. The old master was light in his cart and the driver scarcely more than a rude, overbearing teenager. The horse had heard him in the stables, boasting of his manhood, of his prowess with the whip, of the leaves he chewed and of the hot dreams they brought on. But the voyage should have been routine, and the shaft-horse, though patronizing (he had been to the oracle before the grey was foaled), was friendly enough.

It all happened at such speed. The horses had been half asleep, their eyes closed against the damned flies. Out of breath with the heat and the slight rise which leads to the place where the three roads meet, the two slaves were trotting in the spare shade of the cart. The old man was humming to himself, as he often did, a lullaby to a new-born child, but breaking off, always, as on a jagged tooth. Then the harsh pull on the reins, forcing the horses almost to their haunches. The slash of the whip and the charioteer's high-pitched obscenities. The muffled call of the old man, his bony arms waving in the drumming air. And cutting through it all, a voice which the dappled would never shake out of its ears. A voice strangely like his old master's, but totally different: raw yet resonant, like that of a bronze clarion. A call so brimful of rage that it tore the skin off one's back, but knowing, with a knowledge that was like a knife.

One of the windmill strokes from the traveller's knotted staff grazed the little horse's neck. It was not a direct blow—he had heard the old man's skull crack and the death-rattle of the driver—but of a contemptuous violence. The traces had snapped like dry reeds and the grey had raced for the hills. The sharp flint had galled his hoofs and now, at sunset, the shadows ran cold. Looking back, the little horse had glimpsed a figure running desperately towards Thebes. Was it one of the slaves, or the traveller? He did not know. And began neighing, uncertain of his fodder.

*H*is third record request was for the scratch or, more precisely, for the sibilant swerve (in G minor) of the steel nib on Rudolf Julius Emmanuel Clausius's pen in the instant in which this pen wrote the n in the exponential n minus x to the nth power in the equation of entropy.

Würzburg is not, even at its best, an ebullient town. On that early spring evening in 1863, the rain was streaming down the grimed windows. His lids heavy, Herr Clausius blinked and bent closer to his work-table. A grey film seemed to hang around the gas-lamp, and when the draughts streaked through the curtains, the china globe of the lamp shivered morosely. Clausius observed with annoyance that these same gusts made his dentures throb. Unnoticing he pressed the pen-holder against his aching molar. Foxed with the damp, the off-prints of Sir William Thomson's papers on thermodynamics and Sadi Carnot's *mémoire* on the airpump lay at his elbow. Carnot's two equations, for the boiler when the piston was in position a, and when it was in position a prime, hummed, as it were, at the enervated edge of Clausius's awareness. Like two stick-insects, their brittle feelers interlocked. Somewhere in the house, and behind the splattering rain, a clock chimed and rattled. Konstanze had, again, forgotten to wind it.

To the nth power. The nib hovered over the paper, and for an idle moment Clausius's attention wandered, through the armorial and dragon-maze of the watermark. The equation stood. Against reason. Against the long-drawn breath of life. In uncaring defiance of the future tense. Formally, the algebra was nothing but the proof, at once abstract and statistical, of the unrecuperability of caloric energy when turned to heat, of the degree of loss in all thermal and thermodynamic processes. That is how Clausius would entitle and describe his paper when dispatching it to the *acta* of the Prussian Academy of Science (Section IV: Applied Science). But what he was staring at—and the sensation was rather more distant, more indifferent than that of his bruised gums—was the determination, irrefutable, of the heat-death of the universe. The n minus x function would not be bought off. Entropy meant run-down and the transmutation of spent energy into cold stasis. A stillness, a cold past all imagining. Compared to which our own deaths and the decomposition of the warm flesh are a trivial carnival. In that equation, the cosmos had its epitaph. In the beginning was the Word; at the close was the algebraic function. A pen-nib, bought in a scrolled cardboard box at Kreutzner's, university stationer, had put *finis* to the sum and total of being. After the downward right-hand stroke of that n came not infinite blackness, which *is* still, but a nothingness, an unfathomable zero. Unthinking, Clausius started tracing a line beneath the equation. But the nib had gone dry.

he custodians of the sound-archive are not prudish. They know how often hearing is overhearing, and brought him his fourth disc unblinking.

A petty nightmare of a day. The first flight cancelled at Brussels Airport because of a work-to-rule by French air-controllers. Planes stacked over Europe like stale rusks in holding patterns and the fog thickening. He had rung her apartment; she must have left minutes before. Which meant she was already at the railway terminal. His change ran out as he tried to reach the station and have her paged on the public address system (knowing how incensed she would be at the grossness of hearing her name loud-hailed, though it was a coded sobriquet, he was almost glad he had not succeeded). As through cotton wool, he heard the announcement of a possible departure to L. from the other terminal. He bounded awkwardly along the escalator and connecting tunnel, only to find a dozen other stranded passengers at the stand-by counter. When he finally took off, it was late afternoon. The hotel room had been booked in an assumed though, God knows, transparent name and she would not be able to claim the reservation. Would she have the spendthrift nonchalance to take another room in the same hotel? She would bridle at that.

With the fog slow to lift, the airport at L. was teeming and the lines at the passport-window interminable. He reached the hotel almost hysterical with exasperation and guilt. No sign of her. He lacked the nerve to inquire whether a lady of singular radiance (or so she was to him) had left her overnight bag with the *portier*.

The streets and squares of the city were awash with tawdry snow and patches of black ice. The flicker of neon lights dazzled him as it bounced off the tramcar-rails and shop windows. He circled aimlessly, back to the hotel lobby. Once more across the gusting bridge. Now obliquely and towards the cold flatness of the lake. He detested the place. He had loved it beyond words when last they had arrived there, the lights of the station underpass caught in her live hair. Now towards the hotel again, his hands trembling.

He found her. At the bottom of the unlit alley below the steps to the old town. She heard him running and turned. They stumbled, like drunks, into the solid dark of an arched doorway.

The sounds came in a soft rush. That of her fingers in his perspiring hair as he knelt. Of the buttons slipping out of the braided hooks of her long coat. The rustle of her skirt, like the leafy edge of summer, as she drew it up her thighs. And when his tongue came home to her, from above his dizzied head and shoulders, that laugh, distant at first, over-arching, then closer than his own skin. The hushed chime of her laugh (it was this he had requested from the archive) as he drank of her. A note which left the soul singing and crazy with peace.

*T*here is, so far as is known, only one (and imperfect) tape extant of the otherwise lost Trio in F Major for crumhorn, double bass and Sumatran conch-bells which Sigbert Weimerschlund composed in the year of his death. The choice of instruments, though perhaps *recherché*, had seemed to Weimerschlund inevitable. As deputy curator of the palaeontology collection in the Atheneum in Second Falls (Ohio), he had long been spellbound by the serpentine, delicately rifled contours of certain immemorially ancient horned beasties. His heart attack in the cruel winter of 1937—a serious hiccup, some years later, was to cause his decease—had left Weimerschlund with a singular aural vestige. At certain moments, in the face of a prairie wind, under professional stress—the Second Falls Chamber of Commerce, though sympathetic, recurrently put in question the value of the Atheneum and, more especially, of its fossil cabinets, which the new Estes Polk Memorial High School was, in any event, prepared to house—or when sheer lonesome gluttony had seduced him into bringing to his boarding-house room and consuming at one go a whole quarter-pound of chopped herring, Weimerschlund would hear, inside the echo-chamber of his ventricles, a low syncopated thrumming. A dense beat, a second beat echoing the first, then a vibrato. Tremolo and reprise sounding from the shadow-left of his heart. Though alarming, the sequence had its eerie charm, and Sigbert sometimes found himself hesitant to reach for the assuaging pills. Hence, after the crumhorn, the double bass.

The conch-bells, not bells really but nacreous, iridescent sea-shells suspended on a bamboo frame and graduated according to the pentatonic scale, did, he knew, represent an extravagant touch. Weimerschlund had never, of course, been anywhere in range of Sumatra. But he had heard the chiming glitter, the sea-arpeggios of conch-bells through a tent-wall on the night when Hubbard's Circus and Raree Show had stopped in Second Falls. Weimerschlund scarcely remembered what improbable impulse had taken him to the fairground. He fled in nausea from the eyes of the caged timber-wolf and the cackle of the pink-haired Tom Thumb. Looking for an exit, he heard that crystal scale; as if the wind had made the snow sing. Riveted, he pressed his ear to the muting canvas. He squirmed still at the recollection of his indiscreet gesture: Sigbert Weimerschlund, deputy curator and Shriner, down on all fours, prizing loose the sodden tent-flap to peer inside. Where he glimpsed, by the sheen of a greying light-bulb, only the back of the player. It was, he later thought, the back of a boy or very young man (The Indian Rope-Trick Performed by Tamu the Blind Pearl Diver).

The precise circumstances under which the Trio had been recorded by the three brothers—he was now listening to a tape taken from the 78—are a matter of mild musicological dispute. Nor should one advance exaggerated claims for the quality of the piece. It is, after all, amateur work. Weimerschlund appears to have overlooked that *pizzicati* on a double bass produce awkward effects when in counterpoint to the nasal register of the crumhorn. No, what remains memorable is the devoted performance. Zeppo manages to draw from the crumhorn not its customary sedate buzz, but a desolate and oracular hum. His breath-control, his variations of pitch and flutter, are those of a virtuoso. On the double bass, Harpo has lapses. It is not he, however, who is to blame when Weimerschlund calls for a *glissando* at the start of the last movement and, unreasonably, marks it *presto*. In Chico's hands or, more accurately, under the felt mallet as Chico wields it, the Sumatran chimes are magic. It is they who prelude, by means of a subtle *rubato*, the transcendent moment in the Trio: the return to the dominant, nineteen bars from the close. A moment in which the ache of the horn, the heart-thrum of the double bass, itself like a footfall on a winter path, are fused by the almost imperceptible yet rhythmically-binding flicker of the bells. This, he fancied, as he listened in the studio, might well be the music played, and these the performers, in the waiting-room for the Last Judgement.

he painting which occasioned his sixth and final selection is little known. An unreliable mimeographed check-list is all that is made available, morosely, by the semi-private collection in the French Savoie in which it is hung. Labelled 'By the Master of the Chambéry Passion', it is a Crucifixion on gilded panelling which can most plausibly be dated mid-fourteenth century and ascribed to one of the workshops in the Turin area. The taut, angular grouping with St Damian at the edge, the motif of crossed lances and gonfalons against a dullish burnt-earth background and empty sky, suggest the influence either of Baldassare Ordosso himself or of one of his apprentices (a number of these are known to have journeyed the Alps into France after 1345). The torn features of Christ, the somewhat rhetorical gesture of the Mother of God—observe her heightened knuckles and the touch of sweat around her azure head-band—are well executed but iconographically routine.

It is the red-headed lad in the attendant crowd, the fourth figure from the left, who arrests attention. He is whistling. On two supple fingers inserted, shepherd- or street-urchin-style, into a corner of his full lips. Whistling, either to himself or to some listener—a crony, a sheep-dog, a girl—outside the scene. There can be no mistake. The whistle is a loud and joyous one, as of a thrush on a spring upland. The whistler's firm, green-hosed legs tell us that, as does the merry swelling of his throat and cheeks. And though his lips are pursed, there can be no doubt as to the smile and dawn cheer which gives them breath. Yet the young man's eyes are on the Cross, on the twisted flesh and the petals of bright blood around the nails. The eyes are unwavering as he whistles, as the pure clear merriment rises into the paschal air.

What he asked for from the sound-archive was the recording of that whistle.

Strangely enough, it was not this request which proved most difficult to satisfy.

This year's essential reading
(no one will lend you their copy)

Third World Affairs 1986 addresses itself to vital issues such as survival in the nuclear age; Reaganomics and its impact on the Third World; the debt crisis; democracy in Latin America; Marxism in Africa; foreign policy alignments of the developing countries; the effects of energy on the environment; religion and politics; new directions in Third World cinema.

Order your copy now and receive the South Atlas FREE

The only Atlas in the world to project accurately the real size of the developing countries in relation to those of the North.

ISBN No: 0 907962 34 3

Order Form

☐ Yes, please send me _____ copies of **Third World Affairs 1986** at £20.00 / U.S. $26.00 per copy (inc. p&p)

Name _____

Organisation _____

Address _____

_____

_____

☐ I enclose cheque for £/US$ _____
(made payable to Third World Foundation)
☐ I would like to pay by credit card

Name of card _____

Name of Cardholder _____

Card Account No _____

Signature _____

Date _____

86BT

When completed please return this card with your payment to the Circulation Department, Third World Foundation, 13th floor, New Zealand House, 80 Haymarket London SW1Y 4TS, England.

A leader in educational innovation since 1852 offers in London an accredited

INDIVIDUALISED M.A. IN CREATIVE WRITING

which gives you the freedom to design your own syllabus in line with your personal interests and career requirements, and to study on a part-time basis.

Write for further details:
Antioch University
Regent's College
Inner Circle Regent's Park
London NW1 4NS
Phone: 01-486 9605

Inside Asia
the radical bimonthly voice on Asian Affairs

Issue 8 out now:

Walden Bello on where the Philippines goes from here – the anti-dowry movement and a decade of women's struggles in India – Mongolia's Soviet style development – landless people strike back in Bangladesh – Hongkong's democracy movement under threat – and who will succeed Suharto in Indonesia?

Previous issues have included Noam Chomsky, Ben Kiernan and Michael Vickery on Kampuchea; Praful Bidwai on Bhopal; Sumanta Banerjee on India's Left. Plus Anthony Barnett, Hanif Kureishi, Amrit Wilson, Dilip Hiro, John Gittings...

Sample issue on request

Subscriptions (for six issues)
- £10 (individuals) and £18 (institutions) in UK, Ireland, Europe, Asia (excluding Japan) and the rest of the Third World
- £15 (individuals) and £20 (institutions) in Japan, USA, Canada, Australia and New Zealand

Inside Asia, 242-244 Pentonville Road, London N1 9UP

Longman are proud to announce two exciting new series of outstanding writing

NEW

Longman Caribbean Writers

The Dragon Can't Dance *Earl Lovelace*	£2.95
A Brighter Sun *Sam Selvon*	£2.50
Ways of Sunlight *Sam Selvon*	£2.50
Lonely Londoners *Sam Selvon*	£2.50
The Jumbie Bird *Ismith Khan*	£2.50
Plays for Today *Edited by Errol Hill*	£2.95
Black Albino *Namba Roy*	£2.95
Summer Lightning *Olive Senior*	£2.50

Available in your bookshops now

Longman African Classics

Hungry Flames *Edited by Mbulelo Mzamane*	£2.95
Fools *Njabulo Ndebele*	£2.95
Scarlet Song *Mariama Bâ*	£2.95
Tales of Amadou Koumba *Birago Diop*	£2.95
Sundiata *D. T. Niane*	£1.95
The Last Duty *Isidore Okpewho*	£2.95

To be launched Monday 16 June 1986

Full details of both series are available from

**Promotion Department
Africa and Caribbean Division
Longman House, Burnt Mill
Harlow, Essex, CM20 2JE
(0279) 26721**

Longman

There's so much interesting
reading every week in

THE LISTENER

SPECIALLY COMMISSIONED ARTICLES...
on aspects of contemporary life and thought
PREVIEWS...
the highlights of TV & Radio drama, music
and films for the week ahead
REVIEWS...
of outstanding past broadcasts and
The Listener Review of Books
...and much more

Britain's
best-written
weekly

EVERY
THURSDAY
70p

For details of subscription
write to:
BBC Publications,
144/152 Bermondsey St,
London. SE1 3TH
or telephone 01-407 6961

Lobbying—a new act for the arts
Malcolm Davies
Raymond Snoddy Paying for TV at the checkout
The social security time-bomb

JAMES FENTON
THE SNAP
REVOLUTION

I
THE SNAP
ELECTION

HIS EXCELLENC
PRESIDENT FERDINAND F

The Project is Thwarted

A man sets light to himself, promising his followers that he will rise again in three hours. When the time has elapsed, the police clear away the remains. Another man, a half-caste, has himself crucified every year—he has made a vow to do this until God puts him in touch with his American father. A third unfortunate, who has lost his mother, stands rigid at the gate of his house and has been there, the paper tells us, for the last fourteen years, 'gazing into an empty rubber plantation.'

I don't know when it was that I began noticing stories like these, or began to think that the Philippines must be a strange and fascinating place. Pirates came from there last year to attack a city in Borneo. Ships sank with catastrophic loss of lives. People came from all over the world to have psycho-surgeons rummage through their guts—their wounds opened and closed in a trice. There was a Holy War in Mindanao. There was a communist insurgency. Political dialogue was conducted by murderers. Manila was a brothel.

It was the Cuba of the future. It was going the way of Iran. It was another Nicaragua, another Cambodia, another Vietnam. But all these places, awesome in their histories, are so different from each other that one couldn't help thinking: this kind of talk was a shorthand for a confusion. All that was being said was that something was happening in the Philippines. Or more plausibly: a lot of different things were happening in the Philippines. And a lot of people were feeling obliged to speak out about it.

But still at this stage, although the tantalizing little items were appearing daily in the English press, I had not seen any very ambitious account of what was going on. This fact pleased me. I thought that if I planned well in advance, engineered a decent holiday and went off to Manila, I would have the place to myself, as it were. I would have leisure and space enough to work away at my own pace, not running after a story, not hunting with the pack of journalists. I would watch, and wait, and observe. I would control my project rather than have it control me.

Photo: Alain Keler (Sygma)

But I had reckoned without the Reagan administration and the whims of a dictator. Washington began sending urgent and rather public envoys to Manila, calling for reforms and declaring that time was running out. There was something suspicious in all this. It looked as if they were trying to fix a deal with Marcos—for if they weren't trying to fix things the alternative view must be that they were destablizing the dictatorship, and this seemed out of character. Then Marcos went on American television and announced a snap election. And this too smelled fishy. I couldn't imagine that he would have made such a move had he not been certain of the outcome. For a while it was uncertain whether the snap election could or would be held, for the terms which the dictator offered to his people appeared unconstitutional. The constitution required that Marcos resign before running again for office. But Marcos would not resign: he would offer a post-dated resignation letter only, and he would fight the presidential election in his role as president.

In other words, the deal was: Marcos would remain president but would hold a fair election to reassure his American critics that he still had the support of his people; if, by some fluke, it turned out that he did not have this support, the world had his word of honour that he would step down and let somebody else be president. And this somebody else, in all probability, would be the woman who was accusing Marcos of having murdered her husband. So if he stepped down, Marcos would very likely be tried for murder.

It didn't sound as if it was going to be much of an election.

What's more, it was going to wreck my dream of having Manila all to myself. Indeed, my project was already in ruins. By now everybody in the world seemed to have noticed what an interesting place the Philippines was. There would be a massive press corps running after every politician and diplomat. There would be a deluge of background articles in the press. People would start getting sick of the subject well before I had had the chance to put pen to paper.

I toyed with the idea of ignoring the election altogether. It was a sham and a fake. It would be a 'breaking story'. If I stuck to my original plan, I would wait till Easter, which is when they normally hold the crucifixions. I wasn't going to be panicked into joining the herd.

Then I panicked and changed all my plans. Contrary to some expectations, the opposition had united behind Corazón Aquino, the widow of the national hero Benigno 'Ninoy' Aquino. She was supposedly an unwilling candidate, and supposedly a completely inexperienced politician. But she was immensely popular— unwillingness and inexperience, it appeared, made a refreshing change. The assassination of her husband in 1983, as he stepped off the plane in Manila airport, was a matter that had never been cleared up. So there was a highly personal, as well as political, clash ahead.

(Not everybody believes, I was to discover, that President Marcos personally authorized the murder. At the time, one is assured, he was having one of his relapses. A man who was involved in the design of the presidential dentures told me, meaningly, that at the time of Ninoy's death Marcos's gums were very swollen— which was always a sign. And he added, intriguingly, that whenever Marcos's gums were swollen, the gums of General Ver, the Chief of Staff, swelled up in sympathy. Marcos was in the military hospital at the time, and I have it from someone who knew one of his nurses that, when he heard the news, Marcos threw his food-tray at his wife, Imelda. Others say he slapped her, but I prefer the food-tray version.)

In addition to the growing opposition to Marcos in the Philippines, there was the discrediting campaign in the United States, which began to come up with some interesting facts and theories. Marcos's vaunted war record had been faked. His medals were fakes. His property holdings overseas were vast. He was shifting huge sums of dollars back to the Philippines to finance the coming campaign. He was seriously ill from lupus erythematosus. He had had two kidney transplants, but whether he still had two kidneys was another matter. His supporters painted slogans around Manila:

WE ♡ FM

His opponents, many of whom had a rough sense of humour, changed these to

LUPUS ♡ FM

At the outset of the campaign he was obviously very ill. One day his hands were mysteriously bleeding. Had he received the stigmata? He was carried into meetings on a chair. Perhaps he would be dead before the campaign was through.

Foreign observers had been invited to see fair play in the elections. There was Senator Lugar and his American team, and there was an international team. Around a thousand journalists arrived, plus other freelance observers. So that when I boarded my plane at Gatwick on 30 January, it was with a sense of being stampeded into a story. I had no great hope of the elections. I was going just in case.

A Loyal Marcos Man

There's a special kind of vigilance in the foyer of a press hotel. The star TV correspondents move through, as film stars do, as if waiting to be recognized, spotted. When they come back sweating and covered with the dust of the road, they have a particular look which says: See, I have come back sweating, covered with the dust of the road. When they leave in a hurry on a hot news tip, they have a look which says: What? Me leave in a hurry on a hot news tip? No, I'm just sloping off to dinner. Everyone is alert to any sudden activity— the arrival of a quotable politician, the sudden disappearance of a rival crew, the hearty greetings of the old hands. When the foyer is full, it is like a stock exchange for news. When it is empty, you think: where *are* they all? what's going on?

I was frisked at the door of the Manila Hotel. It was government-owned, and nobody was taking any chances. The bellboys came past wheeling massive displays of flowers. In the brown air beneath the chandeliers, obvious agents were keeping a track of events. The hotel telephone system was working to capacity, and there was trouble with crossed lines. But I finally got through to Helen, my main contact in Manila, and we agreed to meet in the Taproom.

Here the atmosphere was green from the glass reading-lamps on the bar. A pale, shrunken face was knocking back some strong mixture. Hearing me order, the face approached me and made itself unavoidable. 'You're English, aren't you? You see? I can always tell. What you doing?'

'I'm a tourist.'

That made him laugh. 'Tourist? I bet you're M.I.Sixteen.' I thought, if he wants me to be M.I.Sixteen, that's fine by me. I stared into my whisky as if to confirm his analysis. By now he was rather close. I wondered how long it would take Helen to 'wash up and finish a few things.' My companion ordered another Brandy Alexander. He was going to get very drunk that night, he said, then he would get him a girlfriend.

He was English like me, he said, only he had been deported at the age of eight. Now his Filipina wife had left him, and at midnight it would be his birthday. Could he see my matches? Those were English matches, weren't they? I passed him the box. He was, he said, the only white man to have worn the uniform of Marcos's bodyguard.

Or maybe he said palace guard. He was wearing a *barong tagalog*, the Filipino shirt that you don't tuck in. He'd been at the palace that day—he'd just come from there—and he'd been in big trouble. Hadn't had the right clothes. Just look, he said, there are darns in my trousers. His wife had left him and she had taken all his clothes—everything. Now he was going to get drunk, get him a girl and go home at midnight.

Since it was my turn to talk, I suggested that he find the girl first, then go home.

'It's my *birthday*,' he said, staring at his watch under the reading-lamp to see how long he had to drink till midnight. He had five hours in hand. His car was parked outside. I suggested he take a taxi home. He told me he had the biggest police car in Manila. I suggested he get a policeman to drive him home. He ordered another Brandy Alexander. The waiters smiled nervously at him and called him colonel. I began to think he might be for real.

He lurched forward confidentially. 'I'm a loyal Marcos man,' he said, 'but this election . . .' He shook his head. 'He'll win it,' he said, 'but it'll be a damn close thing. He'll lose in Metro Manila. Marcos is a great man, but it's the people around him. There's so much corruption at the palace. So many corrupt people . . .'

I didn't want any more of his confidences. I'd been here a couple of hours, and I wasn't going to be drawn. I said: 'Tell me about your ring.' It was as big as a stud-box.

'Oh,' he said, 'it started off as a piece of jade, then I had my initials put on it, then the setting'—it seemed to include diamonds—'and then the stone fell out and I stuck it back with superglue.'

I thought it must be superglue, I said. In addition to the ring he had a heavy gold watch and an identity bracelet, all gross and sparkling.

'The Queen gave me a medal,' he said. 'And my wife threw it in the trash-can! She threw it away! Look, she tied a knot in the ribbon!'

He fished the medal out of his trouser pocket. 'That's a George III medal,' he said. 'I'm English and proud of it. Any time I want, I can go back to Cheshire and eat kippers.'

Then he said: 'Would you do me a favour?'

I panicked a little.

'Those matches,' he said, 'English matches. Would you give them to me? You see, if I show these at the Palace, everyone'll be surprised. They won't know where I got them from. We don't have them here.'

I gave him the matches. 'What are you doing this evening?' he asked.

'I'm afraid I have a dinner appointment.'

He laughed at these little panics he knew how to create, and told me not to worry. He wasn't going to barge in on my night out. We returned to the subject of his wife. He produced a letter and told me to read it out loud.

It was very dark in the bar, so we had to huddle together by the reading light. The letter was from the Minister of Tourism: 'Dear ____,' I read, 'Please remember that ____ is your husband and the father of your two children. Please give him back his clothes so that he can recover his self-respect.'

'Read it out,' said the colonel, 'read it out loud.'

Then he told me that Marcos could do nothing to help him. His wife had taken everything, the children, his clothes, the lot. The case was in a civil court and Marcos could do nothing about it.

This was the first time I had heard of a court beyond Marcos's control. I could see what the colonel meant about going back to Cheshire and eating kippers.

Pedro's Party

When Helen arrived the colonel looked startled and impressed. I was impressed too. I hadn't expected Helen to look like Meryl Streep. The colonel shot me a look and I shot one back. He wanted to tell Helen about his wife. 'I'm sorry,' I said, 'but we're late for our meeting.' Then I took the surprised Helen and propelled her across the foyer.

'What's going on?' she said. I was just afraid we might be landed with him all evening.

It turned out, though, that there *was* a meeting in hand. That is, one of Helen's friends, Pedro, was giving a party, and if I wanted to go, if I could stay awake after dinner, I was welcome. Pedro's family were squatters, and I noticed—without realizing how customary this was in the Philippines—that at the end of the meal Helen and I had together, she packed up the remains of our food and took it with us for Pedro's children.

I was impressed by Helen: she seemed to know everyone on the street, and most of them by name. People greeted her from the café as we passed, and the cigarette vendors called out to us. We turned down a little alley-way and into a garden beneath a mango-tree. Pedro's hut consisted of a single room with a covered extension. There was a large fridge outside, painted green, with a 'Bad Bananas' sticker, and posters advertising a performance of Antigone and a concert by an American pianist. Helen disappeared indoors to talk to the women and children, while the rest of us drank beer around a table. There were reporters, photographers and theatre people, and members of the foreign press corps, also friends of Helen. I was beginning to get the idea. We were all friends of Helen. She had a whole society of friends.

The great conversation topic was what had just happened in the Manila Hotel. There had been a press conference. As Marcos had been brought in, the *Paris Match* photographer had held his camera in the air to get a shot of him. Two of Marcos's bodyguards had tried to snatch the camera, and the photographer had tried to elbow them away. He had been hustled out of the room and into the hotel

41

kitchen, where the bodyguards had taken turns beating him up. The chef who had been passing was knocked over in the mêlée, and dropped the special cake he had prepared in Marcos's honour.

The party grew, and grew noisy. People taught me the political signs. The Laban sign was an L made with the thumb and first finger. That was the sign for Cory's campaign—'Laban' was Tagalog for 'fight'. The sign for the KBL, Marcos's party, was a V. If you turned your hand over and rubbed your thumb and fourth finger together, that was the sign for money, the bribe, the greasing of the machine. The boycott sign was an X, two fingers crossed, or two clenched fists across your chest. Many of the people present were solidly, and others liquidly, behind the election boycott. 'We're all partisans here!' shouted one guy. He was wearing a red baseball cap with a red star, and an embroidered badge saying 'Don't shoot journalists.' No joke, that. Of the thirty journalists killed worldwide last year, half had been Filipinos. Several of the company were wearing the *tubao,* a purple and yellow kerchief which showed, if you wore it, you had probably been to 'the hell of Mindanao', one of the worst areas of the war.

Pedro moved among the guests, and plundered the crates of San Miguel beer. People tied their kerchiefs over their noses and made fearsome gestures, laughing hugely. A guitar was passed around and songs were sung from the war of independence against the Spanish. Helen sang too. She seemed to improvise a song in Tagalog, and this was doubly surprising because she had been complaining of laryngitis earlier in the evening. Now her voice had woken up for the occasion. It was deep and throaty. She was singing about the Mendiola Bridge, where all the big demonstrations ended up, and where the army or the police used to disperse the crowd with water-cannon and tear-gas.

There was another song about the Mendiola Bridge which went simply:

> Mendiola Bridge is falling down
> Falling down
> Falling down
> Mendiola Bridge is falling down
> My First Lady.

The First Lady being Imelda Marcos. I had heard she was very superstitious, always off to the soothsayer. One day she was told the three things that would happen before the Marcos regime fell: a major earthquake would destroy a church; a piece of earth would erupt after a long silence; and the opposition would cross Mendiola Bridge by force. Since that prophecy had been made, Marcos had spent 2.4 million dollars restoring a church in his native Ilocos Norte for his daughter Irene's wedding. A few weeks after the ceremony there had been an earthquake and the fault had run right through the church. Then the Mayon volcano had erupted after a long silence. As for the third condition, some people said it had already been fulfilled when some opposition people had been allowed across the bridge. But others said no: it must be crossed by force. The bridge was the point of defence along the road to the Malacañang Palace. I imagined that, to have achieved such a significance, it must be a great big handsome bridge. I certainly did not think that I should see the crowds swarm over it. But I was wrong on both counts.

The Americans at the party obviously shared Helen's love for the Filipinos, although they had not been here as long as she had. While I sat there blearily congratulating myself on having arrived and actually *met* people, they were thick in an involvement which I was yet to feel. I could see that they were really delighted to be at Pedro's house, a piece of somewhat haphazard carpentry. I too felt honoured. But I sensed in the Americans a feeling of guilt about the Filipinos, and when I asked one of them what was happening he said: 'It's all a sordid and disgusting deal. Marcos has everything on his side—the army, the police, the banking system, the whole apparatus. He's going to fix the election, and Washington is going to go along with it.'

Then he gave me a sharp look and said: 'You know what you're suffering from. You're suffering from jet-lag denial.' It was quite true. Pedro found me a taxi to the hotel.

My hotel, the Philippines Plaza, was a big mistake, perhaps my biggest mistake so far. When people heard I was staying there, they couldn't believe my bad judgement. The thing I couldn't explain to any of them was that I had needed the name of a hotel in order to tell the NPA where they could contact me. By coincidence, a friend from Ethiopia had been staying at this place and had dropped me a note. So now I was stuck in this isolated monstrosity, which I had known only by name, in the vain hope that I would receive some message. In order to deliver the message, the NPA would have to get past the matador on the front door. From what I knew of the NPA, that would be no problem. But what about me? I was a bad case of jet-lag denial. The matador, both of him, saluted and opened the taxi door. I paid my fare and stumbled out, at the height of his frogged breeches.

Among the Boycotters

Harry and Jojo picked me up the next morning. I felt fine, really fine. They, less so. Pedro's party had taken it out of them. Harry asked what I had expected of Manila. I paused. 'Probably from abroad you think there are killings going on all the time,' said Harry, 'but you know . . . they do the killings mostly at night.' And he laughed a good deal.

'Why are you laughing, Harry?' I said. 'I don't think that's funny at all.'

'You don't think it's funny. Europeans never think it's funny if someone's killed. But you know, we Filipinos, sometimes there are demonstrations where two or three people are killed, and immediately afterwards people are joking and fooling around. You have to joke in order to keep going. But I've noticed Europeans never joke about these things.'

He had been to Europe on business. Photography was only a sideline for him. He wanted me to know that the people we were about to see this morning, the Bayan marchers, were the most important people in the election. 'At the end,' said Harry, 'once the Cory supporters see that it has all been a fix, many of them will join Bayan, or return to its ranks.' The marches would go on, up and down the country. That was the important thing, and he insisted on the point throughout the day. Sometimes I would look at Harry and think: he's as proud of Bayan as if they were his sons and daughters, as if he were living through their achievements. At other times I felt I was being pressed for a response, a confidence. I couldn't reconcile my idea of Harry the owner of the small export business with Harry the admirer of the Left.

Bayan, the umbrella organization for the legal, 'cause-oriented' groups in the opposition, was said by some to be nothing but a communist front. Others emphasized the diversity of political opinion within its ranks. I asked many people in subsequent weeks what the truth of the matter was. A Communist told me: 'It's not a communist front—it *is* the Communists.' Others strongly rejected this. A Bayan member told me: 'It's like this. When the Communists speak, we listen to what they say. When Bayan speaks, they listen to us. We are neighbours. I never see my neighbour from one week to the next, but when he is cooking, I know what he'll be having for dinner.' It was an open secret, he said, that within four years the NPA would be marching through Manila. When that happened, Bayan would have helped them.

Harry said: 'Maybe there'll be some trouble today as the marchers come into the city. Maybe we'll see something.'

I said: 'I very much hope not.' I enjoyed disconcerting Harry with a resolutely anti-good-story line.

Harry said: 'You know, photographers—they love it when trouble begins.'

I wasn't looking for trouble.

We drove south on the highway, past small businesses, authorized dealers in this and that, scrappy banana palms, pawnshops, factories—some with their own housing estates adjacent—American-style eateries, posh condominiums and slums. As a first impression it offered nothing very shocking.

Just beyond Muntinlupa we met the marchers, about a thousand of them with banners denouncing the US-Marcos dictatorship. Most of them were masked. They looked young, and I would have thought that they were students, but Harry insisted they were mainly peasants and workers. I was asked to sign a piece of paper explaining who I was. Most journalists, I realized, wore plasticated ID tags round their necks. In the absence of this, you were assumed to be from the American Embassy. A masked figure passed me with a megaphone, and shouted: 'Down with US imperialism.'

'They're very well organized,' said Harry. 'You'll see. They're ready for anything.' And it was true—they had their own first aid team and an ambulance. They quite expected to be shot. If Bayan was the legal arm of the people's struggle it was still organized like an army. The march was divided into units, and when they stopped at the Church of Our Lady you could see how the units stayed close together to avoid infiltration. As the march approached Manila they were expecting trouble from goons. It was clear that they were very experienced marchers and knew exactly how to maintain control of their numbers.

The people at the church had not made them welcome, but they took over the building nevertheless. Rice and vegetables were brought from the market, and they ate in groups, or rested in the cool of the building, under the crucified figure of the Black Nazarene, whose wavy brown wig reached down to his waist.

The marchers had seemed hostile at first, and I was in no hurry to talk to them if they didn't want to talk to me. Finally I met Chichoy, who was I suppose in his early twenties, and whose political work, he told me, was in educating peasants and workers towards a state of mind where they did not consider their grievances to be part of an inevitable order of things. It was good work and had produced gratifying results. But, as Chichoy said at one point, 'People like me do not live long. We are prepared to die at any time. The point is not to have a long life—a long life would be a good thing—the point is to have a meaningful life.' His way of speaking combined a serious firmness of tone with a deep sadness, as if his own death in the cause were something that he had often contemplated, very much regretted, but there it was.

Not all of the Bayan marchers struck me like this. Some of them seemed to relish the figures they cut, with their red flags and face-masks, and their way of bringing drama onto the streets in the manner of the Peking ballet. Chichoy talked about how a fair election was an impossibility. He was adamant that the intention of the US was to support a dictatorship either way—if not Marcos, an alternative Marcos. If Ninoy Aquino had not been killed, maybe he would have become the alternative dictator. Firmly in his mind was the equation of the US with dictatorship. The Americans had to be overthrown. Their bases had to be closed down. The Philippines would become non-aligned, 'and that will be our contribution to world peace.'

The march moved off. It was one of a series converging on the city, and it joined with another group under the highway at Muntinlupa. People shouted: 'The Snap Election is a fake. So what. We're going to the mountains.' There were few police in sight, and nobody tried to stop the teams of girls with paint pots, who scrawled hurried slogans on the kerbs and walls. On a house which was decked with Marcos posters, I noticed a window full of boycott placards being waved wildly by unseen people. Bayan had its supporters—over a million of them in the country, it was said. But the crowds did not join in. It was as if these demonstrators were on a dangerous mission of their own. The people watched them and kept their own counsel.

We were marching underneath the raised highway, and the acoustics were tempting. When the firecrackers started exploding, the demonstrators cheered. For my part, I became extremely anxious. We had been expecting trouble, and I couldn't tell whether it was the demonstrators who were lobbing the firecrackers or the crowd. I didn't yet know that this was part of the Bayan style. I asked Harry, 'Who's throwing those things?'

'I don't know,' he said, clicking away. He hadn't caught the sense of my question.

The Bayan style was to make each demonstration look and sound as dangerous as possible. When the marches converged on Manila that evening, and the demonstrators sealed off roads by linking arms, the speed and drama with which they operated made it look as if a revolution was in the offing. The defiance of the slogans, the glamour of the torches, the burning tyres, the masked faces—it was a spectacular show. But the state was adopting an official policy of Maximum Tolerance, and the demonstrators had the streets to themselves.

The next day they came together and marched towards Malacañang. And so we arrived at the famed Mendiola Bridge, where the barricades were up, a massive press corps stood in waiting, and the military blocked the way. The bridge was insignificant enough: you wouldn't have noticed it if you had not been looking for it. On the side streets, US Embassy men with walkie-talkies were giving up-to-date accounts of the action. 'You ought to have a mask,' said Helen, 'there may be a dispersal.' But the tear-gas was not used, and the water-cannon was only there for display. They burned effigies of Reagan and Marcos at the front of the barricade. Reagan caught alight easily, but Marcos was slow to burn.

Overheard

The telephones in the Manila Hotel were somewhat overloaded. Here is a conversation Helen overheard on a crossed line on Sunday, 2 February.

Voice One: This is the problem, *compadre*. We're planning to go to Central Luzon and Tarlac on Monday. I'm sure you understand my position as the chairman. I can't just support the campaign for Marcos by words alone. I need the paper.

Voice Two: Yes, yes. Go ahead.

Voice One: We need at least 10,000 pesos deposited by Monday to take care of the people there.

Voice Two: Well, I'll see what I can do.

Voice One: If it's possible, I'd really like to pick up at least part of it this afternoon or early this evening. You know, if I could, I would just go to Malacañang to ask, but I don't want to go ask the President himself at this time. You know what I mean? Do you think it's possible?

Voice Two: OK, come on over.

Voice One: I don't really want to call again. It's difficult on the phone. It's better if I see you. Oh, one more thing, Mr ——, I've got some news. I've just come back from —— and the word there is Marcos-Laurel.

Voice Two: Well, anyway, the important thing is that Macoy himself gets back in. If the VP needs to be sacrificed that doesn't matter. Right? (*They both laugh and say goodbye.*)

The Marcos-Laurel idea was much in the air at the time. Marcos's own vice-presidential candidate was Tolentino, but the theory was that if a close election was engineered in which Cory lost but her vice-president Doy Laurel won, the Americans might feel that honour had been satisfied. Marcos could say: You see? It is as I told you. The people would not vote for a woman president, let alone a completely inexperienced politician.

Rival Rallies

I never found out whether it was actually true, but people said in a very confident way that Marcos had seeded the clouds in the hope of producing a downpour for Cory's *miting de avance*. If he did, it was another of his miscalculations—like the calling of the Snap Election. The Laban supporters had asked for the grandstand in Luneta Park, just by the Manila Hotel. They weren't allowed it, and were obliged to put up their own platform facing the opposite way. The park filled up. The grandstand itself filled up. The meeting overflowed. People tried to guess how many there were in the crowd—a million, two million? It was impossible to tell. It was the biggest rally I'd ever been in, and one of the friendliest and funniest.

I sat among the crowd just in front of the platform. We were jammed so tight that sitting itself was very difficult. But if we stood we got shouted at by the people behind us, whereas if we shouted at the people in front of us to sit down they literally could not do so. It was very painful, and went on for seven or eight hours. What a relief when the dancing girls came on, or when we all stood for a performance of 'Tie a Yellow Ribbon round the Old Oak Tree,' Ninoy's old campaign song. The idiom of the rally was distinctly American, with extra-flash gestures, like the priest on the platform who ripped open his soutane to reveal a yellow Cory T-shirt, or Butz Aquino in his Texan hat, or the yellow-ribboned pigeons and the fireworks overhead.

It was not easy for a newcomer to tell the difference between the pop-singers and professional crooners on the one hand, and the politicians and their wives and families on the other. Everyone sang—current hits, old favourites, I don't know what. The most electrifying speaker was undoubtedly Doy Laurel, although by the time he came on the anticipation was such that his work was easy. People had said Cory was not a professional politician. She was a professional something, though, taking the microphone and singing the Lord's Prayer. After the rabble-rousing of Laurel, the occasion had turned solemn and moving. When the crowd sang '*Bayan Ko*', the national anthem of the Opposition, you felt all the accumulated laughter and cheering of the day turn into pure emotion. Religion and national feeling were at the heart of what Cory stood for.

The next day, Marcos had to do something about all this. The world's press had seen the great crowds. He had to come up with something equally impressive.

I sat on the balcony of my hotel room, with its view of Manila Bay. Helicopters were passing to and fro across the city. Ships arrived, laden down with people. Army trucks and coaches were busing in the Marcos supporters, who formed up in groups in the hotel forecourt, in order to march down to Luneta.

Helen arrived with Jojo and Bing, another of her gang. They'd come down from Quezon City, where the streets were alive with anger. The Marcos supporters were being stoned as they arrived from the boondocks. We went back to have a look.

The taxi-man looked faintly nervous. He was carrying a Marcos flag—all the taxis at the Plaza did the same. He said: 'I think we may be stoned.'

I said: 'Wouldn't it be a good idea to remove that flag?' As soon as we were out of sight of the hotel, he did.

Along the road the 'noise barrage' had begun—long and short blasts on the horn, for *Co-ry*. Groups had gathered at street-corners to jeer the buses as they passed. From the car in front of us people were handing out Marcos T-shirts to the other drivers. When a busload of Marcos supporters came past, we found they were all leaning out of the windows making the Laban sign and calling for Cory. Helen asked them what they were up to. Oh, they said, we're all Cory supporters here—we're only doing it for the money. And they laughed at us: we were going to have to pay for our taxi, they said, whereas they were being paid to ride in their bus. They all treated the occasion as a tremendous joke. It was worth their while attending a Marcos rally for a couple of dollars. Such sums were not easy to come by.

Bing and I were walking towards the meeting. An enormous number of people in T-shirts were already walking away from it. Bing asked them, straight-faced, 'Has Marcos spoken already?' No, they said. Then why were they leaving the meeting? They looked at him as if he were mad. They'd already had enough.

And now the clouds broke, and people really *had* had enough. As we ran for shelter in the Manila Hotel, the hired supporters (not one of whom would normally have been allowed to set foot in it) realized that they could hardly be turned away in their full Marcos paraphernalia. They stormed the foyer, pushing their way past the security guards and treating the whole occasion as a wonderful joke.

Marcos had been due to speak in the evening, but at this rate there wasn't going to be anybody left. So they brought him forward for an earlier rant.

And afterwards, no doubt, they called for the guy who had been told to seed the clouds, and gave him a very nasty time indeed.

Helen on Smoky Mountain

'Within that American body,' says Jojo, 'there's a Filipino soul struggling to escape.' Or another way of putting it was: 'Helen is the first victim of Filipino imperialism.' She has found herself in another language, and indeed she is in some danger of losing her American identity altogether. Among the circle of friends to whom she introduced me, she speaks English—when she speaks it—with a Filipino accent. Or perhaps it is more a matter of intonation. She will say: 'There's going to be viol*ence*.' She leans towards the end of the sentence. Instead of saying, 'They were *shooting* at me,' she says, 'They were shooting at *me*.' And she has forgotten the meaning of several English words.

English people sometimes find life relaxing in a foreign language if it means that they can lose their class backgrounds. Americans, rather lacking this incentive, don't seem to like to unbend linguistically. Whenever I meet really good American linguists, I always assume they're on a journey away from something. I don't ask Helen very much about her past. It's not that I'm not impertinent. I pride myself on being just as impertinent as the next man. But whenever I garner little details about her past, it's so dramatic that I don't know what to say. If I said, 'So what does your little sister do now?' she would be bound to come up with something like, 'She was eaten by a school of barracudas.' And then I wouldn't know where to look.

She is essentially companionable and generous, and this leads her to do something I've never seen anybody do. She doesn't drink, but she enjoys the company of drinkers, and, rather than lag behind as they get drunk, she gets mentally drunk first. One *calamansi* juice and she's slightly squiffy. After a couple of glasses of iced water she's well away.

Another unique feature: she's both a tomboy and a woman's woman. 'What do you mean by a woman's woman?' she said one day, bridling. Well, what I meant was that she's the kind of woman women like. She goes into a house and within seconds, it seems, there are fascinating conversations taking place in the kitchen. Then suddenly all the women are going off to the cinema for a soppy movie in Tagalog. Helen has got them organized.

The tomboy side of Helen comes out in her professional life. The Filipino press corps is her gang, and she often says that it was a difficult gang to join, to be accepted by. There were suspicions. There were unkind rumours. She had to prove herself before she was considered one of the group. But by now the group in question is so large that going on a demonstration with Helen is like being taken to an enormous cocktail-party which happens, for some reason, to be winding its way through the Manila streets towards the inevitable Mendiola Bridge. Hundreds and hundreds of introductions, slappings on the back, encounters with long-lost friends, wavings across a sea of heads.

Everything turns into a party around Helen. You suggest a working dinner *à deux*. By the evening in question it has turned into a feast *à huit*, with further complications about where to go afterwards, because another part of the party is waiting on the other side of the city, a third group is in the offing and there is even a chance that somebody she would like you to meet might turn up at a place which isn't exactly next door to where we are going but . . .

You have to consider this party as an event which is taking place all over Manila—like a demonstration.

One of the things that makes Helen really angry is the brothel aspect of Manila. The mere act of walking down certain Ermita streets is enough to send her into a passionate rage. She cannot relax among the sleaze—that would be a kind of connivance. If Helen's Filipino friends are rather curious to see the bars (which cater largely, it would appear, for Australians) she cannot follow them. Her rage would stand like a bouncer at the door, blocking her path.

She has a heroic conception of the Filipino people. The opposite conception—of an easy-going, lackadaisical, prostituted and eventually degraded nation—this she will fight against. You cannot help noticing that the struggle of the Filipino is carried on in the deepest recesses of her mind. Once she was saying, 'Anyway, even if Cory Aquino were to become President of the United States of America, that wouldn't change anything—'

'Helen, do you realize what you've just said? Cory isn't standing for President of the United States of America.'

'Is that what I said? Oh, so that's really Freudian, *huh*?'

'Yup.' The Filipino struggle is the missing radical wing of American politics. This is Helen's discovery.

The car stops at a red light and the pathetic moaning children beg for money.

'I'm not going to give money to you,' says Helen to a boy. 'You just give it to the police.'

The boy is scandalized and drops the moaning immediately. 'How do you know we give money to the police?'

'Everyone knows the police organize you kids. There's been gossip about it for years.'

'Well if you spread gossip like that, that means *you're* a gossip,' he snaps. Helen laughs. It's obvious that the gossip is true. The police take a cut from the street-urchins, just as they get money from the child prostitutes. Another Manila speciality.

Manila is a city of more than eight million, of whom three to four million live in the Tondo slums. And in some of these slums you see people who are barely managing to remain on the brink of existence. Smoky Mountain, one of the main garbage-dumps of Metro Manila, is such a place. The people live from scavenging plastic or polythene which is then sold to dealers and re-cycled. The mountain itself provides a living for rival communities who take it in turns to go out and sift the garbage. Sometimes there are quarrels over the shifts, and the scavengers actually fight over the tip. The worst work is by night: it is said that the truck-drivers pay no attention to the scavengers and drive over them.

Infant mortality among the scavengers is sixty-five to seventy per cent. The people live in huts at the foot of the tip, by the banks of the filthy Pasig River, a sewer in which they wash. It is here, by the bridge, that they sometimes find the mutilated victims of the latest 'salvaging'.

Coming here with Helen is like trailing in the wake of royalty. Word passes among the huts, the children swarm around her, they all know her by name, and she seems to know a great number of them. She loves making children laugh. She keeps a glove puppet in her camera bag for the purpose.

Up on the burning heap itself, I meet a boy who can say two sentences in English. 'I am a scabenger, I am a scabenger,' he repeats, and 'This is garbage.' He makes me feel the top of his head, which has a perfectly round dent three inches across, where he was beaten up, and he opens his shirt to show me a scar running from his neck to his navel, a war wound from one of the scavengers' battles. In his hand he holds a piece of cloth, like a comforter. He is high on solvent.

He tells Helen of his desperation and asks for her help, but she is severe with him. She says she'll only help him if he gives up the solvent. He says he only takes it because life is so desperate. She says she knows all about that. She's been a drug addict herself. But addiction doesn't help any.

Helen is hard on herself. In work, she likes to push herself to the limit. All the day it's go, go, go until the point when she's about

Opposite: Smoky Mountain.

to keel over. At that moment, all other expressions leave her face, and what you see is panic. When I catch her pushing herself to this point, I want to boss her about, like some Elder Brother from Outer Space.

But nobody bosses Helen about. She has her own destiny.

Election Eve: Davao

There is a way of seeing without seeming to see. Harry had it to a certain degree. An eyebrow moves. A quiet word alerts your attention to the fact that something is going on. But it is no use expecting to be able to follow the direction of a gaze, in order to work out what you are supposed to be taking in. The seer will not give himself away. He is entirely surreptitious.

I noticed it first with Harry among the boycotters in Muntinlupa. We were sitting in the car not far from a peanut stall. What Harry was watching, without seeming to watch, was the behaviour of the policemen standing by the stall, keeping an eye on the Bayan rally. Casually, as they talked, they were helping themselves to the peanuts. The stall-holder made no protest. He was reading a comic. I suppose he too was seeing without seeming to see.

The policemen moved on. Then a plump figure in civilian clothes wandered past and the stall-holder passed him some notes. 'What do you think he is?' I murmured to Harry.

'Looks like a gangster,' he said. The man had been collecting the protection money. A small sum, no doubt, and it wasn't as if the policemen had been stuffing their faces with the peanuts. It was just that these were the kind of overheads a peanut vendor had to allow for.

Davao was quiet on election eve. It felt almost as if a curfew was in force. The sale of alcohol was prohibited, and there was no life around the market. Our driver had told us that there were salvagings almost every day—meaning that bodies were found and the people knew from the state of their mutilations that this was the work of the military. The driver had his own odd code. He told us that he wouldn't go along a certain street because there were a lot of dogs there and he couldn't stand dogs.

The eating-place we found was open to the street, and the positioning of its television meant that the clientele sat facing the outside world, but with their heads tilted upwards. There was a programme of Sumo wrestling, with a commentary in Japanese. Even the adverts were in Japanese. The clientele were drinking soft drinks. Nobody was talking. Everyone was watching the wrestling.

It seemed a hostile sort of place. We chose our food from the counter, but the waitress was slow and indifferent. Behind her on the wall was a Marcos sticker and, for good measure, a Cory sticker. I sat with my back to the street. Jojo and Helen were facing outwards.

At first I didn't notice that Jojo had seen something. Then I turned round and scrutinized the darkened street. Two jeeps had drawn up. I could see a man with a rifle disappearing into a house. Then a confusion of figures coming back to the vehicles, which drove swiftly off. In short, nothing much.

'They're picking someone up,' said Jojo. 'There'll probably be a lot of that tonight.'

As far as I could tell, nobody else in the eating-place had observed the little incident. They were all engrossed in the wrestling. Except I didn't know how many of them had this gift of seeing without seeming to see.

Voting Day in Mindanao

It wasn't hard to tell which areas were going to vote for Marcos and which for Cory. In the Cory areas people were out on the road, cheering and waving and making the Laban sign. In the Marcos areas there was an atmosphere of quiet tension. The crowd, such as it was, did not speak freely. There was a spokesman who explained calmly and simply that Marcos had done so much for this village that there was no support for the opposition. As we could see, the explanation continued, there was no intimidation or harrassment. People were voting according to their own free will. They all supported Marcos.

It was only out of earshot of this spokesman that members of my group were told *sotto voce* that they had been threatened with eviction if they voted the wrong way. Even so, some people said, they were not going to be coerced.

We drove to Tadeco, the huge banana plantation run by Antonio Florendo, one of the chief Marcos cronies. The Cory campaigners were hoping to get the votes from this area disqualified, as the register apparently featured far more names than Mr Florendo employed. He had something like 6,000 workers, many of whom were prisoners. But the register had been wildly padded.

The polling station was at the centre of Mr Florendo's domain. Rows and rows of trucks were lined up, and a vast crowd was milling around, waiting to vote. At the gates, a couple of disconsolate observers from NAMFREL, the National Movement for a Free Election, complained that they had been excluded from the station on the grounds that their papers lacked the requisite signatures. In fact the signatures were there and in order, but the people on the gate insisted this was not so. A sinister 'journalist' began inquiring who I was, and writing down my particulars. 'Oh, you come from England,' he said menacingly. 'Well, that may be useful if we all have to flee the country.' Whenever I tried to speak to somebody, this man shoved his microphone under my nose.

We asked to speak to Mr Florendo, and to our surprise he appeared, with an angry, wiry little lawyer at his side. The lawyer was trying to explain to us why the NAMFREL people should not be allowed in. He had a sheaf of papers to support his case. We introduced ourselves to Mr Florendo, who looked like a character from *Dynasty* or *Dallas*—Texan hat, distinguished white hair, all smiles and public relations. He was a model employer. Everything here was above board. No, the register had not been padded—we could come in and see for ourselves. We asked him why the NAMFREL people had been excluded. He turned to his lawyer and said: 'Is this so? Let them in, by all means.' The lawyer expostulated and pointed to his sheaf of papers. Mr Florendo waved him aside.

Of course the NAMFREL people could come in. There was nothing to hide.

(One of the things they might have hidden better, which my companions noticed, was a group of voters lining up with ink on their fingers: they had already been through at least once.)

We asked if we could take Mr Florendo's picture. 'Oh,' he said, 'you must photograph my son, Tony-Boy—he's the handsome one.' And he called to Tony-Boy, a languid and peculiarly hideous youth. Mr Florendo thought that Tony-Boy could be a Hollywood star. I thought not. Mr Florendo invited us to lunch. I thought not again. Mr Florendo was overwhelming us with his honesty and generosity. He asked the crowd whether he was not a model employer, always available to his workers, and they all agreed that he was indeed a model employer.

In the early afternoon news came over the radio that the KBL had switched candidates, and that Imelda was now stepping in for her husband. 'But they can't do that,' I said. Oh yes they can, said the people in the car. For a while we believed the rumour. Jojo giggled helplessly. 'If Imelda gets in, there really will be panic-buying. Only we've got no money to buy with. We'll just have to panic instead.' And he flopped into a panic as he contemplated the awesome prospect.

Now the returns began to be announced over the NAMFREL radio. The idea was to do a quick count, so that the possibilities of tampering would be kept to a minimum. In precinct after precinct the results were showing Cory winning by a landslide. Around Davao alone they had expected her to get seventy percent of the vote. And this indeed seemed possible. It all depended on what went on in the outlying areas such as Mr Florendo's fief. NAMFREL could not observe everywhere. They simply didn't have enough people. But if they could monitor enough returns fast enough, they might be able to keep cheating to a minimum.

Davao, which features in stories as being one of the murder capitals of the world, had had a quiet day. I think only two people had been killed. The NPA-dominated quarter called Agpao, and nicknamed Nicaragpao, had voted for Cory, although it was plastered with boycott posters, including one which showed the people taking to the mountains.

As the radio continued to announce Cory wins, Jojo came up with an idea. The votes could be converted into different currencies. Cory gets ten million votes, and these are expressed as rupees. Marcos gets five million, but these are dollars. So Marcos wins after all.

Certainly some kind of device was going to be needed.

In the hotel lobby, a desk had been set up to co-ordinate the results. The blackboard showed Cory with a healthy lead.

On the television, it appeared that far fewer of the results had so far been added up. Marcos was doing okay.

The figures in the lobby came from NAMFREL, which was the citizens' arm of the official tabulating organization, COMELEC. In the end it would be the COMELEC figures which counted. But the sources of both figures were the same certified returns. Something very odd was happening.

The head of NAMFREL was called Joe Concepción. The head of COMELEC was Jaime Opinión. The television told us to trust Mr Opinión; the radio, Mr Concepción.

Late that night, the COMELEC count ground to a complete halt. Something had gone wrong—and it was perfectly obvious what.

The NAMFREL Struggle

There were several ways of fixing the election, all of which Marcos tried. The first was to strike names off the electoral register in areas of solid Cory support, and to pad out other registers with fictional names for the flying voters. You could bribe the voters with money and sacks of rice, or, above-board and publicly, with election promises. You could intimidate the solid areas. You could bribe the tellers. You could have fake ballot-papers (a franking machine for these had gone missing for a whole week before the election). You could put carbon-paper under the ballot form, to make sure that an individual had voted the right way before you paid him off. You could print money for his pay-off, and if you printed the money with the same serial numbers there would be no record of how much you had printed. You could force the early closure of polling stations in hostile areas. You could do all these things and you might, if you were Marcos, get away with it.

But what if, after all that, the early returns made it plain that you still hadn't won?

Then you would have to start stealing the ballot-boxes, faking the returns, losing the ballots, shaving off a bit here, padding a bit there and slowing down the returns so that, you hoped, once the initial wave of anger had subsided, you could eventually declare yourself the winner. To explain the delays in the counting of returns, there was a formula which never failed to unconvince. You could say over and over again on Channel Four, the government broadcasting station: 'What the foreign observers fail to realize is that the Philippines is a nation comprised of over 7,000 islands. It takes a long time to collect the ballot boxes. Some of them have to be brought by boat or by carabao from very remote areas.' But in the meantime votes would be taking a mysteriously long time to find their way from one side of Manila to the other.

This second phase of corruption was now beginning, and the people who stood against it were the NAMFREL volunteers and the Church. There was a great deal of overlap. Outside the town halls where the ballot-boxes were kept and counted stood rows of nuns chanting Hail Marys, seminarians grouped under their processional crosses, Jesuits, priests and lay people. Outside Pasay Town Hall in Manila, the day after the election, I asked a Jesuit whether the whole of his order had taken to the streets in this way. He said that the only ones who hadn't were the foreigners, who didn't feel they could interfere. They were manning the telephones instead.

The Jesuit was a cheerful character. He told me that in the past members of his order used to go on retreat with Marcos once a year. He invited them down to a country residence of his in Bataan. They'd been very well catered for—food had come from a posh local restaurant. But Marcos himself had eaten very simply and kept retreat in the most pious manner. He had offered them the chance to go water-skiing, but the coastguard had said there were too many jellyfish.

'What would the Pope have said,' I asked him, 'if you'd gone water-skiing? Would he have approved?'

'Maybe not,' said the Jesuit. 'Skiing yes, water-skiing perhaps no.'

Anyway, these days of retreats with the Marcoses were now over. Not only were the Jesuits out on the streets. There were all kinds of people. At the same place I talked at length to a police cadet who was an ardent NAMFREL supporter. There were poor people and there were extremely elegant ladies—but elegant in the Cory, not the Imelda, style. In the trouble-spots, at Makati Town Hall and in the Tondo for instance, they had kept a vigil over the ballot boxes. They linked arms to protect them. They formed human chains to transport them. They all said, and they said it over and over again, that all they could do was protect the vote with their bodies. They were expecting harrassment and they got it. They were expecting to be beaten up. They were expecting martyrdom and they got that too.

The expression, 'the sanctity of the ballot', had been injected with real force, real meaning. It had been preached from every pulpit and it had sunk into every Catholic heart. The crony press was full of vituperation against the Church. It abominated Cardinal Sin. The Church that had once supported martial law, and had been courted by the Marcoses (Imelda was always swanning off to the Vatican), was now a public enemy. Paul's Epistle to the Romans was cited by the *Sunday Express* against the Church:

> Everyone must obey state authorities, because no authority exists without God's permission, and the existing authorities have been put there by God. Whoever opposes the existing authority opposes what God has ordered; and anyone who does so will bring judgment on himself.

But they did not continue with the next verse: 'For government, a terror to crime, has no terrors for good behaviour.' Which proves that Paul had not envisaged the Marcos dictatorship.

As the NAMFREL struggle continued, and behind the scenes the Marcos men were working out the best strategy for cooking the books, Marcos himself gave a press conference at Malacañang. You couldn't get near the palace by taxi. You had to stop at the beginning of a street called J.P. Laurel, then walk down past some old and rather beautiful houses in the Spanish colonial style. As you came through the gate, you found that the lawns had been turned over to the cultivation of vegetables in little parterres. I wondered whether these were siege rations. What were the Marcoses expecting? Beyond the vegetable garden lay a sculpture garden depicting mythological beings in concrete. It looked rather as if some member of the family had had a thing about being a sculptor, and been indulged in her illusions.

A further gate, a body search, and then you came to the grand staircase flanked by carved wooden figures, leading up to an ante-room where several grand ladies, Imelda-clones, sat chatting. The room's decorations were heavy. There was an arcaded gallery from which, I suppose, members of the Spanish governor's household would have looked down on the waiting petitioners. The ante-room led directly into a large and brightly-lit hall, got up very much like a throne-room. Here the cameras were all set up, and Marcos was in the process of explaining that the delays of the night before had all been the fault of NAMFREL. They had refused to co-operate with COMELEC in what had been intended as a simultaneous and co-ordinated tabulation of results. However, that matter had all been cleared up earlier this morning. As far as the stopping of the count had been concerned, there had been no malicious, mischievous or illegal intent.

Marcos's eyes were lifeless. He could have been blind. Or perhaps he had only just been woken up. His mouth was an example of a thoroughly unattractive orifice.

He had his own set of figures, and he explained at great length how the arithmetic would work out. As he did so, his hand-gestures were like those of a child imitating a plane taking off. He conceded he might have lost in Metro Manila. He conceded he had lost in Davao. But by moving his million-and-a-half votes from the Solid North all round the shop, so that you could never tell quite what he had set them off against, he managed to arrive at a 'worst possible scenario' where he won by a million-and-a-half votes.

I couldn't follow him. Imelda had slipped in at the side and was watching in admiration. Like any bad actress she had a way of telling you: this is what's going through my mind, this is what I'm feeling.

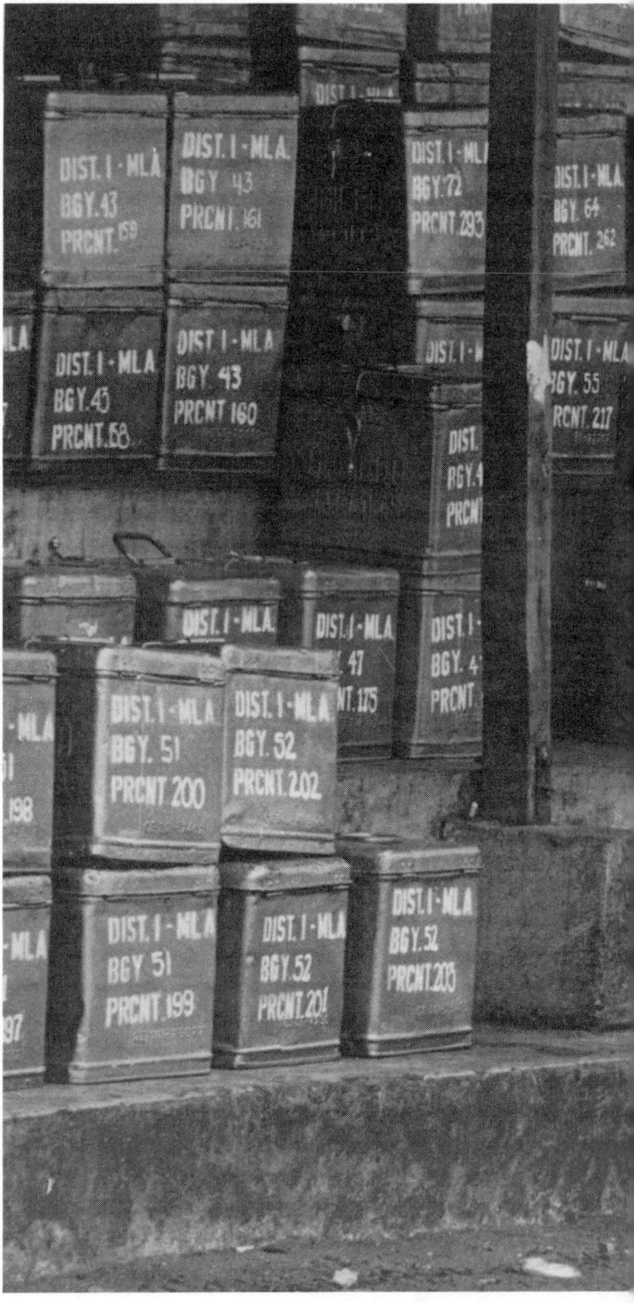

Photo: Associated Press

And the message she was putting across that day was: I've just slipped in, inconspicuously, to watch my husband brilliantly rebutting all the awful things that have been said about him by you foreign meddlers; look at him—isn't he wonderful?—*still*, at *his* age; how deeply I love him and how greatly I appreciate him; why is it that you lot can't see things the way I do? Don't look at me. I'm just sitting here admiring my husband, plain little inconspicuous me.

And she shook her head very gently from side to side, unable to believe how great he was, and how lucky she had been.

The COMELEC Girls at Baclaran

The next evening I was sitting with some Americans in the foyer of the Manila Hotel, wondering whether perhaps we might not have preferred to be in Haiti. There was after all something gripping about the way the people there had dug up Papa Doc's bones and danced on them. And what would happen to all the dictators in exile? *Rolling Stone* suggested a Dictator Theme Park, where we could all go to visit them in natural surroundings.

A chap came up to our table, hovering about three inches off the floor, his eyes dilated. He had taken some high-quality something. 'Listen you guys, nobody move now because the opposition's watching. The COMELEC girls have walked out of the computer count, in protest at the cheating. The whole thing's fucked.'

We got up casually, one by one, and paid our bills. The 'opposition', the rival networks, were no doubt very far from deceived. At the door I bumped into Helen.

'Helen,' I said, 'be absolutely casual. Just turn round and come out with me. The COMELEC girls have walked out of the computer count. Let's get down there.'

But Helen was bursting for a pee. I swore her to secrecy and told her again to act natural. I knew, as I waited for her, that the chances of Helen crossing the foyer of the Manila Hotel without meeting a friend were zero. I dithered, frantic with casualness, by the door.

Helen kept her word, though, and only told one other journalist.

The COMELEC count was taking place in public, in a large conference centre which was one of the Marcoses' notorious extravagances. When we reached the auditorium there was nothing much to see. The girls, around thirty of them, had got up, taking their disks with them, and simply walked out of the building before anyone realized what was going on. The remaining operators were still in place, but because the girls who had walked out occupied a crucial part of the whole computer system, nothing could be done until they and their software were replaced.

A seething general, Remigio P. Octavio, was outside the auditorium. Helen asked him what had happened. Nothing had happened. 'Well, General, there seem to be quite a lot of operators missing.'

Nobody was missing, said Remigio. The girls had needed a rest. People in the gallery had been jeering at them, throwing stones and paper darts, and they'd gone outside for a rest. They were upset. The gallery had been full of Communists. And tomorrow, he said, he would make sure there were enough police down here to prevent a recurrence. He would bring in reinforcements.

'As for the girls,' said the General, 'they will be back again shortly.'

Helen wrote all this down on her pad. When she clicks into her reportorial mode and starts firing questions, it's an impressive sight. She laces her sentences with respectful language, and makes a great show of taking down every detail and improbability. But when somebody is lying to her in the way Remigio P. was, the effect of all this is mockery. I wondered whether the general would realize he was being sent up. If I had been him, I would have shot Helen.

The girls had taken refuge in Baclaran Church, and it was there the press corps tracked them down. By now they were said to be very scared at the consequences of their walk-out. They needed all the protection the church could give them, but they also perhaps needed the protection of the press. Perhaps. Perhaps not. Members of the official teams of observers arrived. There was a great sense that these girls were in extreme danger.

It was the second time that day that I had been in Baclaran Church. In the afternoon it had been jam-packed as Cardinal Sin celebrated mass. Cory had attended. The crowds had spilled out into the churchyard and the street-market nearby. Cardinal Sin had preached a sermon so emphatic in its praise of NAMFREL that he had made its members seem almost saints. Depending on your point of view, they were either heroes or villains. There was no middle ground.

Now the church was about a quarter full. Those who had heard about the walk-out had come to express their support. To pass the time they sang '*Bayan Ko*', and when the girls finally came out in front of the high altar the audience burst into applause.

The cameras had been set up long since and there were masses of photographers angling for a shot. The girls were sobbing and terrified. I could hardly bear to watch the grilling they got. Their spokeswoman said that they would not give their names, and that it was to be understood that what they had done was not political. They were not in fact (although we called them the COMELEC girls) officials of COMELEC. They were computer operators, highly qualified, who had been engaged to perform what they had taken to be a strictly professional job. All had gone well until the night before, when they began to be instructed not to feed in certain figures, so that the tally board giving the overall position was now at odds with what they knew to be the actual total so far.

I remember the word that was used. Discrepancies. Certain discrepancies had crept in, and the girls were worried by them. Finally they had decided that they were being asked to act unprofessionally. They had come out, and they had brought print-outs and disks with them, in order to prove their case.

Earlier that evening the international team of observers had given a press conference at which John Hume, from Northern Ireland, had been the spokesman. He had been adamant that there had been cheating on the part of the KBL, but he had purposely left open the question of whether that cheating had been on such a scale as to alter the eventual result of the election. The reason he had done this was that people feared Marcos might declare the election null and void, using the evidence of the foreign observers. Marcos was still president. He hadn't needed to call the snap election. If he now annulled it he could, constitutionally, go on as if nothing had happened.

Now the COMELEC girls had come out with the most authoritative evidence of cheating so far. People had been killed for much, much smaller offences. The Americans could not possibly overlook this evidence, I thought. There would be no getting around it. That was why the girls were in such danger.

One of the American reporters said to the girls that of course they were entitled to withold their names, but that if they did so Marcos would claim they had not come from COMELEC at all, that this was just black propaganda. For their sakes, they should tell us their names.

At which another pressman snapped, 'It's not for their sakes. You just want to get a good story.'

The press conference drew to a close. I was thinking: so many people have gone so far—they're so exposed—that the Cory campaign must move forward. If it grinds to a halt now, all these people are just going to be killed.

A figure came rushing into the church. It was the Jesuit from Pasay Town Hall, the one who had been so entertained by Marcos. He came up through the press. 'It's very important,' he said, 'it's very important. They *must* give their names. They *must* give their names.'

But the conference was already over, and the girls had gone into hiding.

II

THE NARROW
ROAD TO THE
SOLID NORTH

James Fenton

The Café at Kilometer Zilch

Marcos was from Ilocos Norte. That and the surrounding provinces were his stronghold, and everyone referred to the area as the Solid North. Everyone, that is, except the communists, who called it Ilocoslovakia. From the electoral point of view, Northern Luzon was cut and dried. From the revolutionary perspective, it was quite different.

Fred, my new guide, had been working there for the last few months. There was too much competition among the photo-journalists in Manila. He had to prove himself. He had to get some exclusive stories, and that meant working in the provinces, where the war was. 'My only weapons are my courage and my guts,' he said. He would work from his home province for the next couple of years, and if all went well he would then move to Manila.

The disadvantage of working from near home was that he wouldn't be able to marry his fiancée yet. It was impossible to do so at home without inviting all their friends and relations, and this they simply could not afford. Whereas a wedding in Manila could be a much more modest affair.

Fred had strong aspirations. Obviously he wanted to see a new social order, but as to the question of how that order was to be achieved he was quite prepared to think things over from scratch. He would not brush aside an inconvenient argument. He would dwell on a doubt. He would brood over it and become enveloped in thought. His fundamental conception of society was dynamic rather than static: history in his view never stops.

Talking about photo-journalism one day, he said: 'I would like to cover the guerrillas in China.'

'What guerrillas?'

'Aren't there guerrillas in China?'

'I've never heard of them. Maybe there are.'

'There *must* be guerrillas in China. Thesis—antithesis. If there aren't yet, there must be some soon.'

Most of his life has been spent under Marcos's rule, and his habit of thought was to doubt the story as presented in, say, the newspaper, and to try to guess the story behind the story. As we got on the bus to go north, for instance, he suddenly said: 'Do you think the Americans have finally decided to dump Marcos?' The day's papers would not, on a superficial reading, have given much hope of that, but there was some detail that made him think he'd seen the light at the end of the tunnel. He was always a step ahead of me, and I was constantly being told: 'There, you see, you didn't believe me. Read this.' So I fully expect, in the next years, to discover that there are indeed guerrillas in China, and that Fred is on the story.

The bus was air-conditioned and took the road at a practised lick. I slept and froze and clung to my seat as best I could. In the early hours of the morning we reached the Café at Kilometer Zilch, which was run by a friend of Fred's, a former artist called Johnny. Johnny had put his premises at the disposal of the Aquino campaign, and now that the election was over he was exposed and in danger. The local KBL men had been making threats. There were scores to settle, as there were all over the country. The election violence had not stopped. It had already claimed an illustrious name, that of Evelio Javier, the former governor of Antique. In Manila I had seen the corpse of an obscure beautician called Archie, who had been shot by a sniper while on a Cory rally. The bodies of girls who had worked for NAMFREL had been found, raped and beheaded. Thugs had disrupted the demonstrations around the Parliament in Quezon City. In the 'solid' provinces, those who had conspicuously campaigned for Cory had every reason to be worried.

Johnny gave us a room. The next day, when I looked out across the paddy-fields to the Cordillera, I could see the NPA zone. It would not have been a long walk.

Fred said: 'There's been a dialogue. We just missed it.'

'What sort of dialogue?'

'The NPA came to a municipal hall not far from here and had a dialogue with the military for about an hour.'

It took me some time to realize we were talking about a gun-fight. Fred went off to find out more.

I was sitting in the café reading a book. Associates of the Aquino campaign dropped in during the day. One was an engineer whose family were KBL. He told me how during a previous election he had gone to the house of a relative and watched them faking the ballots. Instead of putting their thumb-prints on the returns, they had removed their shoes and inked their big toes. The engineer was on a drinking spree. He was angry and becoming desperate. A nun sat with him drinking Coke and offering some calm advice.

Johnny came up to my table. He had a farm as well as the café. He had not painted for some time. Now he had an idea for a painting, in which the Filipino people were depicted as prisoners inside a ballot-box. Maybe he would do that.

He was in a deep gloom, and the drink had not relieved it. He was receiving threats. I suggested that he go down to Manila until things cooled off a bit. He said that was impossible. His wife was down there and he had to look after the business. I didn't know what to say. Johnny said: 'Well, if they come for me, I shall defend myself.' And he lifted his T-shirt to show me the pistol tucked into his waistband.

We sat in silence for a while.

When he moved back to his companions on the other table, I picked up my book, put my elbows on my knees and tried to read. There were black and white tiles on the floor. With great force, as if a memory had taken on the power of a hallucination, I recalled what a drop of blood looked like on a tiled floor, something like an ink-blot but more perfectly, regularly pointed. I seemed to be suffering from a mental nosebleed.

Evelio Javier had been gunned down, I seemed to remember, in a café. When he ran wounded and locked himself into the toilet, they came after him and finished him off in there. Perhaps Johnny was thinking of that. Javier had been unarmed. He had foreseen his death, and had gone to the lengths of recording a tape, naming the man who was after him. Javier had come back from the States in order to campaign in the election. Presumably he knew there was no point in being armed. If they wanted to get him, they would.

Fred appeared, and we set off by jeep to the scene of the recent

---

Opposite: 'An obscure beautician called Archie.'

Photo: Toshi Matsumoto (Sygma)

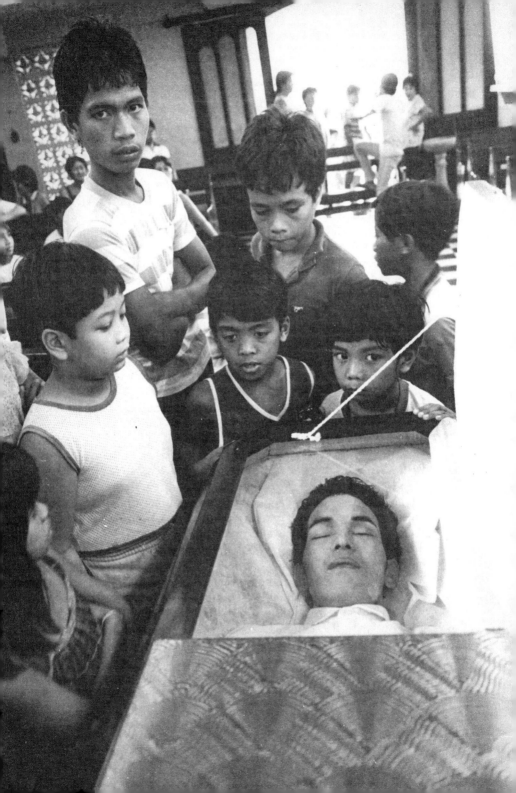

'dialogue', leaving the main road and driving in the direction of the Cordillera. The building in question was a military post at the foot of the mountains. Bobby, the commanding officer, was a friend of Fred's. He greeted us and ushered us into the hall, past the marks on floor and wall where the grenades had exploded.

I felt certain from the moment I saw Bobby, casually dressed and with an easy authority, that he was a very good officer. He was certainly proud of what he had achieved during the dialogue, and he had drawn an elaborate map of the operation. He had heard that the NPA were planning an attack, and had pretended to withdraw some of his troops from the municipal building, taking them down to the other end of the village, and waiting. When the attack had come, he could have taken a direct route back to the municipal building to relieve his men, but reconnaissance by fire told him that ambushes had been set up along that road. So instead (all this beautifully illustrated in different coloured ball-points) he had brought his men very quickly round the back, and convinced the NPA that they were outnumbered. In fact it was he who was outnumbered. He had managed to inflict several casualties on the other side.

His job, it appeared, was to live like this at the edge of the NPA area—that is, at the foot of the mountains—and to prevent the communist infiltration of the villages around. But infiltration went on all the time. (The fact that his feigned retreat from the building we were sitting in had been noticed by the NPA was enough to indicate that news travelled fast in the area.) He had made a list of all the informants and collaborators in the village, had told them he knew exactly who they were and that they were to present themselves to him, admit what they'd been up to and give full details.

'And they did?'

'Sure, they did. They knew I had good intelligence.'

'What happened to them afterwards?'

'They went back to the village. Nothing happened.'

'But they had informed on the NPA. Didn't the NPA do anything about it?'

'No. The NPA just know they can't work here. That's all.'

What kind of reality was represented by this story I did not know. On the one hand, the NPA could well have told the villagers to comply with Bobby's instructions. On the other, it might be just as he said. The two sides knew a lot about each other, and knew that, in such a war, that was inevitable. They might win a village, lose it, win it again. They were fighting a political battle, and this was the way such things go.

'I say to my men,' said Bobby, 'they have to be with the people. They have to be trusted by the people. If not, they're like a fish out of water.'

'But that's Mao,' we all said at once.

'I know it's Mao, that's why I say it.' Bobby's intellectual hero was Hans Morgenthau. I hadn't read any, but he expounded a few ideas, and in his version they sounded a bit like Mao as well. As dusk fell we thought we ought to leave. Bobby said: 'Why don't you stay the night? I'm expecting another attack.'

As it happened we couldn't, and I was sorry. Bobby was a major and the kind of guy, I imagined, who would support Ramos and the movement for military reform. I would have liked to have got him to talk about that as well. He had enough confidence to do so. He seemed also to like his job, which left him, essentially, exposed. The NPA theory was not to attack unless you outnumbered the enemy. Bobby knew that. He had been outnumbered in the last attack and he would be again if anything happened tonight. That was what he was proud of.

That night I returned to my book while Fred read *Granta*. Helen had given him my account of the fall of Saigon, which had been much passed around. I was like a bird of ill-omen in the Philippines; people said, 'So you've come for the fall of Manila, have you?' And indeed there was something eerie about meeting so many foreign journalists whom I had known from Indochina, and watching the past intertwine with the present, the previous and the next *Granta*s coiling like sea-snakes. I was very curious to know what Fred would think of my piece, but he needed time to brood.

'It's changed my mind on one thing, though,' he said before going to sleep. 'I used to think the crucial thing would be the battle for Manila. Now I see the crucial thing is what's going on over there, now, in the mountains.'

James Fenton

A Typical Politician's House

Times are hard for business in the Philippines, so the garden of
Maximo's house has been converted into a lavatory factory, and as
you walk up to the front door you pass rows of freshly-cast pedestals
and squatting-jobs. There is also a sideline in concrete balustrades.

The exterior of the building is unspectacular, but when you step
inside, and look up, you have to be impressed. The whole thing has
been lined with nara wood, the most expensive timber. The design
of the panelling imitates brickwork, and there is a heavily carved
balcony running round three sides of what I think deserves to be
called the atrium.

Below the balcony level nothing has been finished. The stairs
are makeshift. The lower walls are frankly breeze-block. The floor
is concrete. The focus of the furniture is a gigantic television in a
wooden case. There are religious pictures and a glass-fronted case
containing encyclopaedias and school-books. Maximo's office is in
a small recess.

He is away. His wife is just about to leave, but she insists that
Fred and I stay here and treat the place as our home. I compliment
her on it. 'It's a typical politician's house,' she says. She designed the
atrium herself. It had to be large and light because Maximo will have
to entertain. He is a councillor, and he is hoping to become mayor
at the next elections.

But how did she get so much nara? (Nowadays it is illegal to fell
the trees. If you want to buy nara, you have to have friends in the
military, who have an interest in illegal logging.) She explains that
a former mayor of the town had been a great gambler, and he used
to drop round at all hours to borrow money from Maximo. It
seemed convenient to pay him back in nara logs, which they saved
up over a period of fifteen years until they could build a proper
politician's house.

Then came the sugar slump (Maximo is mainly in sugar and
toilets) and the inflation. Diversifying into toilets had kept their
heads above water, but they hadn't liked to borrow money in order
to complete the atrium. There was a little nara left, but somehow
they would have to find some more. The next problem would be the

floor. She wanted marble, but Maximo had said she would be six feet under before they could afford it. So now she doesn't know. She had been apologizing to a priest about the unfinished state of the place, and he had said: 'Don't worry. Rome wasn't built in a day.' She says: 'We're just a typical middle-income-bracket family. Fortunately my husband is an assiduous worker, so we can educate our children.'

Some of her children are in Manila. The oldest is a NAMFREL nun, and all the children in Manila, she says, support Cory. Maximo has been an independent, but now he has just decided to join the ruling KBL.

If you were to say to Maximo, 'Isn't this an odd time to join the KBL?' he would say: 'The fact that I joined the KBL at this moment proves that I'm not an opportunist.' There is some doubt as to whether the KBL will field him as their mayoral candidate. If they don't, Maximo intends to stand as Independent KBL.

There doesn't seem to be great strife in the family over their different political allegiances. I think Maximo takes great pride in his children, although the activities of one of them do cause him to raise an eyebrow. Still, I imagine that if your daughter is a nun you listen to her with respect, and if she is a member of NAMFREL you feel involved in its activities as well. Maximo's view is that the KBL must start introducing thorough reforms. This is likely to be his platform in the forthcoming local elections.

If Maximo stands as mayor, it will be to replace Ultimo, the current incumbent who, just before the presidential election, switched allegiance from KBL to the opposition UNIDO. Ultimo's house is not as grand as Maximo's is going to be, but Ultimo has a luminous picture of the Agony in the Garden, and a parrot trained to shriek 'Mayor!' And he has lovely daughters and nieces who also support Cory, and who, I guess, might have influenced his decision.

Ultimo says: 'How could I have gone on in the thought that my grandchildren and great-grandchildren would grow up in the knowledge that I had supported such an appalling government? I could not! It was a matter of principle.' (He also tells me that, as a KBL candidate, he stood as mayor four times. The principle must have been slow in seeping through.)

Fred asks him whether he will hold a proclamation rally for Cory. Ultimo looks disconcerted. He *would* do so, he says, if he thought the support was there. I don't think Ultimo is going to be very keen to hold a rally for Cory. But he says that if she doesn't win he will resign.

He explains that the KBL produced a great wodge of money in the town, just two days before the election. Something like two million pesos arrived, and there was widespread buying of votes. Some of the teachers involved in the counting received a thousand (fifty dollars) apiece. His niece had been offered five thousand and had refused.

Ultimo's view of the matter is simple: UNIDO didn't have the money to outbid the KBL. 'The way I would have done it would have been to ask—OK, what are they offering? Fine, we'll double it. Ten pesos a vote? We'll make it twenty, and so on.' As he says this, he appears to realize that this was not the way the Cory camp were supposed to be electioneering. He has to justify himself. 'Because I think you'll agree,' he says, 'that the only way to match money is with money. Or with guns. We didn't have the money and we didn't have the guns. What can you do?'

Ultimo could hardly have given me a franker account of the way he likes to run things. Elsewhere I am told that he made himself unpopular recently when he pulled a gun in an argument. The 'real' reason why Ultimo resigned from the KBL was that he had gone drinking with a friend and, unusually for him, had taken alcohol. He had spoken out against the government, and this had got him into trouble with the really big guy around here, the Defence Minister, Juan Ponce Enrile. It had all been a bit more complicated than he had made out. (There is no going against Enrile. And when people hear that Enrile intends to have his son, Jackie, appointed Governor of the region, they look really alarmed.)

There is no love lost between Maximo and Ultimo. Maximo's family tells me that the real indicator of Ultimo's low standing is that when he switched sides, his clan did not go with him. His immediate family, maybe, but not his clan. And they say: 'Did you see his house? It was amazing how quickly he built it after he became mayor.' Whereas Maximo's house—well, Rome wasn't built in a day.

After the Ambush

Filipino English is for the most part very similar to American English. But there are words which have gained an ominous significance and force, whose meaning is not always clear to the foreigner. 'There's been a *dialogue*,' Fred had said, meaning a firefight. 'You ought to have a mask,' said Helen, 'there may be a *dispersal*.' Meaning tear-gas and water-cannon. A *salvaging* is a murder carried out by the *military* (government soldiers) or by *goons*. A *sparrow unit* (two or three members of the NPA) would call their work a *liquidation*. It would be the settlement perhaps of a *blood debt*. *Hamleting* does not appear to mean putting people from a disputed area into strategic hamlets or concentration camps. Rather the military simply clear the village in question and move its inhabitants wherever may be convenient. Thus: 'Many of the families on Smoky Mountain are victims of *hamleting*.' 'We've been *pinpointed*,' said a member of the human rights group, Task Force Detainees (TFD), meaning something like 'We've been fingered', but without the implication of guilt. Pinpointed is a very sinister word.

Fred had heard that there was to be a *fact-finding*—that is, some nuns, some workers from TFD and other human rights people had gone off to the mountains where they had learned that a detainee was being tortured. We hired a jeepney and set off after them. One purpose of a fact-finding was to let the military know that somebody else in the world knew that they had a detainee. In this way it was hoped that interrogation would not end in a salvaging. Of course, people who took part in a fact-finding ran a risk of being pinpointed. That was simply one of the facts of life.

The hilly ground we had been covering must have been deforested long ago. Today it was a kind of grassy downs, except where, in the fold of the hills, a more jungly vegetation thrived. Part of the time I was reminded of Sussex. Then we would hit one of these overgrown valleys, and I would see that this must once have been rain-forest. The further we went into the mountains, the more frequently the forest asserted itself. We had already passed the scene of an ambush where a colonel and his companions had been killed in their jeep a month or so before. Now we came upon a group of military walking along the road and looking very scared. There had just been an ambush, they said, and they checked us out with great suspicion.

The soldiers were wearing Adidas sportswear. They were well armed with a variety of weapons, but mostly M16s. Seeing how alarmed they were, I assumed at first that there was a whole NPA unit in the area, but when we reached the nearest military camp and inquired about the incident, it turned out to be rather strange.

The jeepney before ours (had we left one hour earlier we might well have been on it) had been carrying a soldier and his sweetheart. Half a mile back, two of the other passengers had drawn pistols. One had hit the soldier on the head. The sweetheart, we were told, had fought with one of the armed men, while the other shot the soldier. In the scuffle, she had actually picked up one of the pistols, but it had not been loaded. The two men had taken the soldier's weapons and disappeared. The driver had gone with them.

'That's the sweetheart, over there,' said the commanding officer. The woman was in shock.

The military said that the incident had been the work of a sparrow unit. Attacks on isolated soldiers had been one of the ways the NPA had been able to arm themselves, and on the face of it this seemed the probable explanation. Except the way the operation had been almost bungled—the detail of the unloaded pistol, for instance—seemed out of character. Possibly it was a case of gangsterism. And why had the driver abandoned his jeepney? Had he been part of the plot, or had he feared he would be blamed by the military?

What was most striking was the continued state of alarm in the camp. The soldiers were obviously badly trained. They didn't know how to hold their weapons, and I watched one of them sticking his rifle barrel into the dirt, until an officer reprimanded him. The soldiers were not pleased to see us, and we soon moved on.

Immediately, the landscape looked more jungly, and full of ideal spots for an ambush.

If you hire a jeepney for your personal use (as opposed to joining the passengers on a wildly overcrowded vehicle), you will quite often find that a couple of passengers come along anyway. They may be friends of the driver, or his partners, or there may be some other explanation. Normally I took it as a part of everyday life. But now a fancy formed in my mind that the two unexplained guys we were carrying might also be a sparrow unit. They had a way, when we stopped at a roadblock, of dismounting, dematerializing and joining us again when we were through.

The news of the incident had spread along the road—so, too, had the alarm.

We met the members of the fact-finding team coming the other way. They had been refused access to the detainee, and they were sorry we had not been there to boost their numbers. The wife of the detainee had not been allowed to see him, but she had spoken to him through the wall of the hut where he was being held. Among the things he had asked for had been iodine for his wounds. When his wife had asked him how he had been hurt, a soldier replied on her husband's behalf that he had injured himself on a nail the night before. The detainee had sounded very weak.

Two members of the fact-finding agreed to accompany us to show us the way. Another member, a journalist, warned us to watch out for a very drunken group of soldiers who had gone through all their things and had deliberately dropped his camera. We told him the news from Manila. Cory had called for a nationwide campaign of civil disobedience. She had asked for a boycott of the crony newspapers and—this was the bad news—San Miguel beer. The man was covered with the dust of the road. He groaned, 'Oh no, oh no. Not San Miguel.' He looked as if he could use a beer, and the problem was that there was very little alternative to San Miguel. Crony capitalism was a string of monopolies. The future without San Miguel looked very bleak.

We got back in the jeepney—Helen, Fred, our new companions and my imagined sparrow unit. Before very long we were flagged down by the military. These were the drunken soldiers we had been warned about. I watched the driver's reaction as they told us to drive them back to the last village. He didn't react at all. He was being immensely careful. One of the soldiers examined my press card. The other said that they were scared and that it was very urgent they get back to the village. They were heavily armed and in uniform. One had a JESUS SAVES sticker on his rifle. As they climbed into the back, they said they couldn't see why foreigners like us were allowed to come to places like this. We only caused trouble.

We were all rather worried that we had now become a target. But it was even more worrying to think what these very scared and drunk soldiers might do next. Fortunately, it was to hail another vehicle after a mile or two, and transfer. We turned back yet again. I abandoned the theory about the sparrow unit. The two guys in our jeepney looked as relieved as we were. Now my apprehensions were all to do with the fact that to the right of the road was a sheer drop of several hundred feet. One of the NPA ambush techniques in this area, I later learned, was to hurl great rocks down in front of military vehicles. A swerving armoured car had, not long before, plunged into the ravine.

My awareness of the military, straggled out along the road into the mountains and at the mercy of attacks by the guerrillas, was vivid. One quietly-spoken officer said that he had served in Mindanao and that this place was worse. He wouldn't tell us why, said it was a military secret. I guessed though, from other things I had heard, that the soldiers here knew that they were outnumbered by the NPA.

From the state of the forest, much of which had been planted with bananas, I could see that the jungle had only recently been cleared. I began to think of the Central Highlands of Vietnam. Every time we came to a bridge, it seemed extraordinary to me that it was not guarded, and as night began to fall I thought of the golden rule in Indochina: never be on the roads after dark. The drunken military obviously obeyed that rule. They were as demoralized as the South Vietnamese at their worst.

I thought that the guerrilla war could not be very advanced. If it had been, all of these bridges would have been blown up. But later an NPA soldier said to me, 'Oh no, we like having the military up there. That way we get more weapons.' The whole spectacular landscape was a well-laid trap.

That night the villager with whom we stayed told us what had been going on. The military had arrested a well-known thief from the area. To get out of trouble, he had decided to sing. He claimed to have been an NPA supporter himself and he had pinpointed several villagers as belonging to the guerrillas. And had they? No, said our host, they had all been innocent, but the whole place was terrified now of what the thief might say next. He had got himself into favour with the military and was now living with them.

The villagers were living in the crossfire. Sometimes the NPA came along, and the strong traditions of hospitality meant that you had to entertain them. Then the military came along and the trouble began. There was no justice. The NPA were strong in the area—sometimes you would see a hundred or more of them. The villagers were obviously in a quandary over how to behave towards both sides. A nurse told me they were all suffering from hyper-acidity, and I could see why.

That night, when our driver and his friends, who were not after all a sparrow unit, had had a little to drink, they began discussing the future of the Philippines. What would happen if the American bases were closed down? What would become of all the employees? Oh, said one, they will all become bandits. Another said, There's no reason for that, they can pan for gold in the rivers—the rivers of the Philippines are full of gold.

The next morning we watched the local gold-panners for a while. They were not doing too badly, but there were few of them. This was not a gold rush area. It was in a section of the village which had been haunted by a wailing woman. Some years before, a pregnant girl had died and been buried there. After the hauntings, they dug her up and found that she had given birth after her burial. They had moved the grave and the hauntings ceased.

The military camp was situated in the schoolgrounds, so that the NPA would be unlikely to attack it by day. At the gate a young officer admitted under some pressure that there was a detainee, but of course we could not see him. He had not been tortured and he was eating the same food that they were. The officer was extremely reluctant to talk. As he did so, I noticed he had a twitching muscle below his right eye. He said that the mission of his men was largely political—it was to win the hearts and minds of the villagers here. We asked him if he was going to hand the detainee over to his superiors. 'Oh yes, we will do so,' he said, and then sneered, 'one of these days.'

The detainee's wife said the military had been very angry after yesterday's fact-finding. They wanted to know who had sent for these people, and she had simply replied she didn't know. (The nuns had warned her that she might get into trouble for reporting the case.)

What had happened was this. The thief had pinpointed the man who was now detained. The military had come to arrest him and found four other visitors in the house. The military had begun straight away to torture the detainee, whose father, seeing this, had tried to escape. He had taken his *bolo*, his long knife, and cut a hole in the roof of the hut in order to climb out. There had been a scuffle and one of the soldiers had been slightly wounded. As the father ran away, the soldiers shot him dead. The four visitors had also been arrested, but had since been released. There was nothing on them, not even the word of the thief.

The hut was a sorry affair. These people were obviously very poor. In the darkness sat the widow, the mother of the detainee. She was rigid with grief.

The Crossing

The crossing itself is nothing. That is, you hardly know when it has happened. It's not as if a uniform suddenly bobs up, or there's a roadblock to pass, or a document to be shown. I couldn't tell you where I crossed because I don't know myself. For all I knew, I had crossed and re-crossed more than once in the last few days. I didn't know, and wasn't interested in knowing, which of my new companions belonged to which sort of organization.

We laughed and joked. Children followed us and had a good look at the plastic bag of food and cigarettes I was carrying. They noticed that the cigarettes were locally made. We went through the porch of a church, then out at a west door, down a road to the water, where a boat was waiting. A well-dressed and handsome woman, who had joined the passengers, passed Matthew—the contact—a note. I tried not to watch the transaction. The note was written in a

The widow.

minute hand, and folded intricately, like a Japanese paper-game. In the shallows, before we came to the beach, a man stood strangely. I wondered if he was mad: his body jerked to and fro. But he was searching for shellfish with his toes. He was just a fisherman.

At the House of Pablo Rosario

'A message is being sent to the NPA,' said Matthew. 'They'll come soon. Would you like to visit the house of Pablo Rosario?'

We had just seen the place where Pablo Rosario had been shot in the days before the election. He had been in favour of the election boycott. We walked through the village and came to his fine stilted house, with its naturally polished hard plank floor. A man said, and said proudly, 'If Pablo Rosario had not been shot, these foreigners would never have come here.' Notebooks and a tape recorder were produced, and I listened to the story of Pablo Rosario's last days. A strange mood had come over me. I knew that I was in the house of a great local figure, among his sons and relatives. I knew that the death of the great man was fresh in their minds. And I could follow the account of the efforts of the local police and politicians—could just follow it—as they had tried to locate him, perhaps tried to intrigue with him, and had then decided to kill him. But I couldn't bear to ask more about the story than I was being told, and so I could not really understand the story. I wished the notebooks and the tape recorder had not been around. But it was too late for that.

Matthew said afterwards: 'You don't seem like a writer.' I asked him what a writer was supposed to be like. Well, I hadn't written anything down. No, I had not, and I had not produced my notebook. I find in such circumstances that producing a notebook has much the same effect as producing a gun.

We walked along a beach and I was asked again about Cambodia. I tried to explain what kind of fighters the Khmer Rouge had been. We were by a narrow river, and I pointed to the opposite bank. 'Imagine that we, sitting here, are the military, and the Khmer Rouge are in that field. I saw them once in a place just like this, and they were defending their foxholes. The military on this side had been calling in artillery, so the field opposite was exploding all over the place. Just here beside us there was an APC, and it was mounted with a recoil-less rifle. They were trying to shoot the Khmer Rouge out of the foxholes. If they aimed too low, the shells hit the water and bounced off into the air. If they shot too high it was useless. They also had machine-guns. There was a fantastic noise.

'On this side of the river there was a great crowd, civilians as well as soldiers. People were laughing and fooling around. Every now and then the Khmer Rouge fired at us with their AKs, and people used to throw themselves on the ground as if it was all a great joke. Our side was giving them everything they'd got. *They'd* clearly got only a few bullets left. And finally, one by one, they got up and tried to run for it. Their nerves had gone. And they would run through the field, zig-zagging like rabbits. Shells were exploding all around them, and I remember one of them had just reached the treeline when it exploded on him.

'All the time this had been happening, the people on this side, where we are sitting now, were shouting out to the soldiers—left a bit, right a bit, there's another one, things like that. Then one Khmer Rouge made a run for it and he was carrying his mortar-tube. He was running quite well, but he was so dazed he was going in the wrong direction, and he came right down to the river-bank before he saw his mistake. Most of the people had never seen a Khmer Rouge in their life. But this guy really impressed them, because they knew that none of the military would have bothered to carry a mortar with him when he was running away. But for the Khmer Rouge things like that meant *everything*.'

They were the bravest soldiers you could have hoped to have on your side, but the war drove them mad.

I had tried to impress upon Matthew what it would be like if full-scale war erupted in the Philippines, and if you had to fight with small against heavy arms. But he already had a sense of this: he had seen an area where bombing had taken place, although such events were exceptional in Luzon. I still could not banish from my mind, as I stared at the afternoon landscape, the thought of what it would all look like devastated.

When we got back to the house, the NPA were waiting for us. The women were very friendly, and I was amused to see that one of them was wearing a Mickey Mouse T-shirt. Comrade Nicky appeared shy on first meeting, and he remained in the background, talking to the villagers. There was also an eight-year-old boy, 'our youngest comrade'.

The conversation was slow at first. Somebody said that I had remarked that the NPA were more sophisticated than the Khmer Rouge. Why was that? asked the girls. 'Well, for a start, the Khmer Rouge didn't wear Mickey Mouse T-shirts,' I said. They looked puzzled. I *was* a puzzle to them. I was a bit of a puzzle to myself. Why did I want to know about the NPA?

I explained to them that most of the articles written about the Philippines began with the fact that the communists were now increasing in strength, and it was clear that the Americans were worried. To write about the place without having met the NPA would be a great pity. I'd managed to meet all kinds of people so far: I'd met a real crony, some goons, the loyal Marcos man, scavengers, nuns, seminarians, jesuits, a KBL mayor who had defected to the opposition, and an independent would-be mayor who had just joined the KBL. I'd seen remarkable events, but there was still one thing missing, and I didn't have much time left, unfortunately.

'But what do you want to know about the NPA?'

By now the large living-room of the house was filling up with villagers. It was difficult to talk in front of so many people. I said that the things I wanted to know would not be very complicated—the normal details of everyday life would be strange enough to me.

The life of the farmers, for instance?

Indeed, the life of the farmers.

By now an old man had occupied the centre of the room, and the discussion instead of being general turned into a rather formal interview. But the formality was rather enjoyable—it seemed to derive from the custom of the village rather than the difficulty of the occasion. The old man had been called upon, I thought, because this was the kind of thing he could and should handle best.

His manner when he began was at odds with his subject-matter. 'There is no justice,' he said resonantly, and a charming smile slid to one side of his face as he thought what to say next. He had worked hard all his life, he said, and now he was old and getting weak. And as he talked about getting weak, he giggled, and the villagers giggled, as if there really were something funny about old age and weakness. He told a story against himself, about how he had been told that some kind of chicken-feed was particularly good for giving old men strength, and how he had tried it a while before consulting a doctor, and how the doctor had laughed at him. He giggled again.

Then he gave us his view on doctors: they put you on pills in order to make you ill, before then giving you something to cure you. The point was, he concluded, that an old man like him was a fool. He had had no education. It had stopped because he had married young. Then he had had—I forget exactly—something like nineteen children. This again seemed funny. And then we got down to the reason why he was in a downward spiral.

His land was going from bad to worse. If he wanted to buy fertilizer, he would have to borrow at the beginning of the season. If he went to the bank, the rates were extortionate enough, but he would also need to pay a whole string of extras such as life insurance and legal fees before the money was forthcoming. If he went for a private loan, the extras were reduced. But the interest was phenomenal. If he borrowed one hundred pesos, he would have to pay back 250 at the end of the season say, three or four months later. He was in the grip of usury.

That was why, he said, there was no justice in the world. All one could do was trust in God.

Our host, also an old man, invited us to eat. He had provided a large meal, and it was prefaced with a long grace in Ilocano. During the meal, a very vigorous debate began in which the farmer who had been talking about justice started quoting chapter and verse of the gospels. The family was mulling over the evidence that the Last Signs had already been seen, and that the end of the world was at hand. The farmer turned out to be a convinced and well-educated Jehovah's Witness.

We talked quite a bit after dinner about the end of the world, and the Last Signs. Our host was not a Jehovah's Witness—'I'm just a Christian,' he said firmly—but he was a very good sparring partner for the farmer. They obviously knew each other's theology backwards. They discussed subjects like the class background of the disciples, how many of them were bourgeois and how many peasants.

'Are you a Christian?' our host said to me suddenly.

'No.'

'Do you believe in God?'

I thought I'd better come clean. 'No,' I said.

'If you don't believe in God then you must believe in science.'

'Yes, perhaps.'

'Do you believe in Darwin?'

'Yes.'

'Darwin said we are descended from monkeys.'

'Darwin was right to say so.'

The farmer smiled and giggled. Our host said very firmly: 'If you don't believe in religion at all, then there is no reason to discuss these things. *You* must now start a new subject and we will talk about that.'

There was a noise as if someone was clambering over the roof, and the whole house shook. People looked up momentarily. I asked what was happening. Oh, it's an earthquake, they said.

It was a very small earthquake, and I seemed to be the only person present for whom an earthquake was a novelty.

I tried to think of a good broad subject for debate.

I said to the farmer: 'Well, let me ask you a question. Who was the worst—the Spanish, the Americans or the Japanese?' The question was translated for the benefit of the packed room.

'The Spanish were the worst,' said the farmer, 'because they wouldn't let us read the Bible.'

Several people insisted that the proper form of the question was: who was worse—the Spanish, the Americans, the Japanese or the Filipinos? And more than one of them said: the Filipinos.

'But the Spanish were worse,' continued the farmer, 'because they killed José Rizal.' At which the young men laughed at him.

'The Japanese weren't too bad,' he went on, 'but they worshipped the sun. They did. I saw them. They worshipped the sun. The Americans were bad because they stole our independence after the Spanish, and they killed a lot of people'.

'But the Spanish friars also killed a lot of people. The Church killed a lot of people,' I said.

The farmer and our host laughed. It seemed I had secured a good debating-point.

Now it was time to leave. Our host said to me: 'You can't go without saying what you believe is the answer to the question.' But I wasn't sure what the answer was. I realized, however, that it was time for me to make a serious contribution to the debate.

I said: 'Well, let me say just this. I think the worst thing the Americans have done recently, but I'm only talking about recently, has been over this election. To push Marcos for reform, to insist on an honest election when he offered one, to watch people go out and risk their lives and actually get killed in the hopes of an honest election—and then to turn around and pretend nothing has happened—I think that's purely cynical. I think that what Reagan said about there having been cheating on both sides was absolutely wicked.'

As we prepared our baggage, one of the old men said: 'Where are you going now?'

'To the next barrio,' said the NPA.

Our host came up to me. 'I am the father of Pablo Rosario,' he said simply. There was a silence between us.

'I have heard about your son,' I said, 'and from what I have heard he was a fine man. He acted according to what he thought right, and that is all we can do. You should be proud of him.'

'Yes,' said the old man, coming as usual straight to the point, 'but he's dead.'

Moon and Farm

It was not quite true that we were going to the next barrio. We were instructed not to use our flashlights unless told to, and never to point them upwards. There was a full moon, and the trek along the paddy dyke presented no great problems. Nobody spoke. We passed some outlying houses, from which there came no sound. Then the path led us up into the hills. We followed a stream, and I began to regret that I had worn the rubber soles of my shoes quite smooth. We passed over a piece of open ground, where the NPA feared we might encounter a military patrol, then into the woods.

And now we really began slithering. One of the girls told us we might use our flashlights. The mud was not deep, but it was, well, muddy. I felt a complete fool, and was only cheered when I heard one of my companions falling over the way I had just done. I was carrying a shopping bag full of instant noodles—not a difficult task, one might have thought—and with my other hand I was trying to keep my sombrero on my head. Perhaps the sombrero had been a mistake. It seemed to make a terrific noise, brushing against the undergrowth. Nobody else was making the kind of noise I seemed to be making.

We left the track and scrambled through the undergrowth. We were among thickets of bamboo, handsome plants with stems three inches across. I swung on a few creepers to negotiate the mud. Then I abandoned that little experiment. Now we slithered down and around, and around again. I began to think: in a few moments we will arrive back at the house of Pablo Rosario. They've just laid this on as an adventure holiday.

Now we had come to a new stream with a bed of flat rock. The banks rose steeply on either side. It was quite enclosed. The leaders of the party began to call out in Ilocano: 'Moon! Moon!' And a voice called back: 'Farm!'

We climbed again, past a bamboo cooking hut of a kind I recognized from Borneo. From here there were steps cut into the mud, but they weren't much help to me. The soldier ahead offered his hand and hauled me up the steepest bits. At the top of the hill stood a smiling figure with a bandoleer and an M16. He was smiling at my exertions. 'Congratulations, comrade,' he said. We had reached the camp.

In the Forest

It was not a fighting unit, although everyone was armed. This was the propaganda unit's base camp. They spent most of their time in the barrios, and only came up here for periods of paperwork and for special meetings. The bamboo structures were not elaborate: there were no trenches or defensive positions and there was no stockade. The roofs of the huts alone told you something of the level of military activity to be expected in this area. They were made of plastic table cloths with flowered patterns. There was no attempt at camouflage. The air war had not reached here.

'Are you afraid to be here?' asked a soldier.

'Not in the least,' I said.

'But what if the military attacked?'

'I assume you know what you are doing and you would be able to look after us.'

The soldier considered this. He obviously wanted me to be a bit afraid, so that he could tell me there was no *need* to be afraid. But I wasn't going to give him this opportunity.

'But what if it was a really big attack?'

'I'm never afraid,' I said airily, 'when I'm among soldiers who know what they're doing. It's when people panic that I start to get nervous. The other day on the road, the military were in a real panic. That made me afraid because I didn't know what was going to happen next. But here, no.'

All this was translated back to the soldier. I'd stolen his lines and he didn't know what to say next. Coffee had been doled out and the NPA had made doughnuts in our honour. (It is said that in Mindanao the guerrillas have their own bakeries. Here the catering was modest but good.)

'Are you afraid when you go into battle?' I asked the soldier.

'No,' he said. Two could play at this game.

'What do you do, how do you prepare yourself before a really important fight?'

'I think of how what I'm going to do will further the revolution,' said the soldier. There was a little laughter among his comrades, as if this was slightly too glib an answer, too heroic.

'Do you say your prayers?'

'No.'

'Do you write a letter home?'

He had not seen his family for years.

'Is there some special, personal thing that you like to do before going out to fight?' This question was very difficult to put across. The soldier was shy anyway, and I could tell that he was trying to think what the correct revolutionary answer would be. Whereas I was trying to ask a question to which there would be no correct answer. I wanted to get him away from the rigmarole. 'I'm sure,' I said, 'that every soldier has some little thing he likes to do before a big fight.'

'There isn't time,' he said, 'there's so much to plan. You have to say to yourself: I must kill and not be killed. There are all the details to think about.'

I was so hoping for a small thing, an eccentricity or a superstition, that I didn't take him up on the big thing he had mentioned—which was of course the answer to my question. You have to get yourself into a killing frame of mind. Before he went into a fight he said to himself: It's either them or me. But how did he think about *them* in order to make himself really want to kill them?

Before they went on what they called a strategic offensive, the NPA normally had a cultural programme—songs, theatricals, speeches, a good meal and so forth. And after the strategic offensive there was another cultural programme, at which one of the important elements was a commemoration of those who had died, and an analysis of why they had died, what purpose their deaths had served.

I could see why they put such emphasis on this. The difference between the NPA and the military was that the NPA gave a meaning to everything in a soldier's life and death. They demanded enormous sacrifices, but if asked the purpose of these sacrifices would not be short of an answer. You don't have to subscribe to their aims in order to see that an army which has a clear idea of what it's doing is superior to one that doesn't. The military might say: But we're fighting communism. But if you asked them: On behalf of what are you fighting communism?—how many of them would have had an answer? The correct answer, in many parts of the country, would have been: On behalf of warlordism. The private soldier of a warlord does not have a *purpose* as a soldier. He merely has a feudal mentality.

To say that a soldier had an overriding purpose which gave meaning to every action in his life and death was not the same as to say he was a fanatic. The NPA I met were not fanatics at all. They were far too empirically-minded for that. In many ways they were ignorant of the world, but they knew that. They chafed against their ignorance. They wanted news. They wanted books. They even wanted advice.

I was saying: 'I don't see how you're going to manage the next stage. Let's say you manage to capture enough weapons to arm the 50,000 people you are supposed to have ready. In that case, the Americans will step up arms supplies to the military. You are going to need anti-tank weapons and missiles.'

'Yes, we know,' they said, 'where do you think we should get them?'

I didn't know. 'Still,' I said, 'people achieve amazing things with very little. I heard of a tribesman in Laos who aimed his crossbow at a helicopter and happened to hit the hydraulic system and—'

The soldier guffawed: 'Oh, that's just *Rambo*. It's impossible.'

'You've seen *Rambo*?'

Sure, they'd *all* seen *Rambo*.

'Where?'

'On the Betamax.'

'Betamax!' Somewhere in the mountains they had a Betamax. They'd seen quite a lot of films. '*State of Siege*' had made a big impression. They had film shows and then discussions afterwards.

'So what did you think of *Rambo*?'

'Super-incredible,' said the soldier. He'd obviously had a good laugh. I was beginning to wish I'd seen *Rambo* too.

One thinks of guerrillas as living thoroughly austere, remote lives. But of course, although these people spent much of their time in the mountains, they had comrades in the cities, and they sometimes went on leave to Manila. Some had their families there. There were facilities for conjugal visits. It wasn't as if there was one world of the jungle, pitched against another world of the wicked city. You had to think of the NPA as the kind of guys you might bump into at the Jollibee Yumburger in Quezon City or the Dunkin' Donuts in Cubao.

'Once in a blue moon,' said one of the girls, 'we have a party. Once in a blue moon. But then there's everything'— and she reeled off a list of drinks which ended with Gilbey's Gin. Then, she said, they would make their *own* Dunkin' Donuts, and if they forgot the baking powder they called them Tonkin Donuts (no reference to Vietnam—it meant 'hard doughnuts' in Ilocano).

I was finding it difficult to adjust my image of the NPA.

Suddenly I saw them all, in the remote Cordillera, with their feet up in front of the Betamax, watching *Rambo*, eating Dunkin' Donuts and drinking Gilbey's Gin. It sounded great. But where did ideology come in?

Actually it was rather difficult to pin them down ideologically. Their movement had its roots in Maoism, and much of the talk about the masses was what you'd expect from a Maoist group. But when you asked which authors they studied, the answer was really, or appeared to be, that they studied their own Filipino ideologues. They emphasized a Filipino solution to Filipino problems. Had I spoken to the Communists in Manila I might have got an entirely different impression. There was a large element of chance in this. But I was very intrigued to come across one guy who had only the vaguest notion of Ho Chi Minh, but knew all about General Giap. The NPA were an essentially self-financing organization, and they were not beholden to any foreign power. They were not in debt to Russia. They didn't have Cuban or Chinese advisers. The war they had fought so far was quite unlike anything in Indochina, because it was essentially still a guerrilla war, not a conventional war as Giap had fought at Dien Bien Phu. The reason I had asked what the next phase of this war might be was simply that, at the moment the NPA became dependent on some foreign supplier of sophisticated arms, their political character might congeal.

There was a theory that the NPA wouldn't need to enter a conventional phase of war in order to win the Philippines. It went like this. At the beginning of the struggle, the guerrillas had been hampered by the fact that they were spread over so many islands. But as their forces grew, geography would work in their favour. If they managed to develop evenly over the whole archipelago, they would tie up the military on a multitude of fronts. There would then be no possibility of operations on a divisional level. Suddenly there would be a co-ordinated uprising, in every city, on every island. The war would explode as if out of nowhere.

According to the NPA there was no shortage of volunteers. There were masses of people waiting to join, and it was the proudest day in your life when you were given your first pistol. After that, you might work for a while in a sparrow unit until you had earned or acquired your first rifle—another great day. Most of the rifles were

M16s, although any guerrilla would prefer an AK47. If for any reason you lost your gun, you would be in the doghouse for a year or so. It would be a terrible disgrace.

Every region was supposed to be responsible for arming itself—which was why the NPA really needed to have the military around.

'But isn't there a political problem for you, if you move into the area to recruit the masses and that is immediately followed by the military coming in and committing atrocities?'

Not at all, they said. People see the difference between the way they behave and the way we behave.

'What would happen if you captured something really sensational, like an armoured car? Would you hand it over to some central authority, or would you automatically keep it in your region?'

They said they would report the capture and they'd probably be told to store it away somewhere safe until such a time as it might be needed.

I said: If they were going to need an army of, say, 100,000 men, and the only way of getting weapons was by killing soldiers, they were going to have to kill an awful lot of their fellow Filipinos before they reached their target. They said: Yes, that was a problem, and that was why they much preferred to conduct raids on camps and depots. Daylight raids of this kind were the only occasions when the NPA wore uniform—they dressed up to look like the military, drove into a camp, were normally respectfully received, and then took the place over.

I asked a man who had been on such raids what they did to the common soldiers. He said that sometimes a private would point out the notorious officers. If they were people with a blood debt, they would be liquidated, but ordinary soldiers were not executed simply for being soldiers.

'So what exactly is a blood debt? If I'm an officer and I've led a successful raid against your camp and I've killed some of your best men—is that a blood debt?'

'No. Killing someone in battle is not a blood debt. Murder or torture of prisoners—that's a blood debt.'

'And I understand you also execute cattle rustlers.'

'Yes, if the masses want it. If we catch a cattle rustler, he will be tried by the village. If it's serious, he'll be executed.'

'Let's say I have stolen two carabao from a farmer. What's going to happen to me? I've been caught and I've confessed.'

'Oh, stealing carabao is very serious indeed,' said the soldier, and he drew his finger across his throat.

'But it was only *two* carabao!' I realized I had ianded myself in big trouble. In this part of the country carabao were considered a part of the family.

'If you stole a farmer's carabao, the farmer himself would probably hack you.' Meaning, he would get to carry out the sentence.

'I want a defence lawyer,' I said.

'The NPA would defend you.'

'I don't want to be defended by the NPA!'

The soldier smiled.

I said: 'OK, I'm going to conduct my own defence. It's true I stole two carabao. I admit it and I apologize for it. But I'm a poor man and my life is desperate. My village was hamleted last year. I lost everything. I have no money, no land, nothing. That's why I took to crime.'

'That's easy,' said the soldier. 'If your village has been hamleted, that must mean that we were in the region. So you tell us the name of your village and we will find out whether what you have said is true, whether you were an honest farmer or whether you were just a thief.'

Shit! I thought. I clearly didn't believe my own defence.

I asked about justice. Everyone had talked about justice, but it seemed to me that if you considered the legal and illegal opposition to Marcos as part of a united movement, they were having it both ways. On the one hand there was the demand for bourgeois justice in the courts—with habeas corpus and all the traditional rights of defence and an independent judiciary. On the other hand there was what we had just been talking about—revolutionary justice, village justice, based on a quite different set of criteria.

The soldier with whom I was speaking at the time could not see the problem, and the conversation turned uneasy—as indeed it did whenever we strayed into an area where there might be a real difference of position, or where a person was feeling inadequately briefed. The longest discussion in the two days I spent in the camp was over the American bases. I wanted to know precisely what the objections to the bases were. It seemed the crucial question for the future, and it seemed obvious to me that if there were any way for the Philippines to avoid a direct confrontation with the Americans in the future, it should be tried.

If the objection to the bases was that they guaranteed American interference in internal politics, would it not be possible, I asked, to negotiate a deal whereby the US presence was greatly reduced but not abandoned altogether? The Americans would still have their bases, would still be, as it were, denying them to the Russians. But they would be a token presence, and the size of the US Embassy staff would be severely restricted. What were the insuperable objections to such a scheme?

One of the big objections was that the American presence made the Philippines a nuclear target—and this was hard to deny. The ancillary objections were that the bases could be used in operations against other people's movements in South-east Asia.

'What other people's movements?'

The uneasiness began. 'In Malaysia, Indonesia, Thailand . . .'

I said that if they thought there was any chance for a communist movement in Thailand, after what had happened in Indochina, they were mistaken. It would be absurd for the NPA to risk battle with the Americans on behalf of communist movements which really didn't exist.

'Well,' they said, looking somewhat dismayed, 'they might start up again. And anyway it's not just communists . . .' I tried to say that anything was better than full-scale war. The NPA might take on the Americans, might even win against them, but the cost would be so prohibitively high that it would surely be better to decide precisely what was so unacceptable about US involvement in their country, and what would be—by way of compromise—a working relationship.

It was at moments like this that our conversation was least happy. A knowledgeable friend said afterwards: 'Well, you were asking the wrong people. The NPA would like to find any way to avoid a direct confrontation with the Americans, but this is not the

time for them to put forward a compromise formula, because nobody's asking their opinion on the matter.'

The NPA in the camp said, 'The matter is being discussed by the Central Committee.'

'Well,' I said, 'that's the answer to my question.'

Strong winds and heavy rain had kept us confined to our shelters, where we slept wrapped up in banners left over from a demonstration against the killing of Pablo Rosario. One of the villagers came up, bringing vegetables. We were safe from attack, because if the military had appeared in any of the nearby barrios a messenger would have been sent to warn us. The soldiers talked about the amount they had learned from the villagers. They were always trying to learn from them. When the early recruits had come from Manila, the first thing they had had to do was learn Ilocano. Now they enjoyed talking to the old men about their experiences fighting the Japanese. There were a lot of old bolo-men in the barrios, they said.

Comrade Nicky, whom I had guessed to be the senior member of the group, had spent the last day reading *Granta* 15. It was only just before I left that we struck up a conversation. Not only was he shy. He had not had a chance to use his English for several years. 'Excuse me,' he said, 'what is your class background?'

'Bourgeois,' I said, 'and you?'

'Upper petit-bourgeois,' he said.

It was always hard for me to understand the NPA conception of class. A soldier had claimed to be lower petit-bourgeois—his father had been a truck-driver.

'Did he own his truck?'

'No.'

In Comrade Nicky's case the term upper petit-bourgeois meant that his father had been a government official who was also a businessman, now retired and gone to live in Canada. 'My parents know what I am doing, and they accept it.'

Comrade Nicky and I had a friend in common, who had once worked in the same cell as he. They had been captured, tortured and imprisoned. I was to send her Comrade Nicky's greetings—they hadn't met for years. After his release he had been arrested a second time, but his false papers had saved him. His news to her was that he was married now. Conditions had been so hard for Comrade Nicky's wife in the mountains that she had had two miscarriages. Now she had a son, with whom she lived in Manila. They saw each other from time to time—she came up here, he went down to Manila. One of the things he missed was books. In Manila he had a book on Nicaragua, but he wanted to read anything about what was going on in the world. He pointed to the issue of *Granta* and said: 'Those people in Vietnam and Cambodia—do you think they have a better life now?'

It was a point on which I could give him no reassurance at all. He shook his head and said: 'It's the Russians.'

Comrade Nicky was not the kind of man who blocks his ears to bad news. I thought he had a very clear idea of what he valued in life, and a strong sense of the difficulty of achieving it. He spoke very simply of his own sufferings, and without bitterness. And as for the future, it held no glib solution.

One More Thing

Fred and Helen and I were about to split up. I had an errand in Baguio. After that, back to work in London.

'You look troubled,' said Fred.

'Wasn't the trip good?' asked Helen.

'Oh, the trip was good,' said Fred, reading my thoughts: 'If you've had something to think about—that's good. If you're troubled it's good.'

We'd just heard the news that a congressional panel had voted to cut off military aid to Marcos. But there had been no planes from Manila that day and we couldn't get hold of the latest papers. I knew that there was enough military aid in the pipeline to last for a little while, but I knew too that the military would eventually have to ditch Macoy. I was sorry to be leaving. But Fred was quite right that I was also troubled.

He himself had a lot to think about. That evening as we were lying on our beds he said: 'I seem to have got ahead of my schedule.

I thought I'd be here a couple of years. But I've proved I've got courage and guts. I've proved I can do it. Maybe now I'll go and try to work in Manila.'

It was obviously a good idea. He might even be able to marry.

'Do you have enough for your article?' he asked. 'You said you'd have enough if only you got to see the NPA.'

'Yes, I've got plenty to describe,' I said, putting the bottle of Andy Players to my lips and mentally holding my nose (for it is a truly awful drink). 'I'd just like one more thing.'

'One more thing?' said Fred. 'What sort of thing?'

'That's it. I don't know. Just one more thing to round it off.'

Photo: Associated Press

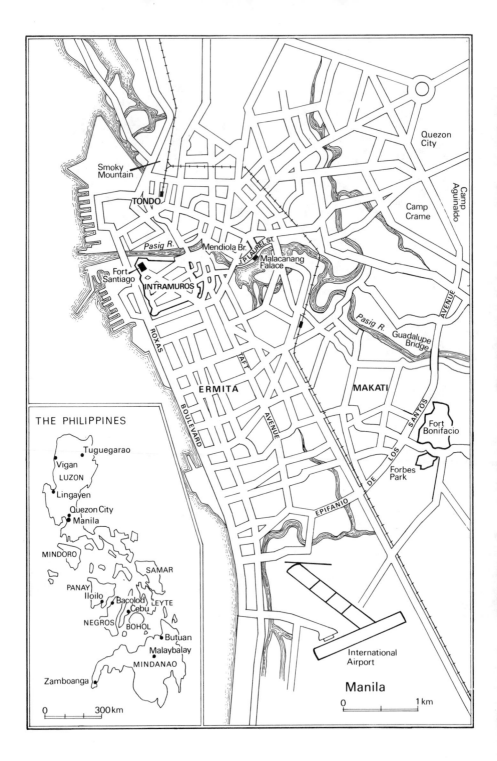

Smoky
Mountain

TONDO

Pasig R.   Mendiola Br.

Fort
Santiago

INTRAMUROS

J.P. LAUREL ST.

Malacanang
Palace

ROXAS

Pasig R.   Guadalupe
Bridge

TAFT

ERMITA

AVENUE

MAKATI

Quezon
City

Camp
Aguinaldo

Camp
Crame

AVENUE

BOULEVARD

Fort
Bonifacio

DE   LOS   SANTOS

Forbes
Park

EPIFANIO

International
Airport

Manila

0   1 km

THE PHILIPPINES

Tuguegarao

Vigan

LUZON

Lingayen

Quezon City

Manila

MINDORO

SAMAR

PANAY

Iloilo

Bacolod

Cebu

LEYTE

NEGROS

BOHOL

Butuan

Malaybalay

MINDANAO

Zamboanga

0   300km

III

THE SNAP
REVOLUTION

Marcos Detects a Plot

When it happens, it happens so fast you can't believe it's happening, and only afterwards can you truly catch up with your perceptions and your emotions. It began on a Saturday and ended the next Tuesday, and I doubt that there was anybody in the Philippines who really felt abreast of events. I wasn't. I was in Baguio when the Minister of Defence Juan Ponce Enrile and the Chief of National Police General Fidel Ramos, having supposedly learned that they were about to be arrested, took refuge in the Ministry of Defence at Camp Aguinaldo. And even the next morning I wasn't quite sure what to make of the news. 'You see what I was saying last night,' said a friend, 'Enrile could be the next president.' We wondered whether Philip Habib, Reagan's latest envoy to the country, had tipped him the wink.

But if it looked like a coup it also looked ominously abortive. Ramos and Enrile were holed up with a small number of men. It sounded as if they were scared as well as cornered. Ramos had said: 'I am calling on the people of the world to help us restore decency, justice, freedom and democracy in this land. There is no justice, no decency, no real freedom, much less democracy in this helpless land. Nobody has indicated any help to us. We are going to help ourselves even with our bare hands.' He had fought for his country, he said: 'I don't have plenty of medals but the hour of reckoning is here and now for me. When you serve your country you have to take risks. Anyway, if I die tonight or tomorrow, Mr Marcos will also die some day. He has no immortality, but at least my heart is clean.'

Enrile has spoken about a hit list which had been drawn up at Malacañang, a list which, according to a report in the London *Times*, featured 3,000 people. The opposition was going to be arrested and liquidated. In withdrawing his support from Marcos, Enrile claimed that in his own region, Cagayan Valley, the KBL had cheated by some 350,000 votes. When asked whether Marcos might reimpose martial law, Enrile had said bitterly that martial law had never been abolished. This was all very striking, coming from the administrator of martial law himself.

111

But it did seem as if very small numbers of soldiers were as yet involved, and it seemed unpromising that it was only after rebelling that the two men had begun to bring arms into the Ministry of Defence.

Also unpromising was the fact that I was due to leave the next day.

I took a taxi to Manila, and the driver insisted on bringing a friend. This man had served in the army, and he knew the military along the first stretch of road. With him in the car, we were less likely to have to bribe our way. These back-handers to the military were nothing to do with the immediate political situation. The problem was simply that the soldiers were in the habit of stopping a long-distance driver and demanding to see his licence. If money was not forthcoming, the soldier would claim some irregularity in the documents and inform the driver that he could pick them up by reporting at such-and-such a place on such-and-such a day. It had happened to me on the way up to Baguio, and it happened again on the way back. You could see why the military were held in such low esteem. For the commercial traffic taking vegetables down from the highlands, bribery was also a fact of everyday life. The farmers who grew the vegetables knew that supplies of fertilizer were in the hands of a monopoly, which kept the price artificially high. The network of bribery was much like the old system in the Mekong Delta. This was how the military earned their perks.

On Sunday evening, when I got back to my room, Marcos was giving a press conference on television. Rows and rows of generals and officers were lined up behind him, demonstrating their loyalty, while Marcos was explaining there had been a plot against his and Imelda's lives. A young colonel, Marcelino Malahacan, was presented before the press, and stutteringly explained that his intention had been not to kill the president but to hold him. The belief of the conspiring officers had been that 'this is the only option left to save the republic from bloody confrontation.'

The colonel blinked and stammered through his confession. I supposed he must have been tortured. What he was actually saying, though, in front of Marcos and in view of the whole nation, seemed immensely brave, because it was surely what vast numbers of people believed. Whereas all Marcos was saying, by putting him on display, was: if you try to rebel against me, this is what will happen to you.

I phoned England and arranged to postpone my return. Then Helen came on the line. She had spent the night at Camp Aguinaldo. Cardinal Sin had called the people out on the streets to form a human barrier to protect the rebel troops, and the crowd had responded with enthusiasm. Now there were tanks waiting to attack, and there was artillery in place and—hold it, she had to go, the tanks were just about to attack again. 'Helen, where *are* you?' I pleaded. She gave me instructions and rushed off to the fray.

By the time I reached the scene, there were no tanks and no attacking troops. Camp Aguinaldo and Camp Crame lay on either side of Epifanio de los Santos Avenue—known as EDSA. This was one of the major urban motorways in Manila, and now it was blocked off by the crowd, which had already swelled to hundreds of thousands. It was really impossible to judge. The Church was out in force. The Cory supporters were there, as were Bayan's—for by now the two had a common purpose. The soldiers manning the perimeter walls of the camps said that all was calm. They were in good spirits. People had brought them food and cigarettes. There were barricades of singing nuns, statues of the Virgin and the Santo Niño, hot dog stalls, but no soft drinks to be had for love or money. It was a festive vigil. To see the soldiers treated as the heroes of the crowd was a novelty for me, and obviously something of a novelty for them.

Late that night Marcos came on the television again, and whereas in the previous press conference he had maintained a gelid calm, now he was angry and almost out of control. It was now clear, he said, that there had been an attempted coup on the part of Enrile and Ramos, and we were not to imagine this was in order to make Cory president. This was a military grab for power which was to eliminate both him and the opposition.

Now Marcos was ranting. 'Some people say the President is incapable of enforcing the law. Let them say that once more and I will set the tanks on them. If they think I am sick I may even want to lead the troops myself to wipe out the Enrile–Ramos group. They may say I'm sick, but I am just like an old war-horse, smelling powder and getting stronger. I have all the power in my hands to eliminate this rebellion at any time we think enough is enough. I am not bluffing. I am telling Enrile and Ramos, if you do not listen to my pleas for discussion let the blood fall on you.' At another moment he said that Cardinal Sin was 'spouting all kinds of sedition' but 'we'll attend to that later on.'

He looked very angry indeed. Whether he looked dangerous I wasn't quite sure.

Maximum Tolerance

'Marcos,' said the taxi-man the next morning, 'is in Guam.'

'Bullshit,' I replied. 'I saw him on the television late last night. About one-thirty. He can't be already in Guam.'

'It was probably a recording,' said the taxi-man. He was the type I would normally have assumed to be working for the secret service.

'So where did you get this information?'

'Oh,' he said conspiratorially, 'military sources.'

He tuned in to the rebel radio. Unconfirmed reports, said a voice, have it that Marcos has been seen arriving in Guam.

'I think we'd better go to Malacañang as quickly as possible,' I said.

The radio was exhorting the people at Mendiola Bridge to be patient. Somebody would be sent as soon as possible to negotiate the removal of the barricades. 'We've waited for this twenty years,' said the voice, 'we can wait another twenty minutes.'

All the cars were sounding their horns in celebration. I thought: maybe it *was* a recording—it was in a studio, no identifying features. The noise barrage increased. The taxi-man was in a good mood. He was right and I was wrong. We reached the point on J.P. Laurel Street where you have to walk to get to the palace.

The soldiers at the gates were wearing white arm-bands. Journalists had been asking them what these were for, but the soldiers weren't talking. Everyone looked faintly shifty. I met an old colleague I'd last seen in Korea. 'You've heard of course,' he said, 'Marcos is already in Guam.' He had some more convincing details. We asked the commanding officer if we could come in. By now a small crowd had gathered and the soldiers were getting nervous. They moved us gently back down the street as a couple of limousines came in through the gates.

Then a very confident journalist arrived and said to the commanding officer: 'General Ramos has called us to a press conference here. Perhaps you will let us through.' The man let us through and through we rushed.

'What was that?' we asked this fine man.

'Oh,' he said, 'I made it up. I was just bullshitting him.'

Something very odd was happening. Where the vegetable garden had been (it had been planted on Imelda's instructions, as part of some pet scheme), they were now laying a lawn. And the sculpture garden too—all the concrete statues were being smashed and carried away. The workers watched us as we passed. There were tanks by the next gate, and the security check was still in operation. 'It's extraordinary, isn't it,' someone said, 'the way they keep going on as if nothing had happened. That platform—they must have been told to put it up for the inauguration. Now Marcos has gone and they're still putting it up.'

As we came through security, a voice began to speak over the public address. It was giving instructions to the military to confine itself to the use of small arms in dealing with attacks. It was outlining Marcos's supposed policy of the whole election campaign— Maximum Tolerance.

'Whose voice is that?' I asked.

'It's Marcos. It must be a recording.'

We ran up the grand staircase and turned right into the ante-room. And there sat Marcos himself, with Imelda and the family all around him, and three or four generals to the right. They had chosen the ante-room rather than the main hall, for there were only a few journalists and cameramen, and yesterday's great array of military men was nowhere to be seen. I looked very closely at Marcos and thought: it isn't him. It looked like ectoplasm. Like the Mighty Mekon. It was talking in a precise and legalistic way, which contrived to sound both lucid and utterly nonsensical. It had its left hand under the table, and I watched the hand for a while to see whether it was being deliberately concealed. But it wasn't.

So Marcos was still hanging on. Indeed he was back in his calm, lawyer's frame of mind. I remember somebody asking him whether he was going to go ahead with his inauguration the next day, as planned. Marcos replied that it was his duty to do so, as laid down by the constitution. The inauguration had to take place ten days after the proclamation by the National Assembly. If he'd been pressed any further in the matter he would have started quoting acts and statutes. That part of his brain was functioning perfectly. The bit that wasn't functioning, it appeared, was the bit that should have told him the game was up.

At first I felt embarrassed, as if I had been caught red-handed by Marcos, trespassing in the palace. Then I felt embarrassed because, there being so few pressmen around, I might be expected to ask the president a question. And I couldn't think of a thing to ask. People hovered around the microphone, and whispered to each other, 'D'you want to go next?' Very few people did. One journalist actually went to the side of the room, sat down and buried his head in his hands, as if overwhelmed by the irreality of the occasion.

General Ver was quivering and in an evident panic. I wondered whether his gums had swollen. He stepped forward and asked for permission to bomb Camp Crame. There were two government F-5 jets circling over it, he said. (Just outside the palace someone had told me that the crowd at Camp Crame appeared to think that these jets were on their side, for they cheered every time the aircraft came over.) Marcos told Ver they were not to be used. Ver's panic increased.

'The air force, sir, is ready to attack were the civilians to leave the vicinity of Camp Crame immediately, Mr President. That's why I come here on your orders so we can immediately strike them. We have to immobilize the helicopters that they got.' (Marcos had sent helicopter gunships against the camp, but the pilots had come out waving white flags and joined the rebels.)

Marcos broke in with tired impatience, as if this had been going on all through the night and he was sick and tired of Ver. 'My order is not to attack. No, no, no. Hold on; not to attack.'

Ver was going wild. 'Our negotiations and our prior dialogue have not succeeded, Mr President.'

Marcos: 'All I can say is that we may have to reach the point we may have to employ heavy weapons, but you will use the small weapons in hand or shoulder weapons in the meantime.'

Ver said: 'Our attack forces are being delayed.'

The *Christian Science Monitor*, at my elbow, said: 'This is absurd. It's a Mutt-and-Jeff act.'

Ver said: 'There are many civilians near our troops, and we cannot keep on withdrawing. We cannot withdraw all the time, Mr President.'

All this was being broadcast live on Channel Four, which Marcos could see on a monitor. Ver finally saluted, stepped backwards and left with the other officers. I forget who they were, just as Marcos, when he introduced them to us, had forgotten all their names and needed prompting. Now the family withdrew as well.

An incident then occurred whose significance I didn't appreciate at the time. The television began to emit white noise. A soldier stepped forward and fiddled with the knobs. The other channels were working, but Channel Four had been knocked off the air. The rebels had taken the government station, which Marcos must have realized. But he hardly batted an eyelid. It was as if the incident were some trivial disturbance, as if the television were simply on the blink.

For me, the most sinister moment of the morning had been when Marcos said that if the rebels continued they would 'be chewed up by our roaming bands of loyal troops.'

Someone asked why the troops at the gate were wearing white arm-bands. They had said, he told Marcos, that it meant they would surrender to the rebels.

Marcos explained that this was not so. The arm-bands were a countersign.

A soldier in the audience said that the countersign was red, white and blue.

The questioner then said, 'No, these were plain white arm-bands.'

Marcos said, a trifle quickly, 'The colours are changed every day.'

Somebody asked him whether he was going to leave the country. 'No,' he said, 'as you can see, we are all still here.' And as he said these words he turned round to discover that there was absolutely nobody standing behind him.

I thought: Kapuściński has scripted this. I looked around for him. It was like his account of the fall of Haile Selassie, only speeded up so that what had taken a year or so—a gradual elimination of the court—seemed to be happening in seconds. There were soldiers in the audience, but they seemed unusually pensive. Imelda was now standing at the side, talking quietly to some journalists. I went over, but again, when I reached her, I was completely stuck for a question. When asked about when she would leave, she looked in the direction of her husband and said: 'You'd better ask him.' One of my colleagues must have spent the last two nights at Camp Aguinaldo. He stank of old clothes, and I noticed the moment when Imelda smelled him, turned up her nose and decided enough was enough: she was going to leave the room.

I met up with Bing, who had been photographing the whole occasion. We walked out together in a daze. It was the first time Bing had seen the inside of Malacañang, and it was all too much to take in. The disappointment that Marcos had not yet left, coupled with the gradual realization that the rebels were on the offensive, made the moment extremely hard to comprehend. We tried to solve the mystery of the countersign and the allegiances of the palace guard, but the man we spoke to was simply close to tears. From the gate, a broad, empty avenue led down towards Mendiola Bridge. There were soldiers there, and water-cannon. Beyond the barricade stood the crowd.

The soldiers started firing into the air. Bing threw up his hands, waved at the soldiers and shouted, 'Hey, you guys, wait for me! Wait for me!' And he ran down the centre of the avenue towards the gunfire. I followed him at a more leisurely pace, sticking to the side of the street. When we were at the barricade, and order had been restored among the crowd, I heard behind me, from the direction of the palace, a kind of popping sound that seemed familiar.

It was a helicopter gunship taking a pot-shot at the presidential quarters.

People's Power

'So it's true,' said Helen, sombrely.

'I swear it.'

'Did you actually get to see him?'

'I was practically within spitting distance. And Imelda was there too. I was so close I could even tell you what perfume she was wearing.'

Now I could hear Helen at the other end of the line, telling Jojo the bad news. Up in Quezon City they had all thought the press conference had been a fake. We agreed to meet up at Camp Crame in the afternoon.

I put down the phone. 'So what does she wear?' said the receptionist.

'I'm sorry?'

'You said you could tell what kind of perfume Imelda wears.'

It was true. I had been lying. 'Guerlain,' I said, and then kicked myself. I should have said Poison.

Helen and Jojo were sitting on top of the Camp gates. I was hoisted up to them by the crowd. So much had happened since I had last seen Jojo that we hardly knew where to begin. 'I've got something to tell you, Jojo: there's been a revolution.'

This seemed to me rather a witty remark at the time. As far as you could see, EDSA was jammed with people. They were all listening to the rebel radio for the latest news. Everyone had been called out onto the avenue, and it had taken me hours to get up here through the traffic. It was said that four miles of broad motorway were crammed full of people, and I could well believe it. How many people were involved? Four million? Five million? Ten percent of the population of the Philippines? Or more?

Helen had had no sleep. 'I'm revolutioned out,' she said. She seemed miles and miles and miles away.

Jojo pointed out that the soldiers were wearing their shoulder-patches upside-down, which was the sign for revolution. We wondered where we should be next. Cory had said that she would come to Camp Crame, but there was also talk of fresh Marcos troops advancing from a place called Guadalupe. Perhaps General Ver was still trying to get through the crowd to kill the rebels.

We went out the back of the camp and found a taxi. As we drove off to Guadalupe, Jojo pointed to a small building in the camp and said, 'That's where I was tortured.' I didn't say anything. The remark had been very off-hand.

The roads from Camp Crame were by now so well barricaded with nuns that it was almost impossible to get out, but eventually we found our way down to a stretch of the Avenue where the attacking soldiers were supposed to be.

Their vehicles were pointed in the wrong direction and they were well and truly stuck in the crowd. I went up to the officer in the first jeep and asked him what was happening. He was rather tight-lipped. All they wanted to do, he said, was go back to their base at Fort Bonifacio. But the people wouldn't let them. As he said this, the soldiers in the back seat were making Laban signs at me. The crowd had given them bags of bread rolls.

The officer seemed to think the people were being thoroughly unreasonable. But what could a mere four truckloads of them do against all these millions? People were coming up and cheering them and saying: 'You are our brothers. You're Filipinos like us.' Jojo asked one soldier whom he supported.

'I don't know,' he said. 'I'm confused. We have two commanders, Ramos and Ver. We don't know which to support.'

We went to the next truck. Jojo asked a soldier: 'Are you confused? You seem to have two commanders.'

The soldier said: 'No, I am not confused. We have only one commander.'

Jojo said: 'So which is your commander—Ramos or Ver?'

'I don't know,' the soldier said.

These men had been brought in from Mindanao, and they were supposed to be pretty ruthless types. One of them said: 'I just want to go back to Zambo.' (Zamboanga.) They were absolutely loaded down with bandoleers of bullets. They had machine-guns—they had everything—and they were entirely nonplussed. At the back of the stranded convoy sat one such soldier, visibly teetering on the edge of defection. A man came up to him and said, 'Here, take my watch, take it as a souvenir. Please, go on. We are all Filipinos and we

shouldn't kill each other.' The soldier was terribly embarrassed. It was a gold watch and the man had tears in his eyes. Only yesterday I had seen my taximan bribing a soldier just like this one. This gesture of the man's was like an honest bribe. It was half sordid, half heroic. The crowd told the soldier to take the watch, but the soldier could only shake his head. If he was going to come over to the people, he couldn't come over on a bribe. The gesture was a rebuke to him. It said so much about the relationship between the military and the people.

And it was part of the genius of the Filipino revolution that it moved forward on simple gestures like this. It was essentially a confrontation between a cynical and a heroic view of the national character. Marcos had opted quite openly for cynicism. Filipinos, he had said, both before and after polling day, were great ones for joining bandwagons. And he had calculated that the right expenditure would achieve this effect. There was really nothing covert about his operation: everyone had known what the deal he was offering amounted to.

Opposed to Marcos were the people wearing T-shirts with Ninoy Aquino's slogan: 'A Filipino is worth dying for.' Their approach was essentially idealistic. If Marcos said, But Cory is a completely inexperienced politician, this cut no ice at all, because Marcos had already defined what a politician is. Nobody wanted a politician any more. They wanted heroism. Marcos had always said that he had been a hero. But nobody believed that story any more either. They were fed up with brothel-politics.

Marcos was terminally out of touch. That evening, in another weird press conference delivered over the radio and (without pictures) on one of the remaining crony television channels, Marcos was asked whether there would be a curfew. 'Now you come to mention it,' said the dictator, who had already declared a state of emergency, 'I hereby declare a curfew.' It was to last from six p.m. to six a.m. But what about night-workers? asked the crony interviewer. Oh, they would be OK, as long as they could explain themselves.

I have never seen a curfew more blithely defied. This was the kind of curfew where you have dancing in the streets, the kind of curfew where people camp out rather than obey the curfew. More

people were out and about during that curfew than on any other night of the revolution.

We returned to Camp Crame, having heard that two thousand Marines were on their way up a certain street, with bayonets fixed. Helen was now completely zonked. Jojo and I left her in the car and went to investigate. In order to get past the human barricade you had to walk along a tricky wall with a deep drop on one side, and it was typical of the organization of these barricades that there were people with flashlights in place to make sure that no one fell and was injured. We reached the relevant place, but discovered that the news, like much else that day, had been an exaggeration. Some Marines had been along, been turned back and had *threatened* to return with 2,000 men with fixed bayonets. That was all. I no longer believed in these famous Marines.

Further down the road, a mere fifty yards, was a military camp of engineers. We went to the gate and asked for the commanding officer, who told us that their instructions were to remain in the base and do nothing. That was what the general had said. But whom, we asked, did the general support? The officer could not say. He wished us well and bade us goodnight.

It wasn't hard to see what was happening. You only had to turn to the liberated Channel Four, where news of the defections was being relayed by Enrile and Ramos. You could see soldiers arriving in the studio and announcing they had joined the rebels. They gave their names, ranks and class year. This business about class years was very important. It was as if you were watching Sandhurst or West Point changing sides, in the intimacy of your hotel room. The great news was that the Philippines Military Academy *itself* had gone over, and this was considered the most significant event of the day.

It was very fascinating but I was very tired. I left the revolution running, and flopped onto the bed.

Opposite: a soldier defects and joins the rebels at Camp Crame.

James Fenton

Rival Victors

At four-thirty a.m. on 25 February, June Keithley, whose efforts on the rebel radio had earned her the complimentary title of General, came on Channel Four to tell us to get up, say our prayers and go out on the streets to prevent any dawn raids on Camp Crame or Channel Four itself. 'Remember,' she kept saying, 'the darkest hour is before dawn.'

I wasn't sure that I believed in these notional dawn raids, but it seemed wise to check. I roused a sleeping taxi-driver and set forth on the rounds.

Nothing at Mendiola Bridge. At J.P. Laurel Street, where the Marines had fired over the heads of the crowd during the night (slightly wounding two people), all was calm again. Channel Four appeared well-protected by the crowd, although I think some tanks had been turned away. The nuns' barricade by Camp Crame was still perfectly in place, candles burning. One of the defenders told me how a car full of goons had tried to pass, and he had spoken to them and convinced them to turn round. 'Nice guys to talk to,' he said, '*with your balls in your throat.*'

Manila was quiet. The 2,000 Marines with their fixed bayonets had not materialized. The crowds had been able to sleep on EDSA, among the litter and the stench of urine. At six o'clock they all stood up, and prayers were broadcast from the loudspeaker vans. Everyone remained rigidly at attention, and at the end of the service we all raised our hands in the Laban sign and sang '*Bayan Ko*' once again. By now I almost knew the words, but I had only the vaguest idea what they meant. Strange then that there was one particular line that always brought tears to my eyes. I had been utterly gripped by the mood of national aspiration.

After the service came the by-now routine announcements on the radio about the deployment of nuns and seminarians around the city, an appeal for wine and large hosts in one quarter, paper cups in another. Today Cory was to be inaugurated as President. And today also, although the radio did not bother to mention it, Marcos would be sworn in at the Palace. Ideally I should have liked to cover both ceremonies.

126

Cory had chosen to hold her inauguration at the Club Filipino in Greenhills, apparently a place with nationalist associations, but also symbolic to most people of the rich exclusive society to which she belonged. The rebel military, it was said, had wanted her to hold it at Camp Crame, which for many would have acknowledged her debt to the crowd, but for others, might have made it look as if Enrile and Ramos had taken over her movement. It was important to emphasize that she had won the election first, and that they had finally acknowledged this.

So Enrile and Ramos came to the club, along with the elder statesmen and the architects of her victory, and a multitude of Cory-clones in elegant but simple dresses and simple short hair-dos. There were two kinds of hair-do among the ladies of standing in Manila. There was Cory style and there was Imelda style. Looking around the room, I noticed that only one Imelda-clone had secured an invitation to this exclusive gathering.

I suddenly thought: this is absurd, I'm in the wrong place. What on earth is the point of standing behind a bank of cameramen listening to the ceremony, when I shall be able to hear it on every car radio in the street? I had to phone Helen and get down to the palace.

I left the ballroom and found a phone by the poolside. As I was dialling, a voice came through. 'Mr Lopez here. I want to know whether I can have lunch.'

'I'm sorry, Mr Lopez. I can't help you.'

'Give me the receptionist.'

'She's not here.'

'I want to check my lunch reservation.'

The place was swarming with rebel soldiers.

'Mr Lopez,' I said, 'could you call back in an hour?'

'Give me a waiter,' said Mr Lopez. I was getting desperate. Helen had said she would await my call.

I replaced the receiver and tried to dial again. But Mr Lopez kept coming through. His telephone technique was obviously better than mine. 'What's happening there?' he asked crossly.

'Oh, there's a revolution, Mr Lopez. I wonder if you could—'

'My lunch.'

He had every right to his lunch, and I had no right to use the phone. So we fought.

Back at J.P. Laurel Street, the road one normally took to Malacañang, the Marines were under orders not to let any journalists into the palace. A crowd of street-urchins had gathered to taunt the 'sip-sip' brigade (the arse-lickers or cock-suckers— translations were various) who were being brought in by jeepney for the inauguration. The limousines were arriving as well, ferrying in the loyal elements of the upper military echelons.

The journalists were disconsolate. We pleaded with the commanding officer to let us through. Around us the crowd were managing to turn away several of the vans full of Marcos supporters, and when anyone came out from the direction of the palace they were jostled and jeered at mercilessly. This was not a nice sort of crowd to be on the wrong side of.

A few moments later we were let through. Along J.P. Laurel Street, there were dumpy ladies with Marcos badges, who were saying things like: 'No one paid us to come. We are real Marcos supporters. It's you foreign press who have ruined everything, meddling in our country.' People were in tears and very angry.

Then someone with a radio said: 'Imelda's started to speak.' And we ran, as somebody shouted from the pavement: 'CIA.'

When I got through the palace gates I saw that the new-laid lawn was already dry and shrivelled. Lunch-boxes were being unloaded from trucks. People had planted their Marcos flags in the lawn in festive clusters. We ran down past the sculpture garden, which had been almost completely dismantled, and through the gates to where the crowd had assembled.

As I moved among them, people nudged each other and pointed to the fact that I was carrying the radical opposition paper, *Malaya*. It was one of a bundle, but there was no way of concealing it now. If I was seen concealing it, that would make matters worse. I could hear the scandalized reaction of the crowd. Many people came up to me, saying that no one had paid them to attend—this was for real. I suppose there were 5,000 of them, and where there was not anger there was a frightening mixture of levity and menace. People offered me flags to wave or badges to wear. I couldn't stand the thought of taking them. So I kept laughing back at them, as if the occasion was indeed all part of a great joke.

On the platform stood a very fat, short fellow with a loud hailer. He was singing snatches of song, apparently anything that occurred to him, and then shouting a few slogans or making jokes, whipping up the crowd. For his rally Marcos could still get a small crowd of T-shirted supporters, but he couldn't lay his hands on any pop-stars. Instead there was simply this grotesque, possibly mad, individual, trying to raise a good noise for the ageing dictator, whipping through 'My Way' at triple speed. Who was he? The palace cook? A torturer? An expert ballot-stuffer?

I and the other journalists had made our way to the platform, and now we were ordered to sit together on one side. Great, I thought, I can sit on *Malaya* and somehow lose it. Then we were told to move further back, and as soon as we had done so they made us get up and move to the other side. Back and forth, up and down we went, obeying the insane instructions with as much good humour as we could manage to feign. A friend said to me: 'It feels like being a hostage in Iran.' I wished he hadn't said it. We were issued with Marcos badges in a very meaning way. I thought: if I throw *Malaya* away, they'll see that I read the *Inquirer*. If I throw the *Inquirer* away, they'll see that I read the *Manila Times*. I hadn't got a single crony news-sheet.

The people in the crowd had been at pains to point out that no one had paid them to attend, and yet, when they saw the chicken-dinners being handed out at the other end of the grounds, whole sections of them detatched themselves and ran off. Maybe they were not all such convinced fascists.

'Martial law!' they shouted, when Marcos appeared on the balcony with Imelda and Bongbong and the rest. 'Martial law!' 'Catch the snakes!' was another slogan, meaning, Get Enrile and Ramos. But the strangest of their cries, to English ears, repeated over and over, was 'Give us back Channel Four!' We didn't then know that, while the Marcos inauguration was just beginning to be broadcast and as the commentator from inside Malacañang was saying, 'And now ladies and gentlemen, the moment you have all been waiting for,' the rebels had knocked them off the one remaining television channel available. Marcos had no broadcasting facility left. He had only the balcony and the crowd. And he must have known this as he came out to us. We were his last audience.

Photo: Jeanne Marie Hallacy

He looked somewhat puffy and less unactual than the day before, less like the Mighty Mekon. He could still rant—and he did so—but there was less power in the baritone voice. You felt that the members of the audience were carrying him along, rather than he exerting his power over them, and this sense of a man faltering in his performance was underlined by Imelda at his side. She was acting out her emotions again, as she had done the first time I saw her, and today's emotion seemed to be: Look what they've done to him, the dear, great old man. Had they no pity? Had they no loyalty? Had they no memory of his greatness?

Marcos's idea had apparently been that this would be his answer to People's Power. People's Power, he said, was for the rich, but he had always been the champion of the poor. Imelda's idea was much the same. It was said that one of the forbidden topics in Malacañang was *Evita*. To William Deedes, who had once made the comparison, she had said: 'Well at least I was never a prostitute.' But here she was in her long white dress, the figure of glamour, the focus, she always felt, of the aspirations of the poor. And when she gave her speech, and the audience began to sing her song, she languidly took the microphone off the stand and led the final encore. The song was called 'Because of You'. For the Marcoses and their faction it was the second national anthem. When they came to the final bars, Marcos himself joined in, froglike, for a few notes. The conjugal dictatorship embraced before the crowd.

Imelda's dress had a slit up the back, and, somewhat inelegantly from our point of view, she reached into this slit for a handkerchief. She dabbed her eyes. She blew her nose (rather too loudly). She looked again at the crowd with a look that said: My *people,* oh my *people,* you are the ones who have always supported us, you are the ones who have always understood. Marcos was gently helped from the balcony, but Imelda gave a version of not being able to bear the thought of leaving the crowd. She came back to the microphone and said words to the effect that at least there was still some spirit among the Filipino people and she would never forget them.

People had indeed been weeping. Valediction was in the air. As for the press, I think we all thought the sooner we got out of this place, the better. We were the enemy as much as Ramos and Enrile,

Photo: Peter Charlesworth

the CIA, the NPA and the rest. As we walked back to the barricades along J.P. Laurel Street, the limousines and jeepneys were leaving the palace, and when we reached the crowd outside it had grown appreciably nastier. Before, they had banged the cars with their hands. Now they began stoning them. Those who left Malacañang on foot were really made to run the gauntlet, which they did defiantly and in a furious temper. The dumpy, angry ladies; the aged goons; the young bloods—they were all in for a bad time. But they kept their badges on and they were ready for a fistfight if provoked.

In the crowd, people seemed to be working themselves up to that point where they could kill a Marcos supporter. There was much the same mad jocularity as there had been at the inauguration.

A boy who had been threatening one of the departing goons turned to me and said: 'He—he—he very very bad man.'

'Who is he?' I said.

'I don't know. Just very very very bad.' And as he said this, a shiver ran down his body that was so strong it lifted him in the air. I'd never seen anything quite like it. He took off from the pavement on a little rocket of disgust.

'We've Beaten Poland!'

Fred and I were trying to think what the next thing would be. As far as we could tell, the only thing left was Malacañang. The rebels were going to have to move in and take it at some stage, and it seemed extraordinary that nothing had been done about it so far. We were in my studio at Boulevard Mansion, not far from the US Embassy. It was dark. Helicopters came over. 'That's the Americans taking Marcos,' said Fred. I didn't think so. A kind of slack wisdom told me to say: 'Have a look if they're twin-bladed. If they're Jolly Green Giants, it's the Americans.' (I was back in Saigon.)

So Fred ran to the end of the corridor to look from the fire-escape, and then I thought I'd better do the same, and the fire-door swung shut behind me and we were trapped on the stairs. By now I was beginning to think Fred might be right again. The helicopters were definitely coming from the direction of the US Embassy. But it took a few minutes to get us back into the building.

Jojo was on the phone from nearby. He had heard that the marines at Malacañang had suddenly said there was no point hanging around any more and they were going back to barracks. We'd better get round there quickly, before the crowd moved in. I phoned Helen at home in Quezon City. It would take her half an hour to get down, and I told her we'd meet her in J.P. Laurel Street.

The noise barrage was on again. Everyone must have suspected that this time Marcos really had gone. We cursed the taxi-man for his slowness and argued about the best way to the palace. There were two ways of approaching J.P. Laurel Street, and Jojo had chosen the nearer end. Then as we crossed the river, Fred saw a helicopter coming from the Palace towards the Embassy, and he wanted to photograph it. 'Oh Fred it's not a photograph. It's just a tiny fucking helicopter in the moonlight.' I doubt if Fred will ever forgive me for losing him that shot.

Jojo led us down some darkened streets, past a few youths with sticks on their way to the palace. He was right. We got right to the gates very quickly, but we soon realized that we were in the wrong crowd. It was the Marcos crowd. The remainder of the thugs who had attended the inauguration were now, in the absence of soldiers, manning the gates. We knew that some of them had guns. Others were carrying great lengths of wood for clubs. A journalist at the gate asked to be let in and was told fiercely, No, that it was foreign press who were to blame. Nobody knew what was happening. We explained to the by-standers that Marcos had left by helicopter and the Marines had gone home. 'Let's get into the palace,' said one youth, 'there might be some money.'

The thugs were panicking. I could see it in their eyes, and I could see Jojo seeing it as well. These people were angry and scared and they were very likely to take it out on us. Some of them thought they were going to be killed, and indeed as we stood there a horribly battered body was brought through the gates. Others apparently believed that Marcos had left the Palace and its treasure for them, and their job was to defend it. Others no doubt just could not believe that Marcos had walked out on them, and I feared their disappointment very much. I knew from what I had seen earlier that day that the Cory crowd fighting their way along J.P. Laurel Street were not the pacifists of EDSA and Camp Aguinaldo, but street-urchins, the rabble. If we were to go in with the rabble, I wanted to be with the friendly, not the hostile rabble.

Jojo agreed, but it was very hard to convince Fred. His courage and his guts were on the line. To go away now, even in order to come back right away, seemed unthinkable. 'Listen, Robert Capa,' I said furiously, 'if you want to take great photographs you've got to stay alive. Just for a bit.' He smiled.

There was a terrified young man who said: 'Look, I'm neutral. I don't support either side. Can you get me out of here? I only came today because they said there was going to be food.' He'd been after those chicken dinners.

'Come with me,' I said.

'And my friends? Can they come?'

'How many friends do you have?' I said, drawing a breath.

His friends emerged from the shadows, boys and girls, five or six of them. We agreed to stick together. We walked down the middle of the road towards Mendiola Bridge, where a large crowd was waiting but was held in check by the nuns and seminarians praying at the front. I could see the barricades were by now almost denuded of their barbed wire. No one was manning them. We slipped down a side-street and ushered the chicken-dinner brigade to safety.

By now Fred was going wild with frustration, but we finally made our way to the other end of J.P. Laurel Street, which the Marines had indeed abandoned. And now the crowd was moving down towards Malacañang. Here too people were carrying sticks, and some of them held bits of plywood over their heads. You could see the stones flying at the front of the crowd. Fred made a bee-line for the action. Jojo told me, if we were pushed back, to jump into a front yard and stay out of the way. Then he too was off.

I had no interest in being stoned. There were gunshots too, and plenty of firecrackers. The eerie thing about the front of the crowd was the way it was marked by flashing lights. It took me some time to realize that this was where the photographers were concentrated

Photo: Jose A. Duran

with their flashes. It looked like an electric storm, but with the wrong sound-track. After a while we were halted. The Marcos men were holding their ground very well. Indeed we were being forced slightly back.

I took shelter in a side-street with a few others. As I did so, I heard a voice in my skull saying: *He made the classic mistake, during a street-fight, of taking refuge in a cul-de-sac; then he was cut off and hacked to death by enraged thugs.* Where had this belated wisdom come from? People leaned out of an upstairs window and shouted to us to wait. The rebel army was sending some soldiers to establish order. I examined the gates in the street for one I might climb in a hurry. The crowd on J.P. Laurel Street were still being pushed back. The side street had a left turn, but when I investigated it people said: 'It's a dead end.' They didn't want me to go down near their houses.

Then a man who lived at the dead end told me there was a wounded KBL supporter who needed help. We went down together. The street ended at a small canal, pretty much a sewer. The man showed me where he had seen the KBL guy being beaten up by the crowd. He had called out to him to wade across the canal, which he had done with difficulty. The man had helped wash him and had put alcohol on his wounds, but he had nasty gashes on his head and back.

I told the KBL guy that I would try to get him out. He emerged with difficulty from the house, saying 'No ID', by which I presumed he meant that he was not wearing any Marcos paraphernalia. His possessions were in a plastic bag, which I took. He was clutching a walkie-talkie and holding his head with his other hand. He had obviously been very badly mauled.

We walked to the turning, where I immediately saw that what I had feared had happened. The Marcos thugs had beaten back the crowd, and we were cut off. We could see them throwing stones and wielding their clubs. I was back on the wrong side of the action.

A gate opened to my left and someone stepped out for a look. I pushed the wounded guy into the front garden, and followed him, to hear a voice saying: 'Close the gate. Oh, you stupid! Look! You, get out!'

'This man is badly wounded,' I said. 'He needs help.'

The man resisted for a moment, and then said crossly: 'All right, it's a humanitarian act.' So we got indoors, which was nice.

Nicer still, there was a doctor in the house. Nicer than that, there was a beer for me. We sat in a hall at the foot of the stairs, while the doctor gave first aid, tying the man's hair in little knots over the wounds so that they would close up. I was impressed by the determination with which the man held on to his walkie-talkie. The owner of the house said: 'Hmm, a Motorola, the most expensive. What do you need that for?'

'To talk to my friends,' said the wounded man. We gradually realized that what we had here was a goon, but a goon in such sorry shape that it seemed unfair to ask him point-blank: Are you a goon?

Then the house-owner saw the plastic bag and said: 'Who brought that in?'

'I did,' I said, 'it's his possessions.' He looked at the bag as if it was about to explode.

'It's probably loot,' he said.

'I think it's just his clothes.' It was only then I wondered whether the bag contained a gun.

Shots were fired outside, then the battle had subsided. It was obvious the soldiers had arrived and taken control. I thought: And now I *have* missed it. Fred would be in the palace with Jojo and Helen and all the gang, and I'd miss it. And when they said: But what *happened* to you? I'd have to say I was looking after a goon.

The houseowner and I went out into the street. All was quiet again. He had a glass of whisky in his hand. He had been celebrating. 'You don't realize,' he said, 'how deep this goes. Nobody will call us cowards again. We've done it. We've had a peaceful revolution. We've beaten Poland.'

I thought at first he was talking about football. Then I realized he was the first guy who had drawn the comparison which had been regularly in my mind for the last few days. The nationalism, the Catholicism, the spontaneous organization, the sheer power of aspiration—that's what Poland must have been like.

The goon was all patched up and the houseowner gave him his taxi-fare. When we got back onto J.P. Laurel Street we found the statue of the virgin in place in the road, and a barricade of praying nuns. I tapped a nun on the shoulder and handed over the goon. As we said goodbye he smiled for the first time.

James Fenton

Back to Malacañang

Well, I thought, if I've missed it all, I've missed it. That's that.

I turned back and walked down the centre of the road to Malacañang, my feet crunching broken glass and stones. I asked a policeman whether he thought it safe to proceed. Yes, he said, there were a few Marcos men hiding in the side-streets, but the fighting had all stopped. A child came running past me and called out, 'Hey Joe, what's the problem?' but didn't wait for an answer.

As I came within view of the palace I saw that people were climbing over the railings, and just as I caught up with them a gate flew open. Everyone was pouring in and making straight for the old Budget Office. It suddenly occurred to me that very few of them knew where the palace itself was. Documents were flying out of the office and the crowd was making whoopee. I began to run.

One of the columnists had written a couple of days before that he had once asked his grandmother about the Revolution of 1896. What had it been like? She had replied: 'A lot of running.' So in his family they had always referred to those days as the Time of Running. It seemed only appropriate that, for the second time that day, I should be running through Imelda's old vegetable patch. The turf looked sorrier than ever. We ran over the polystyrene boxes which had once contained the chicken dinners, past the sculpture garden, past where people were jumping up and down on the armoured cars, and up onto the platform from where we had watched Marcos on the balcony. Everyone stamped on the planks and I was amazed the whole structure didn't collapse.

We came to a side entrance and as we crowded in I felt a hand reach into my back pocket. I pulled the hand out and slapped it. The thief scurried away.

Bing was just behind me, looking seraphically happy, with his cameras bobbing round his neck. We pushed our way through to a kind of hall, where an armed civilian told us we could go no further. The journalists crowded round him, pleading to be allowed a look. The man had been sent by the rebel troops. He had given his word of honour, he said. He couldn't let anybody past. But it was all, I'm afraid, too exciting. One of the Filipino photographers just walked past the guard, then another followed, then Bing went past; and finally I was the only one left.

I thought: oh well, he hasn't shot them, he won't shoot me. I scuttled past him in that way people do when they expect to be kicked up the backside. 'Hey, man, stop,' said the guard, but as he followed me round the corner we both saw he had been standing in the wrong place: the people in the crowd had come round another way and were now going through boxes and packing-cases to see what they could find. There were no takers for the Evian water. But everything else was disappearing. I caught up with Bing, who was looking through the remains of a box of monogrammed towels. We realized they had Imelda's initials. There were a couple left. They were irresistible.

I couldn't believe I would be able to find the actual Marcos apartments, and I knew there was no point in asking. We went up some servants' stairs, at the foot of which I remember seeing an opened crate with two large green jade plates. They were so large as to be vulgar. On the first floor a door opened, and we found ourselves in the great hall where the press conferences had been held. This was the one bit of the palace the crowd would recognize, as it had so often watched Marcos being televised from here. People ran and sat on his throne and began giving mock press-conferences, issuing orders in his deep voice, falling about with laughter or just gaping at the splendour of the room. It was all fully lit. Nobody had bothered, as they left, to turn out the lights.

I remembered that the first time I had been here, the day after the election, Imelda had slipped in and sat at the side. She must have come from that direction. I went to investigate.

And now, for a short while, I was away from the crowd with just one other person, a shy and absolutely thunderstruck Filipino. We had found our way, we realized, into the Marcoses' private rooms. There was a library, and my companion gazed in wonder at the leather-bound volumes while I admired the collection of art books all carefully catalogued and with their numbers on the spines. This was the reference library for Imelda's world-wide collection of treasures. She must have thumbed through them thinking: *I'd like one of them*, or *I've got a couple of them in New York*, or *That's in our London house*. And then there was the Blue Drawing Room with its twin portraits of the Marcoses, where I simply remember standing with my companion and saying, 'It's beautiful, isn't it.' It wasn't that it *was* beautiful. It looked as if it had been purchased at Harrods. It was just that, after all the crowds and the riots, we had landed up in this peaceful, luxurious den. My companion had never seen anything like it. He didn't take anything. He hardly dared touch the furnishings and trinkets. We both simply could not believe that we were there and the Marcoses weren't.

I wish I could remember it all better. For instance, it seemed to me that in every room I saw, practically on every available surface, there was a signed photograph of Nancy Reagan. But this can hardly be literally true. It just felt as if there was a lot of Nancy in evidence.

Another of the rooms had a grand piano. I sat down.

'Can you play?' said my companion.

'A little,' I exaggerated. I can play Bach's Prelude in C, and this is what I proceeded to do, but my companion had obviously hoped for something more racy. Beside the piano stood a framed photograph of Pham Van Dong, and beside the photograph lay a letter. It was a petition from members of a village, asking for property rights on the land they lived on. It was dated well before the Snap Election. Someone (Marcos himself? The letter was addressed to him) must have opened it, seen it was a petition, popped it back in the envelope and sat down to play a tune. The keys were stiff. I wondered if the piano was brand new.

A soldier came in, carrying a rifle. 'Please co-operate,' he said. The soldier looked just as overawed by the place as we were. We co-operated.

When I returned down the service stairs, I noticed that the green jade plates had gone, but there was still some Evian water to be had. I was very thirsty, as it happened. But the revolution had asked me to co-operate. So I did.

Outside, the awe had communicated itself to several members of the crowd. They stood by the fountain looking down at the coloured lights beneath the water, not saying anything. I went to the parapet and looked across the river. I thought: somebody's still fighting; there are still some loyal troops. Then I thought: that's crazy—they can't have started fighting now. I realized that I was back in Saigon yet again. *There* indeed there had been fighting on the other side of the river. But here it was fireworks. The whole city was celebrating.

Bing emerged from the palace. We decided we must see the crowds coming over the Mendiola Bridge. The experience would not be complete without that. And besides we were both hungry. Somewhere must still be open.

We had grown used to the sight of millions of people on the streets, but there was something wonderful about this crowd, noisy but not mad, pouring across the forbidden bridge. Imelda's soothsayer had got it slightly wrong. He should have said: When the crowds pour over the Mendiola Bridge, that will mean the regime *has already* fallen, not that it is about to fall. Still, that error was minor. The man had been right in broad outline. Many members of the crowd were wearing crowns of barbed wire. Bing snapped out of his dream. 'And now,' he said, 'now they will begin to crack down on the Communists. Now there'll be a real crackdown.'

We went down a dark, quiet street in the university area, found some food and started chatting to others who had been at the palace. They had taken boxes and boxes of ammunition. We sat out on the pavement. I said to one guy: 'Congratulations. You've just had a real bourgeois revolution. They don't happen very often nowadays. You should be pleased.'

He said: 'If it's a bourgeois revolution, it's supposed to bring in socialism.'

I said: 'You read Marx?'

He said: 'No! I read Lenin!' Then he laughed, and said he was only joking. But I didn't think he was joking, actually. He said: 'Cory's a rich woman and a landowner. These people aren't the good guys. You come back for the next revolution. The next revolution it'll be the NPA. The next revolution it'll be the Reds!'

Bing took me to find a taxi, and we said goodbye. He couldn't resist it: he had to go back to the palace. The taxi-man had a linguistic habit I had never come across before. He could survive without any personal pronouns except I, me and my. 'Well James,' he said, as I got in, 'have I been to Malacañang?'

I thought for a moment.

'Have I been to Malacañang, James?' he repeated.
'Yes,' I said. 'I have been to Malacañang.'
'Has Marcos gone?'
Yes, this time he really had gone.
'Marcos is a good man, James,' said the taxi-man, 'but my wife is very bad. Yes, James. Marcos is a good man. But my wife is very bad.'
'Yes,' I said, finally understanding the rules, 'my wife is very bad indeed.'

That Morning-After Feeling

'How did you get on last night, Helen? I heard you'd had a nasty experience.'

'It was horrible, all those thugs—did you *see* the way they beat up the Marcos guy? They weren't Cory supporters. They were just—and the way they were shouting "We're free, we're free." That wasn't free-*dom*. That wasn't a liberation. Nothing's happ-*ened*. Nothing's changed. It was brutal. I hated it. And I hate this job. It's not human.'

Helen had indeed had a nasty experience, and she was still having it now, in the foyer of the Manila Hotel. The look of blank panic had returned to her eyes. She had come looking for us along J.P. Laurel Street and had reached the front of the crowd. Then somehow in the course of the fighting she had got among the Marcos thugs. When things had got really dangerous, she had hidden in a kind of shed, but the thugs had spotted her and knew she was inside. They thought she was a Filipino and a Cory supporter. They thought she was a man. And because her voice is deep and she was calling out in perfect Tagalog, the more she protested, the less they believed her. 'They were firing at *me*!' she said. 'They were firing at *me*!'

Finally, to convince them she was a photographer and not a rioter, she had thrown her camera out of the shed. They told her to come out, and as she did so they began grabbing at her and feeling her up. After that she detested everything she saw, and the friends she met up with were disgusted too. They had seen only idiocy on the rampage. At the old Budget Office, for instance, people had been burning papers, and one man was shouting: 'These are precious documents about Marcos. You're destroying precious evidence.'

One thing at least had changed, however, and we could see it from where we were sitting. The body-searches at the hotel front door had been stopped.

Sitting at our table was a politician who had supported the Aquino campaign and who was now fuming: there had been no consultation with the UNIDO members of parliament about the formation of the new cabinet. He himself, he said, had told the Aquino supporters that he did not want a job. But they would find that they needed the co-operation of the parliament to establish the legitimacy of their new government. Parliament had proclaimed Marcos president. Parliament would therefore have to unproclaim him before Cory could be *de jure* as well as *de facto* head of state. She could have a revolutionary, *de facto* government if she wanted. But in that case her power was dependent on the military. She would be vulnerable. The politician was haunted by the fear that corrupt figures would again be put in key positions, and that the whole thing would turn out to have been some kind of sordid switch. The television announcers were congratulating the nation on the success of People's Power. But all three of us at the table were wondering how real People's Power was.

The previous night, Enrile had made a most extraordinary speech on the television. It had come in the form of a crude amateur video. It looked, in a way, like the plea of some kidnap victim, as if he were being forced to speak at gun-point. And what he had said was so strange that now, the morning after, I wondered whether I had dreamed it. So far I'd not met anyone else who had seen the broadcast. Enrile had begun, as far as I remember, by saying that Marcos was now in exile, and that he, Enrile, was sorry. He had not intended things to turn out this way. But he wanted to thank the President (he still called him the President) for not attacking the rebel soldiers when they first went to Camp Aguinaldo. At that time (and here I am referring to a partial text of the speech) 'The military under his control, or the portion of the military under his control, had the fire-power to inflict heavy damage on us.' But it did not do so. 'And for that alone, I would like to express my gratitude to the President. As officers and men of the Armed Forces of the Philippines, we want to salute him for that act of compassion and kindness that he extended to us all.'

I asked Helen and the politician whether they had heard this, and they hadn't. By coincidence, at that very moment, the television in the foyer broadcast an extract from the speech. The politician was shocked. 'He's only been gone a few hours, and already the rehabilitation has begun.'

I then tried out my theory on the others. When I had woken that morning, the theory was there, fully formed, in my head. In a way I had been quite startled to find it there, so complete and horrible. The theory went like this. We had all assumed that Marcos was losing touch with reality. In fact he had not lost his marbles at all. He had seen that he had to go, and that the only way out for a dictator of his kind was exile. The point was to secure the succession. It could not go to General Ver, but Marcos was under an obligation to Ver, and therefore he could not hand over the presidency to anybody else. In some way, whether explicitly or by a nod and a wink, he had told Enrile and Ramos: you may succeed me if you dare, but in order to do so you must overthrow me and Ver. You must rebel. If you do so, the bargain between us will be: I protect you from Ver, and you protect me; if you let me go with my family after my inauguration, I will permit you to rebel. Marcos was writing his legend again, and the legend was: he was the greatest president the Philippines had ever known. Then his most trusted son, Enrile, rebelled; Marcos could easily have put down the rebellion, *but he still loved his son, he loved the Filipino people and he could not bear to shed their blood.* It was a tragic and dignified conclusion.

The theory explained why Marcos had shown himself, on the television, overruling Ver. It explained why there had been so little actual fighting. And it explained the striking fact that no rebel troops had been brought anywhere near the palace until after Marcos had left.

I asked the politician what he thought, and his first reaction was: 'It's too clever.' But then you could see the theory, with all its ramifications, getting a grip on him, until he said: 'My God, I hope you're wrong.' Helen was prepared to believe the theory. When I put it to Fred, he brooded over it darkly. His own theory that day was slightly different. 'It was scripted,' he said, 'the whole thing was scripted by social scientists.' His idea was that this was a copy-book peaceful revolution designed to be held up to other countries all around the world in order to dissuade people from taking up armed struggle.

One way or another, the people I met the day after Marcos left were incapable of trusting the reality of the events they had witnessed. Not all of them believed the theory, but very few of them could muster a concrete argument against it. It was absolutely possible to believe that, instead of joining the revolution, Enrile and Ramos had hijacked it. And everyone was clearly still in the habit of believing in the genius of Marcos, however much they hated him.

Of course by now it looks different. We know that the flight of Marcos could not have been a clever fix, because the question of Marcos's wealth was obviously so badly botched. But still one could argue that the theory contains a core of atavistic truth. We know that Enrile, after he joined Cory's camp, continued to think of Marcos as President. We know he felt he had to make a tribute to Marcos's 'compassion and kindness'.

The son saw that he had to kill the father. The father saw the son preparing to kill him. And he knew that this was inevitable. He knew that he had to die.

Intramuros

I realized I still hadn't the slightest idea of historic Manila. I hadn't looked at anything old. I hadn't done the sights. Instead of beginning with history and working forwards, as one might expect to do, I'd gone straight into the thick of things. My feet had hardly touched ground. And now, like Helen, I was revolutioned out.

The taxi-man offered to show me round Fort Santiago, the Spanish bastion defending the old citadel of Intramuros. He must have been a bit revolutioned out himself, for he didn't talk much, and I appreciated his silences. He said that the waterlilies in the moat were beautiful. I agreed with him. Then he pointed towards the river and said something about shooting. Since I hadn't heard any shots, I thought he was talking about somebody making a film.

We climbed the walls. On a quay by the river below us, a small crowd was gathered. 'There,' said my driver, 'you see the body.' A ferry was coming in to land, dragging a corpse beside it through the water. Somebody called to ask whether it was a salvaging, but it turned out that some gangsters had knifed a security man before pushing him into the river. Criminal life was back to normal, as was the stock exchange. The peso had rallied. The banks were functioning.

The driver pointed to a warehouse which he said belonged to one of the richest men in the Philippines. I wondered where *he* was today. The richest man I had met here, Mr Florendo, was reported to have done a bunk. We looked over the parapet. Children were sniffing glue. On a stretch of waste ground, beside a packing-case house, a man was soaping himself. To the north lay Tondo, beyond view, and Smoky Mountain. But there were scavengers everywhere around town.

Fort Santiago was where the poet, novelist and national hero José Rizal was imprisoned before his execution in 1896. I wondered whether numerologically-minded Filipinos had noticed that it was now 1986. Marcos's lucky number was seven. He had chosen the seventh for the election, and the twenty-fifth (two plus five) for the inauguration. But the Cory-Doy ticket had seven letters too. He had been out-sevened.

'The Spanish were the worst. They killed José Rizal,' the farmer had said. And people had laughed at him. I walked round the little museum to the poet's memory, with its touching exhibition of the clothes he had worn in Europe. It was in Europe first, not in America, that the Filipinos had sought the ideas on which they founded their claim to nationhood and independence. It was from reading Voltaire and Schiller and Victor Hugo. I'd just been reading as much in the newspapers. They may quote you Jefferson or

Abraham Lincoln, the article had said, but really it is to Europe that they look. There *was* something thoroughly romantic about the Filipinos. I thought of Chichoy saying: 'People like me do not live long . . .' I hoped on that point he would now be able to change his mind.

Another famous prisoner of Intramuros was Ferdinand Marcos. Or so a little placard claimed. He had been put here in a dungeon by the Japanese.

I wondered whether that was true. And how long the placard would remain in place.

Granta Gives a Beach-Party

'I'm fine,' said Helen, 'I was just a bit shaken up yesterday.'

'You'd had a nasty experience. You should realize that. These things take some getting over. Bing had this idea we should all go to the sea for a couple of days. Have a rest. I thought *Granta* might throw a beach-party.'

The reaction at the end of the phone was good. Helen's thoughts were racing. A friend of hers from California had a round hut on a beach up north. It was empty, and we were welcome to use it any time. 'There's just this strip of beach, and the fishermen come up and sell you fish in the evening,' said Helen. Everything started shaping up wonderfully. Helen's old room-mates, Esperanza and Caridad, would join us, plus Bing, Fred and Jojo. 'And don't forget Pedro.' I said. 'Remember you took me to his party the first night.' Then Jojo's mum suggested that she might come along to do the cooking, and if she came Jojo's aunty might come to keep her company, and then—if this was all right—there might be . . . I was beginning to get lost in the intricacies of Helen's friends and relations. There was a man with a jeep nearby who had offered it for a bargain price for the weekend. Everything was set.

Alas, when the jeep arrived to pick me up, Bing was missing. After a sleepless week, he had dosed himself with Valium and was now catching up on his dreams. Fred too had been mysteriously called away. But then it turned out that Helen's old room-mate Esperanza had to bring a bodyguard. She had a Chinese lover who didn't know she smoked; *he* couldn't accompany us yet, because he would be gambling in Manila: but if he sent his bodyguard with her, he would know she was not getting up to anything wrong. The Chinese lover would arrive with his other bodyguards later, and all would be well.

We drove off in what I, by now, knew was the wrong direction. Helen's old room-mate Caridad had another room-mate to whom she had lent some money, but who had not paid up, and Caridad had been obliged to pawn her jewellery. This she had to redeem at once, or all would be lost. We drove to the pawnshop, then back along EDSA, where it was difficult to believe that there had once been barricades. By the time we arrived to pick up Helen, she was triumphant: I was so late. It seemed so out of character for *me*. Eventually the fifteen of us set off for the north.

I felt a bit guilty as we stumbled over the dunes late at night, and woke up the caretaker of the hut. We were unannounced. He was asleep and his wife was pregnant. But later I learned that the caretaker did not enjoy his solitude. The hut had a balcony running all round it, and he told us that quite often the ghosts came and wandered round and round. They were always hearing this wailing woman. Once the caretaker had established that we were not ghosts, we were welcome.

In the meanwhile, Bentot, the driver, had had a secret quarrel with Esperanza. He wanted to be paid extra if he was going to take Esperanza to meet her Chinese lover when he returned from gambling. So Esperanza gave Bentot the slip, and Bentot panicked. He naturally assumed that she had been kidnapped by the military and raped, or this is what he led us to believe. Then Bentot had an idea: he would take Caridad with him to look for Esperanza. Caridad was scandalized. If she went off in the dark with Bentot, her reputation would be ruined. *Ruined.* She appealed to me. I said that if she wanted to go off with Bentot none of us would think the worse of her. Bentot was by now so preoccupied with luring Caridad away that I guessed he didn't really think that Esperanza had been raped. He pleaded with Caridad before the company. He told her it didn't matter if they went off together because his wife was old and ugly.

Every time Bentot made a remark like this, Caridad gave him a scandalized riposte and then flashed her dentures in my direction. I knew she wore dentures because I had found her washing them over a sink full of seaweed. I told her I thought Bentot was a man of honour—which was not what I thought, and not what she thought I thought either. Caridad took all this in good part.

When Esperanza's Chinese lover eventually arrived on the second morning of the beach-party, with two more bodyguards and the look of a man who expected the world to arrange itself around him, Esperanza produced the bundle of live crabs she had set aside in his honour and boiled them up. Helen, disgusted, went off to the sea.

Esperanza was a strange girl. She came from a rich family but lived with Caridad at the YWCA. She was a trained nurse, but unlike Caridad she wasn't working any more. In the old days, when a patient had died in the hospital, the two girls would note the number of the patient's bed, then rush down to the *jai alai* and bet on it. Her lover, being of a rather grand Chinese family, was unable to marry her. But he had bought her a house and installed two servants. Esperanza had refused the deal. She continued living in the YWCA, sending out for food at midday, reading comics, coming alive in the evening and then hitting the gambling dens with her lover. Her parents were supposed to know nothing about all this, but she was beautiful and had refused many suitors and the parents must have guessed something. You can see that her friend Helen and she were rather different types.

Esperanza laid the cooked crabs before her lover, who sat with his three burly chums away from the rest of us. I was called over to join them. After the crabs, the lover snoozed, with Esperanza draped over him.

Helen returned: she loved the breakers, but pronounced them to be dangerous. She loved the sun, but it was harsh on her skin. On the first day she stayed out too long, doing her TM, which she never had a chance to do in Manila. That night she had sunstroke. The next day she stayed out too long again. 'I had a fev-*er*,' she said.

'I know you had a fever, Helen. You gave yourself sunstroke. But I've decided by now not to get between you and your self-destructiveness.'

'So I'm the one who is self-destruct-*ive*?' said Helen. But she smiled as if she quite liked the idea.

Caridad was slicing pork for the barbecue, and mixing it in the marinade of soy and *calamansi* juice. There was a seaweed salad. There would be tuna and *lapu-lapu* and all good things. We had two crates of San Miguel beer, and we genuinely believed the boycott was over. Jojo's relations were preparing meal after meal.

I said to Jojo: 'You remember when we drove past Camp Crame, and you pointed out where you had been tortured. What happened?'

When they had come for Jojo in his house, the soldiers had been quite ruthless. From the way they stuck a gun in his aged grandmother's face, he had known that they wouldn't scruple to kill. They almost had killed the old woman. When they took Jojo and his fellow students to Camp Crame, they had beaten them up and tortured them for several days. They had a photo of Jojo in his martial arts outfit. 'So you're a martial arts expert,' they would say, smashing him in the chest with a rifle butt. They had tied electrodes to his hands and feet, but when they tried to get his pants off to do the same to his genitals, he had resisted, said, No, and held on to his pants. So they hadn't persisted, although they perfectly well could have done, and although they had done so to his two friends.

'What did you tell them?'

'I tried to tell them all the details they knew already, everything that was public. I stood for election in the students' association and got so many votes and the other candidates got so many votes. Things like that.'

'Were you tempted to give them false information, just in order to have something to say?'

'It's very, very tempting, and you mustn't do it. If you tell them where to find somebody, and then they take you along and he's not there, they'll kill you.'

'Did you give in, and tell them things they actually wanted to know?'

'No.'

'How did you manage to resist?'

'One thing is, after a while, you become so angry. But the other thing you have to remember is that, if you do start confessing and giving information, when they've finished with you they'll kill you. Your only chance of survival is to tell them nothing at all.'

As Jojo talked, and was filled with remembered anger at his torturers (who were known to have been involved in other salvagings), his voice turned thin and quiet. I'd known him now for four weeks, and I could see that there was a great survival value in never raising your voice in anger. When Jojo was in danger or a passion, only his eyes spoke, and the muscles around the eyes. The voice trailed off, and you had to strain to hear it. But if you were in danger with Jojo, and you knew what an expression meant, you would be in very good company. Torture had taught him a lot. He was an expert survivor, and he had perfected that art of seeing without seeming to see. It was Jojo who had noticed that arrest in Davao.

'Do you still meet the people who were tortured with you?'

'We used to meet for a while, but I've lost contact with them now. Some people, after they've been tortured, don't want to have anything to do with anybody they've known before. If they were communists, they avoid the communists. It's as if they can't bear anything that reminds them of the past.'

'What were you like when you'd been released?'

'For a year I suffered from paranoia. If somebody knocked at the door, I wanted to jump out of the window.'

'That's not what I call paranoia. What you mean is you were really scared. And it sounds as if you had every reason to be scared. If they'd done it once, they might do it again. Paranoia is when you think there are green men from Mars keeping tabs on you. Your fear was perfectly rational.'

Jojo laughed. 'And all the time I thought it was paranoia. Well, I was like that for a year. I kept on with my martial arts. One thing about being tortured is that afterwards, when you meet this kind of person, you can tell immediately. I can recognize them by the way they walk, even the way they smell. You know, when they were torturing me, they were laughing and joking and fooling around. I got to know them very well indeed.'

I looked down towards the breakers. 'Jojo, if we were walking along the beach now, and some people came along and you recognized them as your torturers, what would you do?'

'I wouldn't talk to them. I wouldn't do anything. That wouldn't be a solution.'

'So what would be a solution?'

Jojo was speaking very softly again. 'Well, to be brutal: they should be killed. They've killed people and tortured people. *They* should be killed. Unless of course . . .' He thought a moment. 'Unless they'd really changed. But it would have to be a *real* change.'

I could guess how he felt about a real change. Before we had left Manila, the television had been showing interminable discussions with time-servers who said they'd changed. Not torturers, of course. Small fry. Pop stars who had sung at KBL rallies and were now getting it off their chest. One of them described how, on his way to Marcos's *miting de avance*, the vehicle he was in had been stoned by the crowd. 'And that was a real eye-opener to me, I mean, man . . .' As if he hadn't noticed anything wrong in the Philippines until somebody picked up a stone and threw it at him.

The glib talk of reconciliation would never bring about a solution, a real reconciliation. A change in the society would have to count as a real change if it was to satisfy people like Jojo or Comrade Nicky, whose whole psyches had been changed by what they had been through, or if it was going to dismantle the slums of the Tondo, stop starvation on Negros or release the peasant from the predators. Everything was yet to be done. Most of the prisoners were still to be released; there would have to be a new constitution; the communists would have to be either co-opted or defeated, if the Aquino government was to succeed in its aims. And I was quite sure that nobody really knew what would happen, or what actually was happening. The communists had got it wrong. Bayan had got it wrong. The KBL had got it most spectacularly wrong. Laban had won but were now in a position where expectations were so hysterically aroused that disenchantment of some sort must follow. The struggle of the future was, quite simply, the battle for the definition of justice.

Jojo glanced at the figures on the beach. 'D'you want a swim?' he said. It was evening and the sand was cool enough to walk on. People were keen to photograph the sunset. I picked up my Imelda towel, and we walked down to the water's edge. Pedro was being buried in the sand, and, for one morbid moment, I thought it odd that all over the world there should be a traditional game of giving yourself a shallow grave. Jojo was thinking something quite different. He took a large handful of sand and fashioned for Pedro a spectacular erection. Pedro lay there and giggled, as the erection shook and cracked and broke.

JAMES FENTON THE FALL OF SAIGON

'As reportage it is funny and acute, but as an account of intellectual and emotional change it is even more – brilliant.'

<u>Time Out</u>

GRANTA 15: £3.95/$7.50

Overleaf: James Fenton.

METHUEN MODERN FICTION

*an outstanding series of new novels
and modern classics*

MAUREEN DUFFY

I Want To Go To Moscow

First published in 1973, her disturbing and prophetic novel of animal rights.

'Maureen Duffy is one of the few British writers of fiction of real class' Martin Seymour-Smith, *Financia Times*

£3.50

BARBARA COMYNS

The Juniper Tree

'A magnetic fusion of sympathy and violence' *City Limits*

'*The Juniper Tree* is Barbara Comyns' first novel for eighteen years and is as welcome as spring . . . delicate, tough, quick-moving, it's a haunting book' *Financial Times*

£3.50

SIEGFRIED LENZ

The Lightship

A brilliant novel of tension and a lucid allegory on the rise to power of Adolf Hitler, by one of Germany's greatest post-war novelists. Now a major feature film.

£2.95

CHRISTOPHER ISHERWOOD

A Single Man

Reissued uniform with his other novels.

'A testimony to Isherwood's undisputed brilliance as a novelist' Anthony Burgess

£3.95

ROSE MACAULAY

Non-Combatants & Others

Her celebrated pacifist novel of World War One.

'The intelligence, light-heartedness, and courage; the dispassionate and good-natured callousness of English youth and middle-age, are all conveyed unobtrusively but with complete success' *Times Literary Supplement*

£3.95

Keeping Up Appearances

A brilliant comedy of sparkling and delicious mirth and merriment.

'The book is written with all Miss Macaulay's angry vivacity; it may not be subtle, but it is acute, it is witty, and above all it is uproariously funny' *Sunday Times*

£3.95

COLIN WATSON

The Flaxborough Crab
Plaster Sinners

Two more classic Flaxborough crime novels.

'To read him is to become an addict' *New Statesman*

'All the virtues one looks for in a crime novel' Julian Symons

Each: £3.50

For a complete list of titles in the Methuen Modern Fiction series, write to: Promotions Department, Methuen London, 11, New Fetter Lane, London EC4P 4EE

methuen

Photo: Jeanne Marie Hallacy

ANGELA CARTER **WHO** LEE MILLER
SANDI RUSSELL **WHO** SUE COE SADE
MIRANDA RICHARDSON ALICE WALKER
WHY KATHY ACKER DORIS LESSING
WHY MAYA ANGELOU MARINA WARNER
BILLIE WHITELAW FLICK ALLEN **WHEN**
KERI HULME WINNIE MANDELA **WHEN**
MADONNA ZORA NEALE HURSTON
WHERE MARILYN FRENCH CATHY BALME
WHERE SUSAN HILLER GWEN JOHN

FIND OUT IN WOMEN'S REVIEW

SUBSCRIBE NOW

All subscriptions are annual

- ☐ £15.00 founding subscription
- ☐ £11.50 standard subscription
- ☐ £17.00 European overseas rate
- ☐ £7.50 unwaged/student rate
- ☐ £20.00 institutional subscription
- ☐ £25.00 USA and elsewhere

name

address

*please make cheques/POs payable
to Women's Review Limited and
send to:*

*Women's Review, Unit 1,
Second Floor, 1-4 Christina Street,
London EC2 Telephone 01 739 4906*

MARK
MALLOCH BROWN
AQUINO, MARCOS
AND THE
WHITE HOUSE

Mark Malloch Brown

The most important, unresolved issue surrounding the Philippine elections and their aftermath is the extent of American involvement. Were the Americans hoping to bolster support for Marcos or get rid of him? What was the American attitude towards the elections themselves—were they seen as a democratic test, however limited, of popular opinion or merely a showcase display to prop up Reagan's old friend in Manila? How much was the American government covertly determining events?

For a number of extraordinary months, I was in the Philippines actively involved in the elections, and I know from my experience there that the new government in Manila has every interest in setting the record straight. In the coming months, both the left and the Marcos right will try to undermine the legitimacy of President Aquino by quoting Reagan's self-serving claims to have successfully supported her and her 'fellow freedom fighters' in the Philippines. It is extremely important that we know what really happened.

A reasonable starting point is October 1985, when Reagan sent his friend, Senator Paul Laxalt, to Manila. Laxalt's job was not merely to tell Marcos that the United States was impatient with the absence of reform in the Philippines, but also to stress that this impatience was felt by both the White House and the State Department. In its content the message was not new, but in the past it had always been conveyed by the State Department. It was also a message that Marcos, a shrewd manipulator of Washington politics, had always dismissed as emanating from his enemies in the American bureaucracy acting without the sanction of his greatest supporter, Ronald Reagan. (Marcos did indeed have enemies and had suspected—correctly—that there was a group of State Department officials who had already decided early last year that his time as president should end, and that it was essential to prepare for the transfer of power; at one point, several key officials even considered organizing a military coup.) Laxalt was the first to impress on Marcos that the American Ambassador in Manila, Stephen Bosworth, and others in the State Department spoke for the whole administration, and it was the administration's view that Marcos should start preparing for free and fair presidential

160

elections to be held in 1987. The intention was that Marcos would not be a candidate. Marcos, instead, announced that he would hold 'snap' elections to prove that he still had the people's confidence. The State Department had no interest in an immediate election—it would take at least until 1987 to establish Marcos's chosen successor at the polls—and, with the opposition in disarray, without a candidate or a clear programme or even, for that matter, access to the media, Marcos had, in effect, trapped the Americans into going along with an election grossly weighted in his own favour.

Marcos knew how to manage Washington. His State Department critics faced an angry right, once Laxalt returned. To Jeanne Kirkpatrick and Henry Kissinger, it was bad enough that Marcos was being pressured to make democratic reforms when communist regimes, with no elections at all, escaped this kind of American scrutiny. To the right, Marcos was saying: 'Your State Department, that bastion of liberals, has been harrassing me. Now I have done more than they asked and am not only holding elections but holding them now. So get them off my back.' And Marcos's strategy appeared to succeed. The American right immediately demonstrated its support. It argued that Marcos's faults of corruption were exaggerated: they were just part of the disfigured face of politics evident throughout the Third World; the liberals were applying double standards. Cory Aquino's inexperience, her position on the US bases and her softness on the communists were held up for inspection by right wing columnists and television commentators. A number of them were ushered round the Philippines and sent home with lots of locker room talk about governing the unruly Philippines being a man's work.

Marcos had, in effect, trapped Washington into appearing to endorse a snap election, and the administration—both State Department and White House—was forced to redefine its position. Originally it wanted Marcos out of power; the State Department now hoped for nothing more than that Aquino would succeed in putting up a respectable performance. She might, despite her inexperience, gain thirty percent of the vote and could hence inflict considerable damage on Marcos's reputation, hastening the final end. There were, therefore, only two objectives now: first, that Marcos should not miss the message of the election—he must begin reforms—and, second, that the election should not be such a farce that Marcos's standing at home and abroad would be worse than ever. Even so, it was clear that Marcos had won.

Except he had not counted on Cory Aquino. Nor had the Americans. The difficulty was in the fact that Americans simply did not understand Aquino. Her popular strength came from her very un-American virtues: a deeply private person and reluctant politician, she was driven by a conservative Catholic nationalism that did not fit easily into any of the categories of modern statecraft. Her diffident manner in public—entirely appropriate for a woman candidate in the context of the Philippines—was lost on foreign observers who seemed to think that women leaders should be tough, uncompromising and brassy. Quite simply, the Americans underestimated her. Ambassador Bosworth went through the motions of keeping in touch—doing a much better job of it than his European or even South East Asian counterparts—but he, like the rest of official Manila and Washington, had sunk into the assumption that the election was no longer going to be the *coup de grâce* for Marcos.

At this point Cory Aquino herself certainly did not view American interest as useful. She was still smarting from an interview she had given to the *New York Times* that had portrayed her as an incompetent housewife. It was the worst example of the patronizing early press coverage of the campaign depicting her as the well-meaning widow with a mission who had fallen among political wolves. There were those on her campaign staff who argued that Washington was a vital second campaign front: that it was no good winning in the Philippines if the Americans so doubted her competence that they would not lean on Marcos to concede. She thought that like Marcos the United States would respond only to overwhelming popular pressure. She would add to her objections about giving yet another American press interview one unrebuttable point, 'There are no votes in America.'

Even so, things did not look good for Aquino: at home, she was kept off the television and much of the radio by Marcos; abroad, she was treated as a political accident.

In the last two weeks of January, however, Aquino mounted a series of escalating attacks on Marcos's bravery, his war record and his honesty that gave him the worst hammering of his political career. The attacks succeeded in overcoming the Philippine press censorship of her campaign: they forced Marcos to respond, however indirectly, before his own media. For although the attacks were initially only reported in the foreign press, once Marcos responded to them the government-controlled media could report Marcos's replies. And it was the news of attacks that the Filipinos were greedy for. As the election approached, Aquino became adept at bouncing stories into the domestic press by way of the international press and Marcos's outraged response. Her huge campaign rallies, which in the Catholic Philippines had initially had more the quality of a mass mass than a political gathering, started to produce crowds desperate for change.

The State Department and the Embassy in Manila were, once again, on the defensive. And, once again, they were forced to revise their assumptions. But their concern was not that Aquino might win—that seemed implausible—but that her suddenly apparent strength would frighten Marcos into a blatant cheat. It was precisely this fear which informed one of the most important questions of the election, one that came to over-shadow all others: should there be American observers? When the issue had been first raised, by Marcos among others, it had seemed an easy way to whitewash the elections: international observers have refined the habit of looking the other way whenever rude electoral fraud threatens to burst into sight—a habit so established that it kept Stephen Solarz, the leading congressional critic of Marcos, from joining an observer team. Yet for a different reason the Aquino forces were also anxious to have observers. A whole nation was preparing itself for an act of collective courage: voting out a dictator through the ballot box. Even a handful of outsiders at the polls could be a crucial boost to morale. So under pressure from both parties—while each said publicly that observers would be interfering in the sovereign affairs of the Philippines—Reagan sent a presidential team. An international team of observers was also sent by the Republican and Democratic parties. And in so doing, the United States was sucked far deeper into the election than it ever meant to be.

With television crews and observer teams throughout the Philippines, it is still astonishing how conspicuous Marcos's massive exercise in electoral fraud turned out to be. There are several reasons for it: the panic Marcos felt witnessing the late surge in support for Aquino; the possibility that Marcos was simply losing his touch and, perhaps most interesting, the fact that, just before the elections, Mayor Yabut of Makati was suddenly rushed into hospital with a stroke. Mayor Yabut was Marcos's campaign chief in the middle-class business area of Manila where there was also the highest concentration of observers and television cameras. With Yabut in hospital, his thugs ran amok to the gratification of the television producers.

I happened to be amid the Cory Aquino supporters on the day of the election. I was also with them later that night when they announced that Aquino had won and that Marcos should concede. I subsequently learned that many people regarded the announcement as an act of bravado or propaganda. This was not the case. Aquino's own campaign computer projections showed that, despite all the cheating, she was winning with about fifty-six percent of the votes: it wasn't the seventy percent victory her supporters felt she would have achieved had there been no fraud, but it was still a win. At midnight her own projections were confirmed by CBS, the American television network, that told her it was about to announce an Aquino victory with fifty-four percent based on its own projections from poll returns. The mood was jubilant.

But then at three o'clock that morning, Marcos's Deputy Minister of Information phoned journalists at the Manila Hotel and called them to a press conference, where he furiously condemned this premature claim. Marcos had obviously been panicked by Aquino's announcement. Aquino soon discovered that the announcement served only to delay a wrap-up of the electoral fraud: it did not prevent it. Marcos's formal win was not announced for another eight days. CBS never announced its exit prediction.

Nevertheless, it was interesting to witness the influence of the American media's coverage of the events that day. At first, many of the observers remained cautious about condemning the practices they had seen. Then they saw how events were being represented in the United States. Observers and television producers were soon falling over each other in condemning election fraud. Of course, the election itself—only one phase of the fraud—was no worse (and probably better) than many previous elections. It was Marcos's bad luck that journalists had done their homework and saw the regions of the country where fraud was worst. Television gave its own momentum to the American political response. From this moment, long term American geopolitical ambitions were governed not by State Department calculations but by the pressures felt from the domestic American public: American viewers saw the bully boys of Marcos, their President's old friend, behaving in a very ungentlemanly way.

After the events on election day, the State Department—with the exception of George Shultz—was no longer involved. The decision-making moved to the White House, which was forced to distance the administration from Marcos. White House strategy was curiously—at times, embarrassingly—ill-conceived. It was not interested in the State Department's campaign against Marcos. If anything, it saw little value in the State Department's effort. As a result, the White House was very uninformed. A few days after the election—with the results still unannounced—Reagan made one of his biggest blunders: ignoring Shultz's explicit and clear pre-press conference briefing, Reagan claimed that there appeared to have been fraud on both sides. His claim flew in the face of what the whole American nation had seen on their televisions.

The State Department responded quickly, saying that Reagan had merely 'misspoken', but its own contribution to managing the crisis was little better. Shultz persuaded Reagan to send Philip Habib, the retired Lebanon troubleshooter, as his special envoy to Manila, initially to give Reagan a little time to recover his step after his gaffe. Officially it was billed as a fact-finding mission but it drove the stake into any lingering Reagan support for Marcos in two ways (and in this at least the State Department could claim a perverse success). First, it enraged Senator Richard Lugar, the chairman of the Senate Foreign Relations Committee and head of the observer team. Reagan had spoken from the hip in his comments on the election before Lugar had had a chance to brief him. Now the distinguished Senator found that Reagan was in effect seeking a second opinion. He became more stridently outspoken than ever about the fraud and the need for the United States to condemn the election. Second, it enraged Cory Aquino: at a televised press conference, she demanded to know why the so-called friends of democracy—prepared to support armed 'freedom fighters' elsewhere—were deserting the martyrs of the ballot box here in Manila. Stand tall for freedom, she concluded. The housewife-widow was in top form: she had deliberately borrowed Reagan's rhetoric to put an American president on the run.

But matters deteriorated even more: what is not generally known is that Habib had a second set of instructions in his pocket—proposing that Aquino should concede. In the meanwhile, between Habib's leaving Washington and his arriving in Manila, the full extent of the fraud had emerged: it wasn't in the election-day thuggery, but in the under-registration of voters in the Aquino areas. And worse—as the vote count indicated more and more the support for Aquino—there was an attempt to manipulate the computer count to turn back the landslide, the most telling scene being when thirty frightened computer operators walked out and gave a midnight press conference before a church altar. And it was in this context that Habib was to meet Aquino, and try to persuade her that she should accept the role of loyal opposition and hang on till the next election. The Aquino people felt they had mortgaged their whole futures on taking on Marcos at the ballot box: they were now exposed and their lives genuinely at risk. Marcos was not the sort of opponent who would give them a second chance. The suggestion of this idea was considered a much greater betrayal than Reagan's gaffe. In a sense they expected no better of him. Aquino made it clear that if Habib attempted to raise such a proposal, she would refuse to speak to him entirely. Wisely, Habib didn't: he contented himself with polite fact-finding.

But Habib's fact-finding was overtaken by events. Aquino announced that she would start a mass campaign of peaceful protest and a boycott of goods and services produced by Marcos and his cronies' companies. To many it seemed an anti-climax, but she knew that it was a test: if those round Marcos saw the extent of her determination, the facade of loyalty would crack. It did sooner than expected: within hours of Habib's leaving the country, Defence Minister Juan Ponce Enrile and Acting Chief of Staff of the Armed Forces Fidel Ramos barricaded themselves into Camps Crame and Aguinaldo. As one of Aquino's aides said at the time: 'Poor Habib always seems to be in a plane flying the wrong way across the Pacific at the crucial moments.'

It is this period—from Saturday afternoon, 22 February, to Tuesday evening, 25 February, when Marcos left Malacañang Palace in a US Air Force H-3 helicopter—that speculation about US involvement is at its most persistent and its most dangerous. There are two commonplace assumptions: first, that, before leaving, Habib told Enrile and Ramos to defect; and second, that the CIA was behind an alleged plot to assassinate Marcos (to the extent that the plot is believed to have existed at all).

Neither assumption has any basis in fact.

The CIA, uncharacteristically, seems to have stayed out of the Filipino crisis because Bill Casey, the head of the CIA, disapproved of any campaign against Marcos, and in part because he thought that any active involvement would backfire: it seemed impossible to keep anything in the Philippines, let alone in Washington, a secret. It is equally unlikely that Habib was involved. The impetus for the defection of Enrile and Ramos did not come from Washington; it came from the Reform the Armed Forces Movement, organized by the younger colonels in January of last year as a pressure group to re-organize the military (Defence Minister Enrile was the Movement's clandestine patron).

The young colonels in the Reform Movement had already expressed their restlessness. It was the colonels, for instance, who had helped to get the computer operators away from the Marcos supporters and into sanctuary. On Friday evening, 21 February, the Reform Movement contacted one of Cory Aquino's closest aides: the Movement had planned a military junta and its members wanted Aquino to join it. The information was not passed onto Aquino at the time, because her party workers were confident that she wanted no part of a coup or junta—it was she who had the public mandate—and because she would not want to cancel the mass rally she was meant to attend the next day in the city of Cebu, outside Manila.

Again, Aquino was forcing others to react to her remarkable resolve. The younger officers—seeing that Aquino was going to see the crisis through to the end—were forced into a final showdown and committed themselves to a plan to assassinate Marcos that weekend. But they were caught. When Marcos produced two suspects later that night on television it was widely assumed that it was a put-up job. It was not.

Throughout, the younger officers seemed to have kept Enrile and Ramos only minimally informed of their intentions. Once their plan was exposed everything moved with extraordinary speed. Enrile was drinking coffee with friends, a Saturday routine, when he was alerted by a number of younger officers that Marcos was about to arrest him and other officers. Enrile had been nervous all Saturday morning since another minister, Bobby Ongpin, had told him that Ongpin's own bodyguards had been mysteriously withdrawn the previous Friday night. Something strange was afoot. It was then that Enrile and Ramos went to Camp Crame and Camp Aguinaldo.

Once locked into the camp, one of Enrile's first calls was to the American Ambassador who had just returned from seeing Habib off at the airport. This was not a call between co-conspirators. Enrile's news was indeed just that to the Ambassador. Enrile had not expected to survive the first twelve hours. He subsequently rang a Filipino friend in New York to say goodbye: he assumed that he would be killed. Even so, throughout Saturday, Enrile avoided speaking to Marcos, knowing how persuasive Marcos could be. Apparently, according to Enrile, Marcos was confident that he would be able to persuade his old supporter to stop all this nonsense, if only he could reach Enrile on Saturday night. But it wasn't until Sunday that they were finally in touch, when Marcos proposed that the Philippines could be governed by a junta run by Enrile. But by Sunday morning the momentum was with the people.

On the Saturday night, Aquino's brother, fearing that Marcos would liquidate all members of the opposition, took Cory into hiding in a nunnery in Cebu. The Americans were starting to panic, and offered sanctuary in their bases and ships to various protagonists—including Aquino herself—during the weekend's power struggle. The offer, typically, was not even considered. At some point in the weekend the Ambassador warned Marcos, on Reagan's orders, not to bomb the camps, which were by then surrounded by nuns, civilians and American television cameras. By then, the tide had turned anyway. But what saved Enrile and Ramos at the beginning—the moment when they were indeed vulnerable—was: first, the reluctance of Marcos to kill old friends; second, the incompetence of General Ver; and, third, the strength of People Power. It was not the Americans.

It was Cory Aquino's moment. On Sunday morning, against the advice of her supporters, she flew back to Manila and later in the day she went to Camp Crame. On Monday, the Americans started steps to get Marcos out.

It was none too soon. By the time Marcos left on Tuesday, his palace guard was deserting and people were firing random shots at the palace. It is interesting that Marcos was to attribute the shooting to his military opponents, whose helicopters, he claimed, were being fuelled by the Americans. However, when he had rung Enrile to beg him to call off the attack on the Palace, he had taken Enrile entirely by surprise: no rebel soldier had fired on Malacañang. It was only later that it was shown that the shots had been fired by students. As in the final scenes of Hamlet, the Americans came like the Polacks to pick up the bodies, but they had been irrelevant to much of the drama that had preceded it.

And that drama was a distinctly Filipino one. Its moving force was an improbable politician—Cory Aquino—not America and its out-of-sync meddling. The United States did not lack the will or the notice to interfere; it was simply that Washington was divided between State Department activists and a President who, having frequently intervened elsewhere, was slow to shake free his loyalty to an old friend. But by the time Washington had finally understood the scenes it was witnessing, the play was almost over.

ON SALE NOW

The Fiction Magazine

★ Exciting new fiction every month

★ 56 pages of stories, translations, interviews, poems, reviews

★ Introducing new writers

★ Among our contributors: Brian Aldiss, Tim Aspinall, Dirk Bogarde, Maggie Brooks, Anthony Burgess, Simon Burt, A.S. Byatt, Raymond Carver, Frank Delaney, Margaret Drabble, Paul Durcan, Lawrence Durrell, Janice Elliott, Steve Ellis, Antonia Fraser, Ronald Frame, Mary Flanagan, Leon Garfield, Maggie Gee, Alasdair Gray, Russell Hoban, Desmond Hogan, Kazuo Ishiguro, George Macbeth, Allan Massie, Deborah Moggach, Amos Oz, V.S. Pritchett, Frederic Raphael, Ruth Rendell, Lisa St Aubin de Teran, Graham Swift, Gillian Tindall, Marina Warner, Hugo Williams

SUBSCRIPTIONS £9.50 per 10 issues (UK)
Airmail £19.00 (Europe), £24.50 (Worldwide)
Seamail £15.00 (Europe), £17.50 (Worldwide)
Please send the Fiction Magazine for 10 issues

Name ....

Address ....

....

....

Cheque/PO to: Fiction Magazine, 12/13 Clerkenwell Green, London EC1R OPD
Telephone (01) 250 1504. £1.50 per copy plus 50 P & P.

JOHN BERGER

THE ACCORDION
PLAYER

Will you play at my wedding? Philippe the cheese-maker asked him. Philippe was thirty-four. People had been saying he would never get married.

When is it?

Saturday next.

Why didn't you ask me before?

I didn't dare. Will you?

Where does the bride come from?

Yvonne comes from the Jura. Drop into the Republican Lyre tonight and she'll be there—her parents have come and some friends from Besançon.

The same evening the accordionist, a man in his fifties, found himself sitting in the café, drinking champagne offered by the bride's father, next to a plump woman who laughed a lot and wore dangling earrings. The accordionist had been looking hard at the young bride and he was sure she was pregnant.

You will play for us? Phillippe asked, filling up the glasses.

Yes, I'll play for you and the Yvonne, he said. On the floor at his feet lay a dog, its coat turned grey with age. From time to time he caressed its head.

What's your dog's name? asked the woman with earrings.

Mick, he said. He's a clown without a circus.

He's old to be a clown.

Fifteen Mick is, fifteen.

You have a farm? she questioned further.

At the top of the village—a place we call Lapraz.

Is it a big farm?

Depends who's asking the question, he answered with a little laugh.

Delphine is asking you the question, she chortled.

He wondered if she was often drunk.

Well, is it a big farm? she asked again.

One winter the mayor asked my father: Have you got a lot of snow up at Lapraz? And do you know what father replied? Less than you, Mr Mayor, he said, because I own less land!

That's beautiful! Delphine said, knocking over a glass as she put a hand on his shoulder. No fool, your father.

Have you come for the wedding? he asked her.

I've come to dress the bride!

Dress her?

It was me who made the wedding dress and there are always finishing touches to make on the 'great day'!

Are you a dress-maker? he asked.

No! No! I work in a factory . . . I just pin things up for myself and friends.

That must save you money, he said.

It does, but I do it because it amuses me, like you play the accordion, they tell me . . .

You like music?

She disentangled her arms and held them wide apart as though she were measuring a metre-and-a-half of cloth. With music, she sighed, you can say everything! Do you play regularly?

Every Saturday night in the café, weddings excepted.

This café?

No, the one at home.

Don't you live here?

Lapraz is three kilometres away.

Are you married? she asked, looking him straight in the eye. Her own eyes were grey-green like the jacket she was wearing.

Unmarried, Delphine, he replied. I play at other men's weddings.

I lost my husband four years ago, she said.

He must have been young.

In a car accident . . .

So quick! He pronounced the two words with such finality that she was silenced. She fingered the stem of her glass, then lifted it to her lips and emptied it.

You like playing the accordion, Felix?

I know where music comes from, he said.

That it was going to be a bad year had been evident to Felix from the moment in the spring when the snow thawed. All around the village there were pastures which looked as though they had been ploughed up the previous autumn, and they hadn't been. In the orchards the fruit trees were growing out of mud instead of grass. The earth everywhere was like an animal whose fur was falling out. All this was due to the invasion of the moles. Some maintained that the moles had multiplied so catastrophically because the foxes had died or been shot the year before. A fox eats thirty or forty moles a day. The foxes had died because of the rabies which had been brought to the region from the distant Carpathians.

Felix was standing motionless in the garden in front of his house. Across his body he was holding a spade. He had been like that for ten minutes. He was looking at the earth just ahead of his boots. Not a grain of soil stirred. Towards the mountain a buzzard was circling, otherwise nothing in sight was moving. The leaves of the cabbages and cauliflowers in the garden were wilted and yellow. With one hand he could have lifted any one of these plants off the earth, as you lift a candlestick off a table. All their roots had been severed.

When he saw the soil stir, he raised his spade and struck, grunting as the spade entered the earth. He kicked the soil away. There were the disclosed tunnels and the dead culprit mole.

One less! he said, grinning.

Albertine, Felix's mother, was watching her forty-year-old son through the kitchen window when he killed the mole with the spade. She shouted to him to come in because the meal was on the table.

With today's sun, she said while they were eating, the potatoes shouldn't be dirty.

They shouldn't be, he replied.

The pup under the table looked up, hoping for a bone or some cheese-rind. He was large and black with blond marks shaped like almonds over each eye which made him look comic.

Ah Mick! said Felix. Our Mick's a clown without a circus, isn't he?

If you like, said Albertine, I'll make potato fritters tonight.

With cabbage salad! He took off his cap and smeared his sleeve across his hot forehead.

Years before, when Albertine had been strong enough to work in the fields, they used to lift the potatoes together. While working they would recite all the ways in which potatoes could be eaten: potatoes in their jackets, potatoes with cheese in the oven, potato salad, potatoes with pork fat, mashed potatoes with milk, potatoes cooked without water in the black iron saucepan, potatoes with leeks in the soup—and, best of all, potato fritters with cabbage salad.

The potatoes, unearthed that same morning, had dried well in the sun on the topsoil of the field. As Felix gathered them by hand into buckets, he sorted them. The small ones for the animals and poultry, the large ones for the table. Sometimes he moved forward stooping, sometimes he knelt between the rows and went forward on his knees, like a penitent. Mick, panting in the heat, lay on the ground, and each time Felix moved forward, he accompanied him. When the buckets were full the man emptied the potatoes into sacks along the side of the field. The sacks were of strong white plastic and had contained fertilizer. When they were full, they looked liked praying drunks in white shirts.

Suddenly the dog became alert, his head down, nose in the broken earth. Breathing out heavily, he started to scrabble with his front paws and to scatter the soil behind him.

Fetch him! Mick, fetch him! Felix sat back on his heels to watch the young dog. He was happy to be diverted and to rest his back which ached. The dog continued to dig excitedly.

You want him, Mick, don't you? You want him.

At last the dog deposited a mole on the earth.

You have him, don't let him go!

The dog tossed the mole into the air. For an instant the little animal in its grey fur coat—measuring fifteen centimetres in length and weighing a hundred and fifty grams, with paws like hands, with very weak eyesight and acute hearing, renowned for his testicles and the exceptional amount of seminal fluid they produced—for an instant the little animal was hapless and alone in the sky.

Quick Mick!

Fallen back onto the soil, the mole, no longer capable of flight, began to squeal.

Have him!

The dog ate the mole.

John Berger

Alone in the house, Albertine asked herself for the hundredth time the same question: when she was gone, what would Felix do? Men, she considered, were strong-backed, reckless and weak, each man combining these essential qualities in his own way. Felix needed a woman who would not take advantage of his weakness. If the woman were ambitious or greedy, she would exploit him and use his strong back and his recklessness to ride him where she wanted. Yet now he was forty and the woman had not been found.

There had been Yvette. Yvette would have cuckolded him, just as she was now cuckolding the poor Robert whom she married. There had been Suzanne. One Sunday morning, just before Felix did his military service, she had seen him caressing Suzanne on the floor beneath the blackboard in the schoolroom—the same schoolroom where he had learned as a boy! She had crept away from the window without disturbing them, but she repeatedly reminded her son, when she wrote to him in the army, that schoolteachers can't sit on milking stools. Suzanne had left the village and married a shopkeeper.

Was it going to be worse for her son to be alone than to have married the wrong woman? Sometimes the question made Albertine feel confused: sometimes unexpectedly helpless.

In the evening Felix emptied the sacks full of potatoes into a wooden stall in the cellar under the house. Potatoes just lifted from the earth give off a strange warmth and in the darkness of the cellar they glow like children's shoulders after a day in the sun. He looked at the heap critically: there were going to be far less than last year.

Did you finish? asked Albertine when he entered the kitchen.

Four more rows to do, Maman.

I've just made the coffee . . . Get under the table! You're not firm enough with that pup, Felix.

He caught five moles this afternoon.

Are you going out tonight?

Yes, there's a meeting of the Dairy Committee.

Felix drank the coffee from the bowl his mother handed him, and began reading the Communist Party paper for peasants and agricultural workers.

Do you know where the biggest bell in the world is, Maman? Not round the neck of one of our cows!

It's called the Tsar Kolokol, it weighs one hundred and ninety-six tons and was cast in Moscow in 1735.

That's a bell I'll never hear, she said.

He went into the stable to start milking, and she took out his suit from the wardrobe which her husband had made one winter when they were first married, and brushed the trousers with the same energy as she had once groomed their mare. Then, having laid the suit on the high double bed beneath her husband's portrait, she did something she had never done before in her life. She took off her boots and lay, fully-clothed, on top of the bed.

She heard Felix come back into the kitchen, she listened to him washing by the sink. She heard him taking off his trousers and washing between his legs. When he had finished, he came into the bedroom.

Where are you? he asked.

I'm taking a rest, she said from the bed.

What's the matter?

A rest, my son.

Are you ill, Mother?

I feel better now.

She watched him dress. He stepped into the trousers with the creases which she had ironed. He put on the white cotton shirt, buttoned at the cuffs, which showed off his manly shoulders. He slipped into the jacket—he was putting on weight, no question about that. Nevertheless he was still handsome. He ought to be able to find a wife.

Why don't you go to a dentist? she asked. He glanced at her, puzzled.

He could arrange your teeth.

I haven't a toothache.

He could make you more handsome.

He could also make us poorer!

Let me see you in your cap.

He put it on.

You're even more handsome than your father was, she said.

When Felix returned to the farm that night, he was surprised to see a car, its lights on, parked outside the house. He entered hurriedly. The doctor from the next village was in the kitchen washing his hands in the sink. The door to the middle room was shut.

If there's no improvement by the morning, your mother will have to go to hospital, the doctor said.

Felix looked through the kitchen window at the mountain opposite which, in the moonlight, was the colour of a grey mole, but he could not see around what had happened.

What happened? he asked.

She telephoned your neighbours.

She won't have to go to hospital.

I have no choice, said the doctor.

You are right, said Felix, suddenly furious. It is her choice which counts!

You can't look after her properly here.

She has lived here for fifty years.

If you're not careful, she may die here.

The doctor wore glasses and this was the first thing you noticed about him. He looked at everything as if it were a page to read. He had come straight to the village from medical school full of idealism. Now, after ten years, he was disillusioned. Mountain people did not listen to reason, he complained, mountain people drank too much, mountain people went on repeating what they thought they had once heard as children, mountain people never recognized a rational process, mountain people behaved as if they thought life itself was mad.

Have a drink before you go, Doctor.

Does your mother have a supplementary insurance?

Which do you prefer, pears or plums?

Neither, thank you.

A little gentian? Gentian cures all, Doctor.

No alcohol, thank you.

How much do I owe you?

Twenty thousand, said the doctor, adjusting his glasses.

Felix took out his purse. She has worked every day of the year for fifty years, he thought, and tonight this short-sighted quack asks for twenty thousand. He extracted two folded banknotes and placed them on the table.

The doctor left and Felix went into the middle room. She was so thin that, under the eiderdown, her body was invisible. It was as if her head, decapitated, had been placed on the pillow.

An expression of irritation, like that on a dog's muzzle when it sniffs alcohol, ruffled her face while her eyes remained closed. When the spasm was over, her face resumed its calm, but was older. She was ageing hour by hour.

Noticing the dog lying on the floor at the foot of the bed, Felix hesitated. She would have insisted on the dog being put out.

Not a sound, Mick!

He climbed onto the bed beside his mother so that he would be reassured by her breathing throughout the night. She stirred and, turning on the pillow, asked for some water. When he gave her the glass, she could not raise her head. He had to hold her head up with his hand, and her head seemed to weigh nothing, to be no heavier than a lettuce.

They both lay there, awake and without saying a word.

You'll get the rest of the potatoes in tomorrow? she eventually asked.

Yes.

Next spring there'll be fewer moles, she said. There won't be enough for them all to eat to survive the winter.

They breed quickly, Maman.

In the long run such troubles correct themselves, she insisted, if not by next year, by the year after. Yet you, you, my son, you will always remember the Year of the Thousand Moles.

No, Mother, you're going to get better.

The next day while he was cutting wood on the circular saw, Felix stopped every hour to go into the house and reassure himself. Each time, lying on the large bed, her arms straight by her side, she opened her eyes and smiled at him.

Everything was ready and prepared, she knew, in the second drawer of the wardrobe. Her black dress with mother-of-pearl buttons, the black kerchief with blue gentian flowers printed on it, the dark grey stockings, and the shoes with laces which would be easier to put on than boots. How many times had Marie-Louise promised to come and dress her if it was she, Albertine, who was the first to go?

That night after Felix had come to lie down beside her, she said: It's years, my boy, since you played your accordion.

I don't even know where it is.

It's in the *grenier*, she said. You used to play so well, I don't know why you stopped.

It was when I came out of the army.

Yes, but you stopped.

Father was dead. There was too much to do.

He glanced at the portrait hanging above the bed. His father had a thick moustache, tiny comic eyes and a strong neck. He used to tap his neck, as if it were a barrel, when he was thirsty.

Would you play me something? Albertine asked.

On the accordion?

Yes.

After all this time I won't get a breath out of it.

Try.

He shrugged his shoulders, took the electric torch off its hook on the wall and went out. When he came back he extracted the accordion from its case, arranged one strap round his shoulder and, slipping his wrist inside the other, started to pump. It worked.

What tune do you want?

'*Dans tes Montagnes*'.

The two voices of the accordion, tender and full-blown, filled the room. All her attention was fixed on him. His body was rolling slowly to the music. He has never been able to make up his mind, she reflected: it's as if he doesn't realize this is his only life. I ought to know. I gave birth to him. And then, carried away by the music, she saw their cows in the alpage and Felix learning to walk.

When Felix stopped playing, Albertine was asleep.

Neighbours came to visit the house, bringing with them pears, walnut wine, an apple tart. Albertine repeatedly declared she had no need of anything except water. She stopped eating. She would take whatever messages they wanted, she would pray with them for what they thought they needed, she would bless them, but she would accept no pity and no competition. She was the next to leave.

To the old man, Anselme, she whispered: Try to find him a wife.

It's not like our time, he said, shaking his head. Nobody wants to marry a peasant today.

I'm glad you say that, she said.

I'm not saying Felix couldn't get married, answered Anselme pedantically. I'm simply saying women of his generation have married men from the towns.

It's the idea of his being left alone . . . she answered.

I've been alone for twenty years! It's twenty years now since Claire died and I can recommend it. He chuckled.

Abruptly Albertine lowered her head to indicate it was his duty to kiss her while she prayed. Anselme obeyed and kissed the crown of her head.

She was now so weak and thin that Felix was frightened of smothering her when he slept. One night he woke up from a dream. He listened for her breathing. Her breath was as weak as an intermittent breeze in grass waiting to be scythed. Through the lace curtains he could see the plum trees his father had grafted. The light of the moon going down in the west was reflected in the mirror behind the wash-bowl.

In the dream he had again been a conscript in the army. He was walking along a road, playing an accordion. Behind him was a man carrying a sheep. It was he, Felix, who had stolen the sheep, or rather a young woman had given the sheep to him on condition that . . . and he had taken the sheep knowing full well—

The dream became vaguer and vaguer as, awake, he saw something else. He saw Death approaching the farm. Or, rather, he saw Death's lamp, bobbing up and down, as Death strode leisurely past the edge of the forest where the beech trees in October were the colour of flames, down the slope of the big pasture which drained badly at the bottom, under the linden tree full of wasps in August, over the ruts of the old road to St Jean, between the cherry trees against which, every July, she asked him to lean the long ladder, past the water trough where the source never froze, beside the dung-heap where he threw the after-births, through the stable and into the kitchen. When Death entered the middle room—where the smoked sausages were hanging from the ceiling above the bed—he saw that what he had taken to be a lamp was in fact a white feather of hoar frost. The feather floated down on to the bed.

Abruptly Albertine sat up and said: Fetch me my dress, it is time to go!

The day after the funeral, when Felix delivered his milk to the dairy, he surprised everyone there by his cheerfulness. Have you ever worked as a butcher? he asked Philippe, the cheese-maker. No? Well, you'd better take a correspondence course—with diagrams! Next year there's going to be no hay, no cows, no milk, no bonus for cream, no penalty for dirt . . . We're all going to be in the mole-skin business! That's what we are going to be doing . . .

The absence of the dead when mourned is as precise as their presence once was. Albertine's absence was thin with arthritic hands and long grey hair gathered up in a chignon. The eyes of her absence needed glasses for reading. During her lifetime many cows had stepped on her feet. Each of her toes had been stepped on by a cow on a different occasion, and the growth of its nail consequently deformed. The toenails of her absence were the yellow of horn and irregularly shaped. The legs of her absence were as soft to touch as a young woman's.

Every evening he ate the soup he had prepared, he sliced the bread, he read the Communist Party paper for peasants and agricultural workers and he lit a cigarette. He performed these acts while hugging her absence. As the night drew on and the cows in the stable lay down on their bedding of straw and beech leaves, the warmth of his own body penetrated her absence so that it became his own pain.

On All Soul's Day he bought some chrysanthemums, white ones the colour of goose feather, and placed the pot of flowers, not by the tombstone in the churchyard, but on the marble-top commode in the middle room beside the large empty bed.

A week later the snow came. The children ran screaming out of school, impatient to build snowmen and igloos. When Felix delivered his milk to the dairy, he repeated the remark that

Albertine had made every year when the first snow fell: Let it snow a lot tonight, let the snow get so high our hens can peck the stars!

Through the kitchen window he stared at the white mountain. Mick was licking a plate on the floor.

The winter's long, it would be better if we could sleep.

The dog looked up.

Who do you think is going to win the elections? The same gang as before, eh?

The dog started wagging his tail.

Do you know what you like and what they manufacture in Bethune? Do you know, Mick?

Felix strode across the kitchen towards the massive dresser. To take something off its top shelf it was necessary to stand on a chair. Its doors, with their square panes of glass and their bevelled window-frames, were big enough for a cow to go through.

So you don't know, Mick, what they manufacture in Bethune? From the bottom shelf he picked up a packet of sugar.

Sugar, Mick, sugar is what they manufacture in Bethune!

Brusquely he threw two lumps towards the dog. Three more. Six. Then he emptied the whole packet. Fifty lumps of sugar fell onto the floorboards in a cloud of dust.

Sugar in Bethune! Milk here! He shouted the words so violently the dog hid under the table.

One day in January he noticed that the floorboards, instead of being bread-coloured, were now grey like slates. He put the dog out, he stoked up the stove with wood, took off his boots and trousers and began scrubbing on his knees. He had left it too long; the dirt was ingrained. He ground his teeth, he filled and refilled the bucket with water from the giant saucepan on the stove. The planks slowly changed colour.

The more he scrubbed, the more he saw the countless washings the floor had undergone as a single instant in an eternity of dust and neglect. He straightened his back and looked up at the dresser. On the top shelf was their best china, decorated with sprays and garlands of flowers: violets, forget-me-nots, honeysuckle.

The way the flowers were painted around the rims of the plates, in the hearts of the dishes, on the flanks of the bowls, made him think of ears, mouths, eyes, breasts.

He put on his trousers and boots, laid down sheets of newspaper and, stepping from one sheet to another, reached the door. Outside it was snowing grey snow. He teetered like a drunk into the stable and there, his forehead resting on one of his cow's haunches, he vomited till there was nothing left in his stomach.

A few days later he beat the cow Myrtille. Myrtille had the bad habit of butting the cow next to her. If he showed Myrtille a stick, this was usually enough to deter her. She glowered at him with her insolently tranquil eyes, and he brandished the stick in the air and said: The bow of the violin, eh? Is that enough or do you want some music!

On the evening in question he forgot the stick, and Myrtille knocked him off his stool while he was preparing her neighbour's teats before plugging the milking machine on to them. Seizing a rake, he beat Myrtille across the haunches with the handle. She put her head down and he beat her harder. He was beating her now because she had reduced him to beating her. She lay down on the floor and he beat her out of the fury of his knowledge that he could not stop beating her.

In the name of God! he spat out the words as if they were his own broken teeth. Nothing! Nobody!

The shock of each blow was transmitted to his shoulders. Then the handle of the rake broke.

It seemed to him that the animal never forgave him.

Towards the end of March the giant bedspread of packed snow began to slide down the roof of the house, a few centimetres each day. In the cellar, despite the darkness and the thickness of the walls, the potatoes were putting out pink, violet shoots. The force of these shoots is so strong they can pierce canvas or denim.

A week earlier the doctor had asked him: Are you still vomiting? Do you want some more pills?

Felix had replied: No, doctor . . . what I need is an extra

pair of hands. Can you give me a prescription for that? Preferably a woman's hands, but I'll accept a man's or even a boy's.

He thus confirmed one of the doctor's favourite dinner-table dissertations: namely that the dearth of women in the valley—the best men having left with the women following them—was pushing the idiots who remained towards homosexuality and even bestiality.

In twenty-four hours a well-fed cow shits a wheelbarrow of dung. The winter had lasted 150 days and Felix had seventeen cows. He recalled the time, before they bought a tractor, when all the winter's dung had to be forked into a tip cart, hauled by the horse and unloaded in heaps, to be spread out again with a fork over the fields. Now he had a mechanical shovel and a spreader. And now he was alone.

Albertine had been right: there were fewer mole hills. Many moles must have died, the strongest eating the weakest. In the morning when he started up the tractor it was freezing. By midday on the hillside with the spreader, he was sweating. This year he refused to take off his sheepskin jacket. If he caught cold and fell ill, there would be nobody else to milk the cows. His solitude had strange ramifications. His trousers caked with cowshit went on stinking until he himself put them in the washing-machine. Sometimes the solitude of the house smelled acrid like cowshit.

Every evening, sitting at the table beneath the clock that was always half-an-hour fast so that he would not deliver the milk too late at the dairy, he decided what to do the following day. Shit till Sunday, Mick, or shall we do the wood?

During the winter it had been a question of killing time. Now time was resurrected. He forgot obvious things. He fed the chickens and forgot the eggs. He hadn't collected eggs from the hen-house since he was seven when his father went away for the second time. The first time his father went away was for his military service, the second time was when he went to Paris to earn the money to re-cover the roof of the house with tiles; it took him four winters to earn enough.

How often had he heard his father tell the story of his time in the army. Soldier Jacquier! Why did you not obey the order given to you? Replied his father: One of you tells me to do this, another of you tells me to do that, another of you tells me to do something else, so what am I to do? Just tell me clearly what you want and I'll do it! Soldier Jacquier! Clean out this room! One of you tells me to do this, another one tells me to do that . . . To every order, cunning old boar, his father replied in the same way. Soldier Jacquier, one month's detention! He was put in a cell. Prisoner Jacquier, are you a good shot? You tell me clearly what you want, and I'll do it. The Company needs a good marksman, Jacquier! He was taken out and given a rifle and five bullets. He scored five bull's-eyes. For the rest of his military service he had no duties and no fatigues. All he had to do was to go occasionally and shoot in the regimental competitions on the rifle range. When his father finished the story, he always added: On this earth, Felo, you need to be clever . . .

In April he planted his potatoes. It was as hot that year in April as it usually is in June. Walking slowly along the drill, he dropped a potato between his legs every twenty centimetres. Sometimes the potato fell badly and he was forced to bend down to place it properly.

There are some who know where to go, Mick, and some that have to be put in their place!

Each time he chose with his eyes the exact place between the clods where he hoped the potato would fall. If he did not do this, it fell badly.

The last potato planted, he climbed towards the house. It was almost noon. Suddenly he stopped in his steps. High above the roof a swarm of bees was flying away from the sun towards the north.

Rushing into the kitchen, he came out with a large saucepan and a metal soup ladle. He ran through the orchard rattling the ladle in the saucepan. Mick was barking at his heels. When he was ahead of the swarm, he drummed harder than ever, and held the saucepan so that it glinted in the sun and flashed like a mirror. The swarm, subject to a single will, made straight for the nearest plum tree and settled on one of its branches.

Now he could take his time. He found an empty hive and rubbed its inside with plum leaves. He strolled over to the outhouse to fetch a saw. He sawed off the branch on which the bees were settled and carried it over to the hive. There he tapped the branch smartly with a plank and the swarm fell off like a wig.

If the queen is there, they'll stay. If not, they'll leave tomorrow.

It was then that he heard his mother's voice calling him by name. The drone the bees were making gave birth to her voice, and at the same time muffled it. The voice went on repeating his name as if the solitude of his days was now in the name itself.

Each season loads up men as if they were wheelbarrows and then wheels them forward to do its tasks. Felix ploughed the field for the alfalfa. One day, when he was twelve, in the field he was now ploughing, his father had said to him: Do you want to come hunting with me? They climbed, both of them, to the forest below Peniel.

We'll wait here, Felo, and do nothing. Shut your mouth and keep your eyes skinned.

His father cut some branches from a beech tree and arranged them like a light screen in front of them. The beech leaves, just unfurled, were as fresh-looking as lettuces. They waited behind the screen for what seemed to Felix an eternity. The bones in his body began to ache one by one because he didn't dare move a limb. His father sat there as patient as if he was listening to music, his gun between his knees. From behind a spruce twenty metres away, a wild boar appeared, hesitated, and then walked, like a confident habitué, across their vision. The father fired. The boar keeled over and lay down as if inexplicably overcome by sleep.

Do you know what's important in this life, Felo?

No, Papa.

Good health. And what does good health give you? It gives you a steady hand.

The father prodded the animal with his boot.

Guard him! he said and disappeared down the path to the village. Felix sat on his heels beside the dead boar whose small eyes were open. When his father returned with a sledge across his back, he was panting hard but grinning. Together they tied the carcass—it weighed a good 150 kilos—on to the light sledge. Then they started the difficult journey down.

Father put himself between the two wooden arms in the position of a two-legged horse. Like this he could pull when the runners of the sledge met an obstacle or when the slope wasn't steep enough, and like this, if they were running too fast over the mud or the new slippery grass, he could brake by digging in his heels and lifting up the front of the sledge so that its weight leaned backwards and the back of the sledge was forced into the ground. Felix followed, holding on to a rope to brake the speed, but in fact being pulled along ever faster. One false step on his father's part and the charging boar and sledge would knock him on to his face and ride over him.

His last run home, Felo!

Not so fast, Papa!

The boy had his father's gun across his back.

When they were down on the road which passes the café, they stopped to give their legs a rest.

It's the knees, isn't it, which feel it?

My legs aren't tired, lied the boy.

There's a man for you!

Along the grass bank by the side of the road the sledge slid gently and easily. The boy let go of the rope and put the gun under his arm, carrying it like a hunter.

They met Louis, who could argue a politician under the table.

The month of May, the season for hunting? asked Louis.

It's no gazelle! said his father.

I'd hide him quick if I were you, said Louis. How many shots?

One shot, only one shot. Felo here is going to be a hunter. His hand's as steady as a rock.

And Felix, although he knew why his father, cunning as ever, had invented this story, was filled with pride.

When they got home and the boar had been hidden in the cellar, his father said: It's time you learned to use a gun. I'll find you one. What do you say to that?

I'd rather have an accordion, replied Felix.

An accordion! Ah! you want to seduce the girls, eh?

One night, a few months later, Felix was in bed and he heard his father come into the kitchen, shouting in the sing-song voice which meant he had been drinking. There were some other men with him who were laughing. Then there was a silence, and suddenly the strains of an accordion being clumsily played. I got it for Felo, he heard his father shout, got it off Valentine. She was glad to be rid of it, now Emile's dead, what could she do with an accordion? Poor Emile! said another voice. She never liked him playing, said a third man, she'd walk out of the room as soon as Emile picked the thing up. How's that? She was jealous, was our Valentine, and Emile encouraged her to be so. He liked to make her jealous! Do you know what he named his accordion? What did he call it? He called his accordion Caroline! Come and sit on my knees, Caroline, he'd say, come and have a cuddle! All you men are the same! Felix heard his mother protest. Come and sit on my knees, Albertine! his father roared. Come here and I'll give you a squeeze! Somebody pressed on the bass buttons and the instrument lowed like a bull. You'll wake up Felix, you will! his mother said.

It was a diatonic accordion with sixteen bass keys for the left hand, made by F. Dedents in the 1920s, red and white in colour. The keys had pearly heads, and the sides were blue decorated with yellow flowers, and the reeds were made of metal and leather. He learned to play it, seated, resting the right-hand keyboard on his left thigh and opening the accordion like a cascade falling towards the floor to the left of the chair—a cascade of sound.

Late in the month of May, the grass grows before your eyes. One day it is like a carpet, the next it is halfway up your knees. Get it scythed, Albertine would say, or it'll be tickling the cunt.

The cows in Felix's stable could smell the new grass. They followed with their insolently patient eyes the two swallows who were building a nest on the cross-beam above the horse's stall, long since empty since the purchase of the tractor. They stared at the squares of sunlight on the north wall which had been in shadow all winter long. They became restless. They lowed for Felix before it was milking time. They wouldn't eat their croquettes quietly while being milked. When they licked each other with their tongues, they did so with a kind of frenzy, as if the salt they were tasting had to be a substitute for all the green grass outside.

They want to be out, don't they, Mick? They don't need a calendar to tell them, and they don't give a fuck what year it is. Tomorrow we'll put 'em out, tomorrow when the grass is dry.

Late the following morning Felix undid each cow's chain and opened the large door of the stable.

Myrtille turned towards the sudden light and felt her neck free. Then she tottered, like a convalescent, towards the door. Once outside, she raised her head, bellowed and trotted towards the green grass she could see in the meadow. With each step she refound her strength.

Hold her back, Mick!

The dog bounded after the cow and barked at her forelegs so that she stopped, her neck stretched out taught and straight, her ears up like a second pair of horns, and her imperturbable eyes staring through the sunshine at the meadow. Immobile, her muzzle, her neck, her haunches and her tail in one straight line, she was like the first statue ever made of a cow. The other cows were pushing through the stable door three at a time.

Calm, for Christ's sake! There's enough for you all. Get back Princesse!

The cows trundled their way down the slope towards Myrtille. Mick saw the whole herd charging down upon him. His mouth open without a bark, without a whine; he slunk to the side of the road as they thundered past and triumphantly swept Myrtille into the field. As soon as they felt their feet in the grass, their stampede ended. Some threw their hind legs up into the air. One pair locked their horns and shoved with all their weight against each other. Others turned slowly in circles, listening. The streams from the mountains above the village, white with froth from so much melted ice, were babbling like madmen. The cuckoo was singing. Entire fields were suddenly changing their colour from green to butter yellow— the dandelions, shut at night, were opening their petals.

Princesse mounted Mireille—when a cow is on heat, she may play the bull.

Get her off her!

Mireille, with Princesse on her back, stood gazing at the mountains. The sunshine penetrated to the very marrow of their bones. When the dog approached, Princesse slid gently off Mireille's back, and the wind from the north-west, from beyond the mountains, ruffled the hair between both their horns.

Felix arranged the wire across the opening to the field, switched on the current, and, plucking a stalk of hemlock, held it against the live wire. After a second his hand shot up like a startled bird. He returned slowly to the house, stopping twice to look back at the happiness of the cows.

He phoned the inseminator to ask him to pass by for Princesse and gave him the code-number of her previous insemination.

In making hay there's a wager. The quicker the hay is in, the better it is. Yet the hay must be dry, otherwise it ferments. At the worst, his grandfather said, damp hay could set a house on fire. If you don't take any risks you'll never get your hay in early. You'll be left with hay like straw. So you bet on the sun lasting and the storm holding off. It's not we making hay, repeated Albertine every year, it's sun that makes the hay.

Each time they won the wager, they had cheated the sky. Sometimes they won by minutes, the first drops of rain falling as the horse pulled into the barn the last cart of hay cut two days before. The hurry, the women and children in the fields, the sweat washed away with spring water, the thirst quenched with coffee and cider, being able to jump from a height of fifteen feet in the barn to land deliciously unharmed in the hay, the hay which he knew how to untangle and comb, the barn as tall as a church slowly filling up until, on top of the hay, his head was touching the roof, the supper in the crowded kitchen afterwards, this had all made haymaking a fête during the first half of his life.

Today he was alone, alone to decide the risks, to cut the hay, to tend it, to turn it, to windrow it, to load it, to transport it, to unload it, to pack it, to level it, to quench his thirst, to prepare his own supper. With the new machines he did not have to work harder than in the first half of his life; the difference was that he was now finally alone.

He had cut half the grass in what his father called Grandma's Field. It was on the slope above the linden tree. The hay had been turned but still needed a good hour's sunshine. It was hot and heavy, the weather for horse-flies. He studied the sky as if it were a clock to tell him how many hours away the storm might be. Then he bent down to pick up another handful of hay, assessing its dryness with his fingers. There were four trailer-loads to bring in. He decided to give it half an hour before windrowing. He switched off the tractor engine and walked over to the edge of the field where there was a strip of shade from a little ash grove. There he lay down and pulled the cap over his eyes. He tried to remember the cold of winter but couldn't. He thought he heard thunder in the distance and jumped to his feet.

Get it in now, Felo.

He walked back towards the tractor along the edge of the unmown half of the field where the grass was green and the flowers still coloured. The compagnon rouge pink like lipstick. The bell-flower mauve head bowed. The tiny vetch scattered like stars of creamy milk. The mountain cornflower, deep blue, its calyx criss-crossed with black lace like the stockings of dancers, which cures conjunctivitis. As he noticed them he picked them. Herb bennett yellow like a scarf. Crepide fausse blathaire, vigorous cropped blond. Fragrant orchid red like a pig's penis. He began to pick quickly and indiscriminately in order to make a bouquet, the first since he left school.

Get it in now, Felo.

He drove the tractor back to the house, unhooked the tedder and attached the windrower. The flowers he stuck into a jam jar which he filled with water from the kitchen tap.

The storm broke as he was bringing the last load in.

Saved by the skin of our teeth, Mick!

In the barn he was stripped to the waist. His stomach and back, so rarely exposed to the air, were as pale as a baby's. When you looked at him you thought of a father as seen by his child. Perhaps this was because his own flesh looked both manly and childish.

When he had unloaded the trailer it was time to begin the milking. He walked out into the rain. He could feel it cooling his blood. It ran down his back into the inside of his trousers. Then he put on his vest and his tartan shirt, threw the blue cap on to his wet hair, switched on the motor for the milking machine and went into the stable. He left the door open for there was little light inside and his eyes still smarted from the hay dust.

The milking finished, he entered the kitchen. He had closed the shutters as Albertine had always insisted upon doing in the summer to keep the room cool. Light from the sunset filtered between their slats. On the windowsill was the bunch of flowers he had picked. On seeing them he stopped in mid-stride. He stared at them as if they were a ghost. In the stable a cow pissed. In the kitchen the stillness with its silence was total.

He pulled a chair from under the table, he sat down and he wept. As he wept his head slowly fell forward until his forehead touched the oilcloth. Odd how sounds of distress are recognized by animals. The dog approached the man's back and, getting up on its hindlegs, rested its front paws on his shoulder blades.

He wept for all that would no longer happen. He wept for his mother making potato fritters. He wept for her pruning the roses in the garden. He wept for his father shouting. He wept for the bobsled he had as a boy. He wept for the triangle of hair between the legs of Suzanne the schoolmistress. He wept for the smell of a woman ironing sheets. He wept for jam bubbling in a saucepan on the stove. He wept for never being able to leave the farm for a single day. He wept for the farm where there were no children. He wept for the sound of rain on the rhubarb leaves and his father roaring: Listen to that! That's what you miss when you go away to work for months and when you come back in the spring and you hear that sound again you say—Thank God in Heaven I'm home! He wept for the hay still to be brought in. He wept for the forty-two years that had gone by and he wept for himself.

When Felix, his boots full of hayseed and his face tear-stained, took his two churns of milk to the dairy, he could see for miles across the valley towards the mountains. Most of the fields were mown. Because he was alone, he would always be the last to finish his hay. The heat gone, the shaved ground lay there in a kind of trance waiting for hares or lovers. He drove faster than usual, cutting the corners. His tyres screeched as he braked. There were already five other cars there.

He kicked open the door as if he wanted to break it down. The cheesemaker and the other peasants who had delivered their milk looked at him quizzically. He poured his churn into the tub on the scales without glancing at the reading. And when he emptied the tub into the vat he did so with a ferocity that wiped the smile off the others' faces. The milk splashed the wooden ceiling. His second churn he emptied the same way.

Everything all right at home, Felix?

Nothing, nobody to complain about.

Have a glass of rouge? Clément, the old man, lifted a bottle off a shelf above the sink. Felix shook his head and left.

For God's sake! muttered one of them shaking his head.

In a year or two, said Clément, he'll start drinking. Men aren't made to live alone. Women are stronger. They merge with the weather. I don't know how.

Find him a wife!

He'll never marry.

Why do you say that?

Too late.

It's never too late.

To set up house with a woman, yes, it's too late.

He'd make a good husband.

It's a question of trust, insisted Clément.

Whose trust?

After forty a man doesn't trust a woman enough.

Depends on the woman.

Any woman.

In God's name!

Suppose he finds an old maid—he'll say to himself: there must be something the matter with her, nobody else wanted her. Suppose he finds a woman who's divorced—he'll say: she did wrong by one man, she may do the same to me. Suppose he finds a widow—he'll say: she's been a wife once, it's my farm she's after! With age we all become a little meaner.

And what if he finds a young woman who's unmarried?

Ah! my poor Steve, said Clément, you say that because you're still young yourself. If Felix finds a virgin—

Virgin!

No matter! Suppose he finds a young woman, he'll say to

himself—and who knows, he might be right?—he'll say to himself: in a year or so she's going to cuckold me as sure as day follows night . . .

The men laughed, Clément handed out a glass of wine, and they watched, idly, the white liquid heating in the copper vat, the white liquid that only starts flowing after a birth. Outside the sky was darkening faintly and the first stars were like sleep in its eyes.

F elix, already back in the kitchen, was reading the Communist Party paper for peasants and agricultural workers.

Do you know where the biggest bell in the world is, Maman?

Not round the neck of one of our cows!

It's called the Tsar Kolokol, it weighs one hundred and ninety-six tons and was cast in Moscow in 1735.

That's a bell I'll never hear, she said.

Suddenly he got up from the table and walked across the bare floorboards into the middle room. From under the large bed he pulled out the accordion case and came back with the instrument in his arms. There was no longer light to read by, yet he did not switch on the light. Instead, he opened the door to the stable and entered its darkness. He felt with his foot for the milking-stool that he kept by the water tap and he sat down on it. Myrtille eyed him, another cow mooed. And in the stable, a yard from the gutter full of the cows' greenish shit, he began to play. The air, hot with the heat of the animals who had spent the day in the sun, smelled strongly of garlic, for wild garlic grows in the field by the old road to St Jean where they had been grazing. The instrument breathed in this air and its two voices smelled of it. He played a gavotte in quadruple time. Gavotte, which comes from *gavot*, meaning mountain-dweller, meaning goitre, meaning throat, meaning cry.

Most of the cows were bedded down. At first they turned their heads to where the music was coming from, and the ears of those who were nearest went up, querying, yet very soon they perceived that the music represented nothing more than itself, and their ears relaxed and they replaced their heads on their own flanks or on a neighbour's shoulder. One of the swallows flew around like a bat, less easily reassured than the cows. As he played, Felix looked towards the small window beside the door.

195

The stars were no longer like sleep in the corner of its eye, but like rivets. His head was rigid, only his body moved with the music.

Now he was playing '*Le Jeune Marchois*', a plaintive wedding march he'd learned in the army from a friend who came from Limoges. Two fingers of his left hand, their nails broken, their knuckles ingrained with dirt, the chapped tip of one cracked by the cold of winters, played a staccato beat which was as high and raucous as the cry of a corncrake. His right hand, raised level with his shoulder, was playing the melody which rose and fell like a chain of hills, a chain of gentle hills, of hillocks, of young breasts. His head was now nodding to the tune, his boot on the cobblestones tapping to the beat. The wedding procession approached and the undulating hills gave way to a hedgerow behind which appeared, disappeared and re-appeared women with glistening stoles thrown over their shoulders. The calls of the corncrake too were transformed. No longer the cry of a bird, they were the whistle of air emitted from a leather bag punctured by the point of a knife. His two fingers hit the keys like rivet chargers. The procession had risen in the east by his right shoulder, now it was midday and was before his eyes. Each woman had removed her stole, and the white linen undulating in the wind caressed the bare shoulders of the woman behind her. The women could see the procession of men approaching. The whistles of air were gasps of breath. Appearing and disappearing behind the branches of the hedgerow the women were undoing their hair. Yet already they were passing to the west. The gasps of breath became again the cry of a corncrake, more and more distant, disturbed, fleeing. The road behind the hedge was deserted. A mist covered the hills.

A cow shat when he ceased playing. A pungent smell of wild garlic was wafted towards him. He remembered the waltz of Rosalie de Bon Matin. He played it as loud as he could, as though he hoped the music would remind the hay in the barn above of green grass and blue cornflowers.

It was due to Louis, who can still argue a politician under the table, that Felix began to play regularly every week in the café at Lapraz. One winter evening, Louis went to try to sell Felix a ticket for a lottery which was being organized to raise money to pay for the transport of the village children to the nearest swimming-pool. The campaign slogan was: 'Everyone born in the mountains should learn how to swim!'

There I was, said Louis afterwards in the café, climbing up through the orchard to Felo's house. It was already dark, and I was glad I had a pocket lamp. At the top of the hill I thought I heard music. It must be the radio, I told myself. My hearing's not as good as it used to be. From the big pear tree beside the yard a white owl flew up. There's not many come up this way at night, I said. The music was clearer now, and it was an accordion. No radio sounds like that. The crafty boy, he's got company, I said. Nearer the house, I couldn't believe my ears. The music was coming from the stable! There was a light in the window and the music was coming from the stable! Perhaps he's dancing with gypsies, perhaps he likes to dance with gypsies and is frightened to let them into the house, thieving good-for-nothings that they are. Who would have believed Felo would dance with gypsies if he wasn't his father's son. I peered through the filthy little window and inside I could make out the dancing figures. No use knocking here, Lulu, I said. So I tried the door. It was locked. To hell with the lottery ticket, I simply wanted to see what was going on. All the doors were locked, and he was with the gypsies in the stable. Then I had an idea. Ten to one, Felix didn't lock the barn door above the house. Up the ramp in five seconds and I was right—it was open. By each trap he'd prepared the hay to fork down to each cow in the morning. Not everyone does that—he's far-sighted, Felix. The music was coming up through the floorboards louder and wilder than ever—a mazurka. I lifted up one of the traps and, lying on my stomach on the little pile of hay, I peered through. There was the cow bedded down, and there was Felix seated on a stool, beneath the one dim electric light bulb, an accordion between his arms. For the rest I couldn't believe my eyes. Lulu, you're seeing things, I told myself. Felix was alone! Not another soul in the stable, playing to the fucking cows! He can play though, can Felix. You should get him to bring his music down here sometime.

And so Felix began to play in the café at Lapraz most Saturday nights. That was ten years ago.

197

On the night of Philippe's wedding, when the sky was
already getting light from the dawn, long after Philippe
had taken Yvonne to bed, and the parents and the
parents-in-law had gone home, a few wedding guests, including
the dressmaker with dangling earrings who liked to laugh and who
worked in a factory that produced wooden handles for house
painters' brushes, a few guests were still dancing and Felix sat
playing on his usual chair, his cap on the back of his bald head, his
heavy working boots tapping the floor as he played. They might
have stopped dancing before, yet one tune had led to the next, and
Felix had fitted them together, like one pipe into another till the
chimney was so high it was lost in the sky. A chimney of tunes, and
the women's feet so tired they had taken off their shoes to dance
barefoot.

Music demands obedience. It even demands obedience of
the imagination when a melody comes to mind. One can think of
nothing else. It's a kind of tyrant. In exchange it offers its own
freedom. All bodies can boast about themselves with music. The
old can dance as well as the young. Time is forgotten. And that
night, from behind the silence of the last stars, we thought we
heard the affirmation of a Yes.

La Belle Jacqueline once more! the dressmaker shouted at
Felix. I love music! With music you can say everything!

You can't talk to a lawyer with music, Felix replied.

Perhaps they are right, those who pretend there are harps in
heaven. Maybe flutes and violins too. But I'm sure there are
no accordions, just as I'm sure there's no green cow shit that
smells of wild garlic. The accordion was made for life on this earth,
the left hand marking the bass and the heartbeats, the arms and
shoulders labouring to make breath, and the right hand fingering
for hopes!

Finally the dancing stopped.

Come on, Caroline, come on, Felix muttered as he packed
the accordion away. It's time to go.

"The most influential, readable and far-ranging magazine now existing in the Western World"

So one of Britain's leading journalists, Peregrine Worsthorne, wrote of ENCOUNTER in 1983, shortly before the magazine's 30th anniversary. Recent issues include:

James Rusbridger
'ENIGMA' & PEARL HARBOUR
Christopher Ricks
ALEXANDER POPE
Ronald Hayman
SARTRE & THE MICE
John Wain
MARSHALL McLUHAN
Jeffrey Richards
THE HOOLIGAN CULTURE
Adrian Smith
LOW & BEAVERBROOK
Michael Charlton
STAR WARS OR PEACE IN THE SKIES?

Stories and poems by William Trevor, Gavin Ewart, Peter Porter, Peter Reading, and many others.

If you are not already a regular reader, why not become one now? We will enrol you as a subscriber for one year (ten issues) for the special rate of £13.50 (USA $29.25 air-speeded) — **a saving of 25% on the normal rate.** Please return the coupon below (or a letter in similar terms)

Encounter, 59 St. Martin's Lane, London WC2N 4JS
Thank you for your offer. I'd like to receive ENCOUNTER for one year and enclose my cheque for £13.50 (USA $29.25 air-speeded).

NAME _____
(Please print clearly)
ADDRESS _____

_____ ZIP (USA) _____
Please charge to my American Express a/c no.:

Granta 3

ff

faber and faber

HANIF KUREISHI
My Beautiful Laundrette
and
The Rainbow Sign

Hanif Kureishi's script of his award-winning film,
with a long autobiographical introduction
The Rainbow Sign.
'Funny and humane, real and surreal, this is a British
winner.' *Financial Times*
£3.95 *paper*

CARYL PHILLIPS
A State of Independence

'His eye for cant and political irony is always
needlingly sharp... Spirit and dash here return to the
political novel.' *Observer*
£8.95

ROBERT COOVER

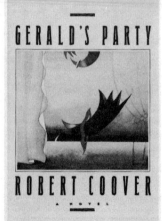

GERALD'S PARTY

'What a novel!... A crazed comic
strip, a zany metaphysical murder
mystery, outrageous satire and humour
at its blackest. Robert Coover's furious
new novel takes on all the queasy
affluence of Reagan's America and hits
it right below the belt. He is unfair, rude,
cruel and murderously funny. A master.'

Angela Carter

£9.95

WILLIAM HEINEMANN

ALICE MUNRO
A QUEER STREAK
PART TWO:
POSSESSION

Dane believes that he has one memory of Violet—his mother's sister—from a time before his mother died. He remembers very little from that far back. He hardly remembers his mother. He has one picture of his mother standing in front of the mirror at the kitchen sink, tucking her red hair under a navy-blue straw hat. He remembers a bright red ribbon on the hat. She must have been getting ready to go to church. And he can see a swollen leg, of a dull-brown colour, that he associates with her last sickness. But he doubts if he ever saw that. Why would her leg be such a colour? He must have heard people talking about it. He heard them say that her leg was as big as a barrel.

He thinks he remembers Violet coming for supper, as she sometimes did, bringing with her a pudding which she set outside in the snow, to keep it cool. (None of the farmhouses had a refrigerator in those days.) Then it snowed, the snow covered the pudding-dish, which sank from sight. Dane remembers Violet tramping around in the snowy yard after dark, calling, 'Pudding, pudding, here pudding!' as if it was a dog. Himself laughing immoderately, and his mother and father laughing in the doorway, and Violet elaborating the performance, stopping to whistle.

Not long after his mother died, his grandmother died—the one who lived with Violet, and wore a black hat, and called the hens in what sounded exactly like their own language—a tireless crooning and clucking. Then Violet sold the farm and moved to town, where she got a job with Bell Telephone. That was during the Second World War, when there was a shortage of men, and Violet soon became manager. There was some feeling that she should have stepped down when the war was over, given the job back to some man who had a family to support. Dane recalls hearing somebody say that—a woman, maybe one of his father's sisters, saying that it would have been the gracious thing to do. But his father said no, Violet did right. He said Violet had spunk.

Instead of the dull, draped, beaded dresses that married women—mothers—wore, Violet wore skirts and blouses. She wore all-round pleated skirts of lively plaid, navy-blue or grey gabardine, with wonderful blouses of ivory satin, ruffled white georgette, pink or yellow or silvery rayon crêpe. The colour of her good coat was royal purple, and it had a silver fox collar. Her hair was not finger-waved, or permanented, but done up in a thick, dark, regal-looking roll. Her complexion was powdered, delicately pink, like the large sea-shell she owned and would let Dane listen to. Dane knows now that she dressed, and looked, like a certain kind of business woman, professional woman, of those days. Stylish but ladylike, shapely though not exactly slender, neither matronly nor girlish. What he took to be so remarkable, and unique, was not really so. This was the truth he discovered about most things as he got older. Just the same, his memory protects her—from any sense of repetition, or classification, or from being in any way diminished.

In town Violet lived in an apartment over the Royal Bank. You had to go up a long closed-in flight of stairs. The long windows in the living-room were called french doors. They opened out on to two tiny balconies with waist-high railings of wrought-iron. The walls were painted, not papered. They were a pale green. Violet bought a new sofa and chair upholstered in a rich moss-green fabric, and a coffee-table with a glass tray that fitted over the wooden top. The curtains were called drapes, and had pull-cords. As they closed over the windows a pattern of shiny cream-coloured leaves rippled out across the dull cream background. There was no ceiling-light—just floor-lamps. In the kitchen there were knotty-pine cupboards and a knotty-pine breakfast nook. Another flight of steps—these were open and steep—led down to a little hedged-in backyard, which only Violet had the use of. It was as tidily enclosed, as susceptible to arrangement and decoration, as any living-room.

During the first two years he went to high school in town, Dane visited Violet fairly often. He stayed overnight in the apartment when the weather was stormy. Violet made him up a bed on the moss-green sofa. He was a skinny, ravenous, red-headed boy in those days—nobody can credit the skinniness now—and Violet fed him well. She made him hot chocolate with whipped cream to drink at bedtime. She served him creamed chicken in tart shells, and layer cakes, and something called gravel pie, which was made with maple syrup. She ate one piece, and he ate the rest. This was a great change from the rough-and-ready meals at home, with his father and the hired man. Violet told him stories about her own childhood on the farm, with his mother and the other sister who lived

203

out in Edmonton now, and their mother and father, whom she called characters. Everybody was a character in those stories, everything was shaped to be funny.

She had bought a record-player, and she played records for him, asking him to choose his favourite. His favourite was the record she got as a bonus when she joined a record club that would introduce her to classical music. It was *The Birds*, by Respighi. Her favourite was 'Kenneth McKellar Singing Sacred and Secular Songs.'

She didn't come out to the farm any more. Dane's father, when he stopped to pick Dane up, never had time for a cup of coffee. Perhaps he was afraid to sit down in such an elegant apartment in his farm clothes. Perhaps he still held a little grudge against Violet for what she had done at church.

Violet had made a choice there, right at the beginning of her town life. The church had two doors. One door was used by country people—the reason for this originally being that it was nearer to the drive-shed—and the other by town people. Inside, the pattern was maintained—town people on one side of the church, country people on the other. There was no definable feeling of superiority or inferiority involved—that was just the way it was. Even country people who had retired and moved to town made a point of not using the town door, though that might mean going out of their way, walking right past it, to the country door.

Violet's move, and her job, certainly made her a town person. But when she first came to that church, Dane and his father were the only people in it that she knew. Choosing the country side would have shown loyalty, and a certain kind of pride, a foregoing of privilege. (For it was true that most of the elders and ushers and Sunday school teachers were chosen from the town side, just as most of the fancy hats and fashionable ladies' outfits appeared over there.) Choosing the town side—which was what Violet did—showed an acceptance of status, perhaps even a wish for more.

Dane's father teased her on the sidewalk afterwards.

'You like the company over there?'

'It just seemed handier,' Violet said, pretending not to know what he was talking about. 'I don't know about the company. I think some fellow had a dead cigar in his pocket.'

Dane wished so much that Violet hadn't done that. It wasn't that he wanted anything serious to happen between Violet and his father—for instance, marriage. He couldn't imagine that. He just wanted them to be on the same side, so that could be his side.

On an afternoon in June, when he had finished writing one of his exams, Dane went around to Violet's apartment to get a book he had left there. He was allowed to use the apartment to study in while she was at work. He would open the french doors and let the smell of the burst-open countryside in, all rank and flowering and newly-ploughed and manured. Dust came in too, but he always thought he could wipe that up before she got home. He walked around and around in the pale bright living-room, tamping down chunks of information, feeling lordly. Everything in the room got bits of whatever he was learning attached to it. There was a dark picture of a dead king and some stately ladies that he would always look at, memorizing poetry. The ladies reminded him in a strange way of Violet.

He hadn't known whether Violet would be home, because her afternoon off varied from week to week. But he heard her voice as he came up the stairs.

'It's me,' he called, and waited for her to come out of the kitchen and ask about his exam.

Instead she called back to him, 'Dane! Dane, I wasn't expecting you! Come and have coffee with us!'

She introduced him to the two people in the kitchen, a man and wife. The Tebbutts. The man was standing by the counter and the woman was sitting in the breakfast nook. Dane knew the man by sight. Wyck Tebbutt, who sold insurance. He was supposed to have been a professional baseball player, but that would have been a long time ago. He was a trim, small, courteous man, always rather nattily dressed, with a deft athlete's modest confidence.

Violet didn't ask Dane anything about his exam, but went on fussing about getting the coffee ready. First she got out breakfast cups, then rejected them, got down her good china. She spread a cloth on the breakfast-nook table. There was a faint scorch-mark on it, from the iron.

'Well, I'm mortified!' said Violet, laughing.

Wyck Tebbutt laughed too.

'So you should be, so you should be!' he said.

Violet's nervous laugh, and her ignoring him, displeased Dane considerably. She had been in town for several years now, and she had made several changes in herself, which he seemed to be just now noticing all together. Her hair was not done up in a roll any more, it was short and curled. And its dark brown colour was not the same as it used to be. Now it had a rich, dull look, like chocolate fudge. Her lipstick was too heavy, too bright a red, and the grain of her skin had coarsened. Also, she had put on a lot of weight, especially around the hips. The harmony of her figure was spoiled—it almost looked as if she was wearing some kind of cage or contraption under her skirt.

As soon as his coffee was poured, Wyck Tebbutt said that he would just take his cup down into the yard, because he wanted to see how those new rose-bushes were getting on.

'Oh, I think they've got some kind of a bug!' said Violet, as if the fact delighted her. 'I'm afraid they have, Wyck!'

All this time the wife was talking, and she went right on, hardly noticing that her husband had left. She talked to Violet and even to Dane, but she was really just talking into the air. She talked about her appointments with the doctor, and the chiropractor. She said that she had a headache that was like red-hot irons being clamped on her temples. And she had another kind of shooting pain down the side of her neck that was like hundreds of needles being driven into her flesh. She wouldn't allow a break, she was like a helpless little talking-machine set up in a corner of the breakfast-nook, her large sad eyes going blank as soon as they fixed on you.

This was the sort of person, this was the sort of talk, that Violet was good at imitating.

And now she was deferring. She was listening, or pretending to listen, to this woman, with an interest the woman didn't even notice or need. Was it because the husband had walked out, did Violet feel a concern about his rudeness to his wife? She did keep glancing down into the backyard.

'I just have to see what Wyck thinks about that bug,' she said, and she was off, down the back steps, at what seemed like a heavy and undignified trot.

'All they are interested in is their money,' the wife said.

. Dane got up to get himself more coffee. He stood at the stove, and lifted the coffee-pot inquiringly while she talked.

'I shouldn't have drunk the amount I already have,' she said. 'Not with ninety percent of my stomach scar tissue.'

Dane looked down at her husband and Violet, who were leaning together over the young rose-bushes. No doubt they were talking about the roses, and bugs, and bug-killer and blight. Nothing so crude as a touch would occur. Wyck, holding his coffee-cup, delicately lifted one leaf, then another, with his foot. Violet's look travelled down obediently to the leaf held against his polished shoe.

It would be wrong to say that Dane understood anything right then. But he forgot the woman who was talking and the coffee-pot he was holding. He felt a secret, a breath of others' intimacy. Something he didn't want to know about, but would have to.

Not so long afterwards he was with his father on the street, and he saw Wyck coming towards them. His father said, 'Hello, Wyck,' in a certain calm respectful voice men use to greet other men they don't know—or perhaps don't want to know—too well. Dane had veered off to look into the hardware store window.

'Don't you know Wyck Tebbutt?' his father said. 'I thought you might've run into him at Violet's.'

Then Dane felt it again—the breath he hated. He hated it more now, because it was all around him. It was all around him, if even his father knew.

He didn't want to understand the extent of Violet's treachery. He already knew that he would never forgive her.

Now Dane is a broad-shouldered ruddy man with the worn outlines of a teddy bear and a beard that is almost entirely grey. He has grown to look more and more like his mother. He is an architect. He went away from home to college, and for a long time he lived and worked in other places, but he came back several years ago, and is kept busy now restoring the churches and town halls and business blocks and houses that were considered eyesores at the time he left. He lives in the house he grew up in, the house his father was born and died in, a 150-year-old stone house that he and Theo have gradually brought back to something like its original style.

He lives with Theo, who is a social worker.

When Dane first told Wyck and Violet (he has forgiven

her—them—long ago) that somebody named Theo was moving in with him, Wyck said, 'I take that to mean you finally turned up a serious girl-friend.'

Violet didn't say anything.

'A man friend,' Dane said gently. 'It isn't easy to tell, from the name.'

'Well. That's him's and your business,' Wyck said affably. The only sign he gave that he might be shaken was in saying 'him's' and not noticing.

'Theo. Yes,' said Violet. 'That is hard to tell.'

This was in the little two-bedroom house on the edge of town, which Violet moved to after she retired from the phone company. Wyck had moved in with her after his wife died, and they were able to marry. The house was one of a row of very similar houses, strung out along a country road in front of a corn-field. Wyck's things were moved in on top of Violet's, and the low-ceilinged rooms seemed crowded, the arrangement temporary and haphazard. The moss-green sofa looked bulky and old-fashioned, under an afghan made by Wyck's wife. A large black velvet painting, belonging to Wyck, took up most of one living-room wall. It depicted a bull and a bullfighter. Wyck's old sporting trophies and the silver tray presented to him by the insurance company sat on the mantel beside Violet's old shell and tippling Scotsman.

All those dust-catchers, Violet called them.

But she kept Wyck's things there even after Wyck himself was gone. He died during the Grey Cup game, at the end of November. Violet phoned Dane, who listened to her at first with his eyes on the television screen.

'I went down to the church,' Violet said. 'I took some things down for the rummage sale, and when I got back, as soon as I opened the door I said, "Wyck," and he didn't answer. I saw the back of his head in a funny position. It was bent towards the arm of his chair. I went around in front of him and turned off the television.'

'What do you mean?' said Dane. 'Aunt Violet? What's the matter?'

'Oh, he's dead,' said Violet, as if Dane had been questioning it. 'He would have to be dead to let me turn off the football game.' She spoke in a loud emphatic voice with an unnatural joviality—as if she was covering up some embarrassment.

When he drove into town he found her sitting on the front step.

'I'm a fool,' she said—her voice still jarring, loud and bright.

Theo said later than many old people were like that, when someone close to them died.

'They get past grief,' he said. 'Or it's a different kind.'

All winter Violet seemed to be all right, driving her car when the weather permitted, going to church, going to the Senior Citizens' Club to play cards. Then just when the hot months were starting and you'd think she would most enjoy getting out, she announced to Dane that she didn't intend to drive any more.

He thought the trouble might be with her eyesight. He suggested an appointment to see if she needed stronger glasses.

'I see well enough,' she said. 'My trouble is not being sure of what I see.'

What did she mean by that?

'I see things I know aren't there.'

How did she know they were not there?

'Because I still have enough sense that I can tell. My brain gets the message through and tells me that's ridiculous. But what if it doesn't get through all the time? How am I going to know? I can get my groceries delivered. Most old people get their groceries delivered. I am an old person. They are not going to miss me that much, at the supermarket.'

But Dane knew how much she enjoyed going to the supermarket, and he thought that he or Theo would have to try to get her there once a week. That was where she got the special strong coffee that Wyck had drunk, and she usually liked to look at the smoked meats and back bacon—both favourite things of Wyck's—though she seldom bought any.

'For instance,' said Violet. 'The other morning I saw King Billy.'

'You saw my grand-daddy?' Dane said, laughing. 'Well. How was he?'

'I saw King Billy the horse,' said Violet shortly. 'I came out of my room and there he was poking his head in at the dining-room window.'

She said she had known him right away. His familiar, foolish, dapple-grey head. She told him to go on, get out of there, and he lifted his head over the sill and moved off in a leisurely kind of way. Violet went on into the kitchen to start her breakfast, and then several things occurred to her.

King Billy the horse had been dead for about sixty-five years.

That couldn't have been the milkman's horse, either, because milkmen hadn't driven horses since around 1950. They drove trucks.

No. They didn't drive anything, because milk was not delivered any more. It didn't even come in bottles. You picked it up at the store, in cartons or in plastic bags.

There was glass in the dining-room window that had not been broken.

'I was never especially fond of that horse, either,' said Violet. 'I was never *un*-fond of it, but if I had my choice of anything or anyone I wanted to see that's gone—it wouldn't be that horse.'

'What would it be?' said Dane, trying to keep the conversation on a light level, though he wasn't at all happy about what he heard. 'What would be your choice?'

But Violet made an unpleasant sound—a balky sort of grunt, *annhh*—as if his question angered and exasperated her. A look of deliberate, even ill-natured, stupidity—the visual equivalent of that grunt—passed over her face.

It happened that a few nights later Dane was watching a television programme about people in South America—mostly women—who believe themselves to be invaded and possessed, from time to time and in special circumstances, by spirits. The look on their faces reminded him of that look on Violet's. The difference was that they courted this possession, and he was sure Violet didn't. Nothing in her wanted to be overtaken by this helpless and distracted, dull and stubborn old woman, with a memory or imagination out of control, bulging at random through the present scene. Trying to keep that old woman in check was bound to make her short-tempered. In fact he had seen her—now he remembered, he had seen her tilt her head to the side and give it a quick slap, as people do to get rid of a buzzing, an unwelcome presence.

A week or so further into the summer, she phoned him.

'Dane. Did I tell you about this pair I see, going by my house?'

'Pair of what, Aunt Violet?'

'Girls. I think so. Boys don't have long hair any more, do they? They're dressed in army clothes, it looks like, but I don't know whether that means anything. One is short and one is tall. I see them go by this house and look at it. They walk out the road and back.'

'Maybe they're collecting bottles. People do.'

'They don't have anything to put bottles in. It's this house. They have some interest in it.'

'Aunt Violet? Are you sure?'

'Yes, I know, I ask myself too. But they're not anybody I've ever known. They're not anybody I know that's dead. That's something.'

He thought he should get around to see her, find out what was going on. But before he got there, she phoned again.

'Dane. I just wanted to tell you. About those girls I noticed walking by the house. They are girls. They're just dressed up in army outfits. They came and knocked on my door. They said they were looking for a Violet Thoms. I said there was no such person living here, and they looked very downcast. Then I said there was a Violet Tebbutt, and would she do?'

She seemed in high spirits. Dane was busy, he had a meeting with some town councillors in half an hour. He also had a toothache. But he said, 'You were right then. So who are they?'

'That's the surprise,' said Violet. 'They are not just any girls. One of them is your cousin. I mean, the daughter of your cousin. Donna Collard's daughter. Do you know who I'm talking about? Your cousin Donna Collard? Her married name is McNie.'

'No,' said Dane.

'Your Aunt Bonnie Hope, out in Edmonton, she was married to a man named Collard, Roy Collard, and she had three daughters. Elinor and Ruth and Donna. Now do you know who I mean?'

'I never met them,' he said.

'No. Well, Donna Collard married a McNie, I forget his first name, and they live in Prince George, British Columbia, and this is their daughter. Heather. This is their daughter Heather that has been walking past my house. The other girl is her friend. Gillian.'

Dane didn't say anything for a minute, and Violet said, 'Dane? I hope you don't think that I'm confused about this?'

He laughed. He said, 'I'll have to come around and see them.'

'They are very polite and good-hearted,' said Violet, 'in spite of how they might look.'

He was fairly sure that these girls were real, but everything was slightly out of focus to him at the time (he had a low-grade fever, though he didn't know it yet, and eventually would have to have a root-canal job done on his tooth). He actually thought that he should ask around town, to find out if anybody else had seen them. When he did get around to doing this, some time later, he found out that a couple of girls of that description had been staying at the hotel, that they owned a beaten-up blue Datsun but walked a lot, in town and out, and were generally thought to be women's libbers. People didn't think much of their outfits, but they didn't cause any trouble, except for getting into some sort of argument with the exotic dancer at the hotel.

In the meantime, he had heard a lot from Violet. She phoned him at home, when his mouth was so sore he could hardly talk, and said it was too bad he wasn't feeling well—otherwise he could have got to meet Heather and Gillian.

'Heather is the tall one,' Violet said. 'She has long fair hair and a narrow build. If she resembles Bonnie Hope at all it is in her teeth. But Heather's teeth suit her face better and they are beautifully white. Gillian is a nice-looking sort of girl with curly hair and a tan. Heather has that fair skin that burns. They wear the same sort of clothes, you know, the army pants and work shirts and boys' boots, but Gillian always has a belt on and her collar turned up and on her it looks like more of a style. Gillian is more confident but I think Heather is more intelligent. She is the one more genuinely interested.'

'What in?' said Dane. 'What are they, anyway—students?'

'They've been to university,' Violet said. 'I don't know what they were studying. They've been to France and Mexico. In Mexico they stayed on an island that was called the Isle of Women. It was a women-ruled society. They belong to a theatre and they make up plays. They make up their own plays, they don't take some writer's plays or do plays that have been done before. It's all women, in this theatre. They made me a lovely supper, Dane, I wish you could have been here. They made a salad with artichoke hearts in it.'

'Violet sounds as if she's on drugs,' said Dane to Theo. 'She sounds as if they've got her spinning.'

When he could talk again he called her.

'What are those girls interested in, Aunt Violet? Are they interested in old china and jewellery and things?'

'They are not,' said Violet crossly. 'They are interested in family history. They are interested in our family and what I can remember about what it was like. I had to tell them what the reservoir was on a stove.'

'What would they want to know that for?'

'Oh. They have some idea. They have some idea about doing a play.'

'What do they know about plays?'

'Didn't I tell you, they've acted in plays? They've made up their own plays and acted in them, in this women's theatre.'

'What sort of play are they going to make up?'

'I don't know. I don't know if they'll do it. They're just interested in what it was like.'

'That's all the style, now,' Dane said. 'To be interested in that.'

'They're not just letting on to be, Dane. They really are.'

But he thought that she didn't sound so buoyant, this time.

'You know they change all the names,' she said. 'When they do make up a play, they change all the names and places. But I think they just like finding out about things, and talking. They're not all that young, but they seem young, they're so curious. And light-hearted.'

'Your face looks different,' said Dane to Violet, when he finally got to visit her again. 'Have you lost weight?'

Violet said, 'I wouldn't think so.'

Dane had lost twelve pounds himself but she did not notice. She seemed cheerful, but agitated. She kept getting up and sitting down, looking out of the window, moving things around for no reason on the kitchen counter.

The girls had gone.

'They're not coming back?' said Dane.

Yes, they were. Violet thought they were coming back. She didn't know just when.

'They're off to find their island, I guess,' said Dane. 'Their island ruled by women.'

'I don't know,' said Violet. 'I think they've gone to Montreal.'

Dane didn't like to think that he could be made to feel so irritable and suspicious by two girls he hadn't even met. He was almost ready to blame it on the medication he still had to take for his tooth. There was a sense he had of something concealed from him—all around him, but concealed, a tiresome, silly, malicious sort of secret.

'You've cut your hair,' he said. That was why her face looked different.

'They cut it. They said it was a Joan of Arc style.' Violet smiled ironically, much as she used to, and touched her hair. 'I told them I hoped I wouldn't end up burned at the stake.'

She held her head in her hands, and rocked back and forth.

'They've tired you,' Dane said. 'They've tired you, Aunt Violet.'

'It's going through all that,' said Violet. She jerked her head towards the back bedroom. 'It's what I have to get to work on, in there.'

In Violet's back bedroom there were boxes of papers, and an old hump-backed trunk that had belonged to her mother. Dane thought that it was full of papers, too. Old high school notes, teachers' college notes, report cards, records and correspondence from her years with the phone company, minutes of meetings, letters, postcards. Anything that had writing on it she had probably kept.

She said that all these papers had to be sorted out. It had to be done before the girls got back. There were things she had promised them.

'What things?'

'Just things.'

Were they coming back soon?

Violet said yes. She expected so, yes. As she thought of this, her hands were patting and rubbing at the table-top. She took a bite of a cookie, and crumbled what was left of it. Dane saw her sweep the crumbs into her hand and put them in her coffee.

'That's what they sent,' she said, and pushed in front of him a card he had noticed, that was propped against her sugar-bowl. It was a home-made card with childishly crayoned violets on it, and red hearts. She seemed to intend that he should read it, so he did.

'Thank you a million, million times for your help and openness. You have given us a wonderful story. It is a classic story of anti-patriarchal rage. Your gift to us, can we give it to others? What is called Female Craziness is nothing but centuries of Frustration and Oppression. The part about the creek is wonderful just by itself and how many women can identify!'

Across the bottom, in capitals, had been written: LONGING TO SEE DOCUMENTS, PLEASE NEXT TIME, LOVE AND GRATITUDE.

'What is all this about?' said Dane. 'Why do you have to sort things out for them? Why can't they just go through the whole mess and find what they want for themselves?'

'Because I am so ashamed,' said Violet vehemently. 'I don't want anybody to see.'

He told her there was nothing, nothing, to be ashamed of.

'I shouldn't have used the word mess. It's just that you've accumulated a lot, over the years. Some of it is probably very interesting.'

'There is more to it than anybody knows! And I am the one has to deal with it!'

'Anti-patriarchal rage,' said Dane, taking up the card again. 'What do they mean by that?' He wondered why they used capitals for 'Female Craziness' and 'Frustration' and 'Oppression'.

'I'll tell you,' said Violet. 'I'll just tell you. You don't know what I've got to contend with. There's things that are not so nice. I went in there and opened up that old trunk to have a look at what was inside, and what do you think I found, Dane? It was full of filth. Horse manure. Set out in rows. On purpose.'

When Dane told Theo this, Theo smiled, then said, 'I'm sorry. What did she say then?'

'I told her I'd go and look at it and she said she'd cleaned it all out.'

'Yes. Well. It looks as if something snapped, doesn't it? I thought I could see it coming.'

Dane remembered the other thing she'd said but he didn't mention it, it didn't matter.

'That's a disgusting trick, isn't it?' she'd said harshly. 'That's the trick of a stunted mind!'

Violet's front door was standing open at noon the next day, when Dane drove down her road, heading out of town. He didn't usually take this route. That he did today was not surprising, considering how much Violet had been on his mind in the last several hours.

He must have come in the door just as the flames started up in the kitchen. He saw their light ahead of him on the kitchen wall. He ran back there, and caught Violet heaping papers on top of the gas stove. She had turned on the burners.

Dane grabbed a scatter-rug from the hall to shield himself, so that he could turn off the gas. Burning papers flew into the air. There were heaps of paper all over the floor, some papers still in boxes. Violet was evidently intending to burn it all.

'Oh, Jesus, Aunt Violet!' Dane was yelling. 'Jesus, Jesus, what are you doing! Get out of here! Get out!'

Violet was standing in the middle of the room, rooted there, like a big bark stump, with scraps of fiery paper flying all around her.

'Get out!' Dane yelled, and turned her around, and pushed her towards the back door. Then all of a sudden her speed was as extraordinary as her stillness had been. She ran or lurched to the door, opened it, and crossed the back porch. Instead of going down the steps, she went off the edge—falling head first into some rose-bushes that Wyck had planted there.

Dane didn't know right away that she had done that. He was too busy in the kitchen.

Luckily, paper in heaps or bundles doesn't catch fire as readily as most people think it does. Dane was more afraid of the curtains catching, or the dry paint behind the stove. Violet wasn't anything like the careful housekeeper she used to be, and the walls were greasy. He brought the scatter-rug down on the flames that were shooting up from the stove, then remembered the fire-extinguisher that he himself had bought for Violet and insisted she keep on the kitchen counter. He went stumbling around the room with the fire-extinguisher, chasing flaming birds that fell down as bits of charred paper. He was impeded by the piles of paper on the floor. But the curtains didn't catch. The wall behind the stove had broken out in paint-blisters, but it didn't catch. He kept at the chase, and in five minutes, maybe less, he had the fire out. Just the bits of burned paper, dirty moth-wings, were lying over everything—a mess.

When he saw Violet on the ground between the rose-bushes he thought the worst. He was afraid she had had a stroke, or a heart attack, or at the very least broken her hip in the fall. But she was conscious, struggling to push herself up, groaning. He got hold of her, and lifted her. With many grunts and exclamations of dismay coming from them both, he helped her to the back steps and set her down.

'What's this blood on you?' he said. Her arms were smeared with dirt and blood.

'It's from the roses,' Violet said. He knew then, by her voice, that there was nothing broken in her.

'The roses scratched me something fierce,' she said. 'Dane, you're a terrible sight. You're a terrible sight, you're all black!'

Tears and sweat ran together down his face. He put his hand up to his cheek, and it came away black.

'Smoke,' he said.

She was so calm that he thought perhaps she had had a tiny stroke, a loss of memory, just enough to let her mind skip over the fire. But she hadn't.

'I didn't even use any coal-oil,' she said. 'Dane, I didn't use coal-oil or anything. What would make it flare up like that?'

'It wasn't a wood-stove, Aunt Violet. It was on top of the gas burners.'

'Oh, Lord.'

'You must have thought you were burning papers in the wood-stove.'

'I must have. What a thing to do. And you came and put it out.'

He was trying to pick the black bits of paper out of her hair, but they disintegrated under his fingers, they fell to smaller bits, and were lost.

'I have you to thank,' said Violet.

'What we ought to do now,' he said, 'is take you over to the hospital, just to make sure you're all right. You could have a rest for a few days while we see about cleaning up the kitchen. Would that be all right?'

She made some groaning but peaceable sound that meant yes.

'Then maybe you'd like to come out and stay with us for a while.'

He would talk to Theo that night, they would have to manage something.

'You'd have to watch me, that I didn't burn the place down.'

'That's all right.'

'Oh, Dane. It's no joke.'

Violet died in the hospital, the third night, without any warning. A delayed reaction, perhaps. Shock. Dane burned all the papers in the backyard incinerator. She never told him to, she never mentioned what she had been doing. She never mentioned the girls again, or anything that had happened that summer. He just felt that he should finish what she had started. He planned, as he burned, what he would say to those girls, but by the time he finished he thought he was being too hard on them—they had brought her happiness, as much as trouble.

While they had been still sitting on the back steps, in the hot, thinly-clouded, early afternoon, with the green wall of corn in front of them, Violet had touched her scratches and said, 'These remind me.'

'I should put some Dettol on them,' said Dane.

'Sit still. Do you think there is any kind of infection that hasn't run its course through my veins, by now?'

He sat still, and she said, 'You know Wyck and I were friends, Dane, a long, long time, before we were able to get married?'

'Yes.'

'Well, these remind me of the way we met, to be friends the way we were, because of course we knew each other by sight. I was driving my first car, the V-8, that you wouldn't remember, and I ran it off the road. I ran it into a bit of a ditch and I couldn't get out. So I heard a car coming, and I waited, and then I couldn't face it.'

'You were embarrassed you'd run off the road?'

'I was feeling badly. That was why I'd run off the road. I was feeling badly for no reason, or just a little reason. I couldn't face anybody, and I ran off into the bushes and right away I got stuck. I turned and twisted and couldn't get loose and the more I turned the more I got scratched. I was in a light summer dress. But the car stopped anyway. It was Wyck. I never told you this, Dane?'

No.

'It was Wyck driving someplace, by himself. He said, stay still there, and he came over and started pulling the berry canes and branches off me. I felt like a buffalo in a trap. But he didn't laugh at me, he didn't seem the least surprised, to find a person in that predicament. I was the one who started laughing. Seeing him going round so dutiful, in his light-blue summer suit.'

She ran her hands up and down her arms, tracing the scratches with her fingertips, patting them.

'What was I just talking about?'

'When you were caught in the bushes, and Wyck was working you out.'

She patted her arms rapidly and shook her head and made that noise in her throat of impatience, or disgust. *Annhh.*

She sat up straight and said in a clear brazen voice, 'There is a wild pig running through the corn.'

'And you were laughing,' Dane said, as if he hadn't heard that.

'Yes,' said Violet, nodding several times, and struggling to be patient. 'Yes. We were.'

GORBACHEV

THE PATH TO POWER
by Christian Schmidt-Häuer

"An invaluable, interesting and timely book ... it is the only useful guide to the subtleties of Gorbachev's mind. The material on Raisa Gorbachev is fascinating, and quite a coup."
Neal Ascherson of The Observer

"This is an excellent book which will last."
Professor John Erickson, Edinburgh University

Publication 13 March   £12.95
ISBN 1 85043 015 2

I.B.TAURIS & C° Lᵗᵈ

3 Henrietta Street, Covent Garden, London WC2E 8PW
Tel 01-836 5814 Telex 261507/3166 Tauris

Through the story of an Arab 'magician'
hounded by the British authorities in the
Palestine of the 1930's, this passionate first
novel illuminates the fate of a whole nation...

THE LORD
SORAYA ANTONIUS

'A moving and heartfelt
account of one of the greatest
tragedies of the twentieth
century'   John Julius Norwich

'Miss Antonius is a new talent
indeed'   Sybille Bedford

£9.95   224pp

hamish hamilton

PARIS WITH PASSION

Treat yourself to a moveable
feast of Paris. Since 1981,
PASSION has been bringing
the best of Paris to readers in
France and around the world.
Each issue offers an editorial
menu as diverse and inviting as
the city it reflects.

From politics to fashion,
photographic portfolios to
works of short fiction,
PASSION is a showcase of
original writing and design
produced by an international
team in Paris. For subscription
information, contact:
PASSION – **The Magazine of
Paris,** 18, rue du Pont-Neuf,
75001 Paris.

SEAMUS DEANE
HAUNTED

On the stairs, there was a clear, plain silence.
It was a short staircase, fourteen steps in all, covered in lino from which the original pattern had been polished away to the point where it had the look of a faint memory. Eleven steps took you to the turn of the stairs where the cathedral and the sky always hung in the window frame. Three more steps took you on to the landing, about six feet long, with the two bedrooms opening off it. It was in those two bedrooms that the nine of us slept—the parents and the seven children.

'Don't move,' my mother said from the landing. 'Don't cross that window.' I was on the tenth step, she was on the landing. I could have touched her.

'There's something there between us. A shadow. Don't move.'

I had no intention. I was enthralled. But I could see no shadow.

'There's somebody there. Somebody unhappy. Go back down the stairs, son.'

I retreated one step. 'How'll you get down?'

'I'll stay a while and it will go away.'

'How do you know?'

'I'll feel it gone.'

'What if it doesn't go?'

'It always does. I'll not be long.'

'You've seen it before?'

'Ever since we came to this house. Before you were born.'

I stood there, looking up at her. I loved her then. She was small and anxious, but without real fear.

'I'm sure I could walk up there to you, in two skips.'

'No, no. God knows. It's bad enough me feeling it; I don't want you to as well.'

'I don't mind feeling it. Maybe I do—it's a bit like the smell of damp clothes, isn't it?'

She laughed. 'No, nothing like that. Don't talk yourself into believing it. Just go downstairs, like a good boy.'

I went down, excited, and sat at the range with its red heart fire and black lead dust. We were haunted! We had a ghost, even in the middle of the afternoon. I heard my mother moving around upstairs. The house was all cobweb tremors. No matter where you walked or what you did, the house rippled. She came down after a bit, looking white.

'Did you see anything?'

'No, nothing, nothing at all. It's just your old mother with her nerves. All imagination. There's nothing there.'

'I can go up then?'

I was up at the window before she could answer, and I looked out at the field, where the gang was playing football on the tilted slope of Drew Stevenson's pitch, and the cathedral beyond that loomed over the dam where a boy from Creggan had drowned. But on the landing itself there was nothing. I stared into the moiling darkness. I heard the clock in the bedroom clicking and the wind breathing through the chimney, and saw the neutral glimmer on the banister vanish into my hand as I slid it down. Four steps before the kitchen door, I felt someone behind me and turned to see a darkness leaving the window.

My mother was crying quietly at the fireside. I went in and sat on the floor beside her and stared into the redness locked behind the range bars.

It was a fierce winter, that year. The snow covered the air-raid shelters. At night, from the stair-window, the field was a white paradise of loneliness, and the wind, coming down from the dwarf stars, made the glass shake like loose, black water, and the sill, misshapen by frost and ice and snow, snored while we slept and while the shadow watched.

The boiler burst that winter and the water came out from behind the fire which went out in a dazzle of hissings. It was desolate. No water, no fire, hardly any money, Christmas coming. My father called in my uncles, my mother's brothers, to help him fix it. Three came—Dan, Tom, John. Tom was the prosperous one. He employed the others. He had a gold tooth and curly hair and wore a suit. Dan was one of those skinny men who looked as though he had once been fat—he had so many folds of skin on his lean face. John, perky but tense, liked to laugh as a way of relaxing. As they worked, they talked, telling story upon story, each one piled on the other until they toppled like a stack of glasses. I knelt on a chair at the table, digging a spoon into a two-pound tin of Tate and Lyle Golden Syrup, watching it come up molten and fall off into little green-gold cobras before disappearing again into the surface. They had stories of gamblers, drinkers, hard men, con men, champion bricklayers, boxing matches, footballers, policemen, priests, hauntings, exorcisms, political killings. There were great events they returned to over and over, like the night of the big shoot-out at the distillery between the IRA and the police when Uncle Eddie, my father's brother, disappeared.

He had been seen years later in Chicago, said one.

In Melbourne, said another.

Or: He had died in the shoot-out, falling into the exploding vats of whisky when the roof collapsed. Certainly he had never returned, although my father would not speak of it at all and turned the conversation as fast as he could.

Then there was the great exorcism that had, in one night, turned Father Browne's hair white, making him old before his time. He had driven the spirit into a bay window of his room and locked it up behind the glass, and then dropped wax from a blessed candle on the snib. No one, he said, was ever to break that seal, which had to be renewed every month, but if anyone, near death or in a state of mortal sin, entered that room at night he would see in the window the stretched face of the devil that would become the face of a child, sobbing and pleading to be released from the devil that had trapped it. But if the snib was broken open, the devil would immediately enter the body of the person who would be possessed and doomed for ever.

You could never be up to the devil.

The boiler was fixed, and they went off—the great white winter piling up around the red fire again.

Hauntings are very specific. Everything has to be exact, even the vaguenesses, and even though the hauntings can never be told the same way twice. Family history is like that too. It comes in bits, and some bits are better told than others, and some bits are better heard, and all sorts of feelings surround their transmission so that when (if ever) a whole saga emerges, the people who originally told a bit of it don't recognize what they hear. Some of the things I remember, I don't remember. I've just been told I remember them, so now I do. My father's family was so mysterious anyway that it has to be reconstructed from scattered pieces. For instance, the feud. Did it really start in that farmhouse at Cockhill outside Buncrana—the one with the raftered ceiling and the walls lined with books? Was it really from the wooden floor of that farmhouse that my father swept up me and my brother and strode out, followed by my mother, into thirty years' silence because he had found out that his sister was not really living in the house but was being treated by her own family as a skivvy and lived in an outhouse, beside the chickens? I remember, I'm told, the great rafters as I rose up in his arms and the dusty road outside when he put me down and their voices above us and the sky above them filling with a great hammerhead cloud off the Atlantic. His mother, long dead, came to our house afterwards, so my mother told me, and stood at the bottom of the bed as my father slept, watching him, and smiled at my mother, and touched the blankets that covered him and was gone.

And then it was only when my father was lying dead in his coffin in the front room that his cousin Eamonn, whom I had never seen before, told me how my father, when his parents died—both in the same week in 1919 during the epidemic of trench flu—lay down in the back of that house on the High Street, among the coal sacks and the chopped wood, and cried for hours on end. Was that my father?

My father. He would have loved to have been educated. When I came down from Belfast the night I got my degree, I came into a kitchen crammed with people and chatter. I'd had a few drinks and was feeling light, so as I came through the door and they looked up expectantly I was about to put on an act of despair and pretend I'd failed when I saw my father behind the door getting off his chair, his face grey, his legs leaden. The rafters came swooping down again and as he straightened, I said, 'I got it. A First.' His huge hand held my shoulder for a second and he smiled.

'A First,' he said and sat down. 'A First,' he whispered to himself, his head down as everybody else began to talk again and my mother nodded at him and said, 'He's—we've been waiting since six for that news. What kept you? It's one in the morning.'

'I had a drink or two in Belfast.'

'A drink or two!' they all echoed, laughing.

'I'd have a drink myself if I didn't have to work in the morning,' he said. He came from behind the door. 'But I'll sleep well tonight.' He went upstairs. He never took a drink in his life. I've reconstructed his vigil behind the door in that noisy room a hundred times since, just as I reconstructed his life out of the remains of the stories about his dead parents, his vanished older brother, his own beloved silence. O father.

The man behind the door, the boy weeping in the coal-shed, the walk down that dusty road, the cousin appearing at the wake looking just like him, his dead mother at the foot of the bed—was that all? In a whole lifetime? How bitterly did he feel, or was he saddened into quietness?

One night we all listened to a boxing match on BBC radio between the British heavyweight champion Bruce Woodcock and a Czechoslovak miner called Josef Baksi. My father knew something about boxing because he had fought professionally for a couple of years. No skill, just a thunderous right hand. This meant he got cut, sliced, jabbed, cuffed, pounded for several rounds before he got through, and for that he was paid peanuts. So he gave it up and always hated the game but loved the sport itself or maybe the men who got into the ring to be hammered for a few quid. At any rate, this was a terrible fight. Woodcock took a pulverizing beating but stayed on his feet the whole way through the fifteen rounds. The commentator was screaming as though someone were standing on his neck; the noise of the crowd seemed to swell the fabric on the radio's speaker. My father listened as though he had a gun in his back. 'Stop the fight,' he said to the radio every so often. 'Stop the fight.' At one point he stood up and switched it off and lit a John Player's Navy Cut cigarette in the ensuing silence and smoked it until the untapped ash broke over his knuckles. Then he switched on again. It was the last round. Woodcock was being driven all over the ring. Then it was over.

'Brave but stupid,' he said, and went out first to the back yard and swept it, and then into the coal-shed and broke the great shale pieces into black diamonds and gleaming ricochets, and hauled out tree blocks and broke them into gnarled sticks while the shed shook with the blows. I came out to look but he shooed me away without turning around. My mother shushed us all up to bed. When she put her finger to her lips, I knew I wasn't imagining his sorrow but I couldn't fathom it. I lay awake all night and heard him go out in the morning at six. I crept to the lobby window and watched him cross the back lane and go down the New Road with his lunch bag in his hand. But it was no help. I could decipher nothing and was so tired at school that day that I fell asleep twice.

'Shush,' said Father O'Flaherty, 'we mustn't talk too loud. We might waken Deane. Maybe we should croon a little lullaby. One, two, three.' His face, when I opened my eyes, was a millimetre away, but I saw only my father. And the blows, when they came, shook in last night's shed and were scarcely felt.

Not long after I found myself in my father's shed. It was a sunny afternoon, the air milky and the breeze scarcely stirring the half-open door. I hauled out two bags of white cement, poured them into a wheelbarrow, took a spade and went round his rose garden, pouring the cement on the flowers until there was a winter scene of grey-white snow. Then I beat the roses down flat with the back of the spade until their petals lay in the dust like blood-flecks. I was choking on the dust when the back door opened and my mother came out. Her hand went out to the window sill for support. After that, my shoes were removed, my clothes confiscated, and I was put to bed to wait for my father. He came in through the back gate and I shut my eyes as I heard his voice. I kept them shut tight until I heard his tread on the stairs, and the bedroom door opened. He stood there in his dark-blue dungarees, a smattering of cement powder still settling on them. His sleeves were rolled back and his arms, thicker than my thighs, were sunburned. He looked at me as I lay there, tightening my toes and drawing my shoulder blades together. Then he left. Not a word. Next day, he stayed off work, dug up the garden and cemented it. We had to use the front door all day while the garden dried from dark to pale grey.

We played a version of miniature football on that cemented stretch for years afterwards. Every so often, our boots would strike a spark from the cement as we kicked or skidded and I would think of the dead roses below, flattened in their grief.

My own first bad haunting happened in Belfast. There was a sectarian fight outside the Drill Hall at the university. Students had attacked a small group of Teddy Boys who had gate-crashed the Saturday night hop and the fight spilled out of the hall on to the patch of lawn outside. The Teddy Boys got away fast but, by then, the fight had become a sectarian one between the students themselves, Protestant turning on Catholic and Catholic on Protestant. A local psychopath, John McCammon, who had started it all, was doing great damage with boot, fist and a broken vodka bottle. He was a tall, fair-haired man, no longer a student, but a dread fixture within the student community. His face was seamed with scars and he smiled as he fought. In the half-light from the dance-hall windows, amid all the heaving bodies and the grunts and slashes of the fight, he dominated the central group, his pale face smudged with violet markings where the light caught the scar tissue.

He saw our small group watching, and moved towards us. We backed off but found ourselves hemmed in by an arm of the battle which had suddenly been flung out behind us and up the steps of the Drill Hall. So we were caught. I don't know how often I was hit. Rain had begun and I was rolling on the grass, scrunched up to avoid the kicks and trying to avoid being pinned along the wall where the kicking was worse and there was no escape. Someone finally felled McCammon. He hit the ground beside me, cursing, the broken bottle-neck still in his hand, his face glistening with sweat and mud and a wrinkle of blood frowning on his forehead. As he made to get up, so did I. Someone must have hit him again because he fell back, his arm out, and I trod on his wrist as I rose, and felt my heel crunch his watch and swivel on it.

Blue lights pulsed and the dying screams of sirens: the police had come. Students ran in all directions and the police, batons drawn, gave chase. A new battle erupted. I ran full tilt into a group of three and went down under a hail of blows. When I came to, I was in Donegal Pass Police Station, in a room crowded with bloodied, groaning students who lay on benches or on the floor, or squatted against the wall, smoking, cursing, their clothes glistening with mud and rain.

It was a long night. We were allowed to go to the bathroom in twos and threes. Several people vomited; two passed out. One fellow, who had been kicked or batoned between the legs was so congested and swollen he couldn't urinate. He was taken to hospital. By four in the morning, our names and addresses taken, we were released. I fell over a cliff into sleep, my body already hurting with the coming impact.

During that sleep, I relived an earlier haunting. First, there were the two police cars, black and white, sitting like spaceships in the early morning light of the street. As they took off, I saw their magpie flash reflected in the dark windows of the house next door. Then, in reverse order, there was the search. A bright figure, in a white rain-cape, came through the bedroom door and stood with his back to the wall, switching the light on and off. He was shouting but I was deaf with shock and could only see his mouth opening. I dressed within this thin membrane of silence. They were, I knew, looking for the gun I had found the afternoon before in the bottom drawer inside the wardrobe of the room next door, where my sisters slept.

It was a long, chilled pistol, blue-black and heavy, which I had smuggled out the back to show to some boys from Fahan Street, up near the old city walls. They had come over to play football and afterwards we had an argument about politics. I had been warned never even to mention the gun which, I was told, was a gift to my father from a young German sailor, whose submarine had been brought in to the port at the end of the war. He had been held with about thirty others in Nissen huts down by the docks, and my father used to bring him extra sandwiches or milk every lunch-time when he was helping to wire up the huts for light and heat. Before he went away the young sailor gave my father the gun as a memento. But we had cousins in gaol and had to be careful. So it was never to be mentioned.

Even as we had been gathered round the gun, hefting it, aiming it, measuring its length against our forearms, I had felt eyes watching. Fogey Campbell, known to be a police informer, was at the end of the lane, looking on. He was a young, open-faced man of twenty or so with a bright smile and wide-spaced, rounded eyes. He looked the soul of candour. He had seen me bring the gun back into the house.

I waited ten minutes and then brought it out again, wrapped in old newspaper, and buried it in one of the stone trenches up the field. Now, here were the police and the house was being splintered open. The lino was ripped off, the floorboards crowbarred up, the wardrobe lay face down in the middle of the floor and the wallpaper was slashed. We were huddled downstairs and held in the centre of the room while the kitchen was searched. One policeman opened a tin of Australian pears and poured the yellow scimitar slices and the sugar-logged syrup all over the floor. Another went out to the yard and split open a bag of cement in his ransacking of the shed. He came walking through in a white cloud, his boots sticking to the glutinous lino and the cement falling from him in white flares. I was still in the silence. Objects seemed to be floating, free of gravity, all over the room. Everybody had sweat or tears on their faces. Then we were in the police cars and the morning light had already reached the roof-tops as a polished gleam in the slates.

Years later, I re-lived the police at our house as a haunting. The door swung open and something came into the room and went round my bed three times. As it moved, I had heard the rice-papery whistle of someone fighting for breath; at another moment, it was the whistle of a plastic cape or coat. Then the door slammed and it was gone. Even in my dream, I woke to find the furniture moved, the mirror turned to the wall, the window bricked up, the bedclothes torn off—and the presence fuming outside the door. Where was the gun? I had had it, I was seen with it—where was it? I needed it now, for defence. I couldn't go out on to the landing, my two arms the one length, to meet this anger that sat there in its cape as in a tent, waiting to rise over me. But I had no gun, there was no gun, it was all a lie. When I finally broke through that door and got down the stairs, I found I was in a kitchen, years later, and I moved among its orderliness in a daze, taking the sleep and fear off my face like cobwebs that would catch you as you moved between high hedges.

Politics was a grief. We seemed to know a lot about it, but could do nothing with it. It smelled of ammonia, as when the police appeared and your hair felt starched and your hands empty. In their black-blue uniforms, they seemed to attract the oxygen out of the air and leave your chest heaving.

One day I saw a boy from Blucher Street killed by a reversing lorry. He was standing at the back wheel, ready to jump on the back when the lorry moved off. But the driver reversed suddenly and the boy went under the wheel as the men at the corner turned round and began shouting and running. But it was too late. He lay there in the darkness under the truck with his arm spread out and blood creeping out on all sides. The lorry driver collapsed and the boy's mother appeared and looked and looked and then suddenly sat down as people came to stand in front of her and hide the awful sight.

I was standing on the parapet wall above Meenan's Park, only twenty yards away, and I could see the police car coming up the road from the barracks at the far end. Two policemen got out and one of them bent down and looked under the lorry. He stood up and pushed his cap back on his head and rubbed his hands on his thighs. I think he felt sick. His distress, as he walked round the lorry, made me feel sick too so that I thought the lorry lurched again. The second policeman had a notebook in his hand and he went round to each of the men who had been standing at the corner when it happened. They all turned their backs on him. Then the ambulance came.

For months, I kept seeing the lorry reversing and Rory Hannaway's arm going out as he was wound under. Somebody told me that one of the policemen had vomited on the other side of the lorry. I felt the sickness again on hearing this and, with it, pity for the man. But this seemed wrong, so I said nothing, especially as I felt hardly at all for Rory's mother or the lorry driver, both of whom I knew. No more than a year later, when we were hiding from the police in a corn field after they had interrupted us chopping down a tree for the annual bonfire on the fifteenth of August, Danny Green told me in detail how young Hannaway had been run over by a police car which had not even stopped. 'Bastards,' he said, shining the blade of his axe with wet grass. I tightened the hauling rope round my waist and said nothing; somehow this allayed the subtle sense of treachery I had felt from the start. As a result, I began to feel then a real sorrow for Rory's mother and for the driver, who had never worked since. The yellow-green corn whistled as the police car slid past on the road below. It was dark before we brought the tree in, combing the back lanes clean with its nervous branches.

Father Regan lit a candle in his dark classroom at the foot of the statue of the Blessed Virgin. Regan permitted no overhead lights when he gave his formal religious address at the beginning of our last year in school. Regan was small, neat, economical. After he said, 'Boys', he stopped for a bit and looked at us. Then he dropped his eyes and kept them down until he said, more loudly this time, '*Boys*'. He had complete silence this time.

'Some of you here, one or two of you perhaps, know the man I am going to talk about today. You may not know you know him, but that doesn't matter.

'More than thirty years ago, during the troubles in Derry, this man was arrested and charged with the murder of a policeman. The policeman had been walking home one night over Craigavon Bridge. It was a bleak night, November, nineteen hundred and twenty two. The time was two in the morning. The policeman was off duty; he was wearing civilian clothes. There were two men coming the other way, on the other side of the bridge. As the policeman neared the middle of the bridge, these two men crossed over to his side. They were strolling, talking casually. They had their hats pulled down over their faces and their coat collars turned up for it was wet and cold. As they passed the policeman, one of them said "Goodnight" and the policeman returned the greeting. And then suddenly he found himself grabbed from behind and lifted off his feet. He tried to kick but one of the men held his legs. "This is for Neil McLaughlin," said one. "May you rot in the hell you're going to, you murdering bastard." They lifted him to the parapet and held him there for a minute like a log and let him stare down at the water—seventy, eighty feet below. Then they pushed him over and he fell, with the street lights shining on his wet coat until he disappeared into the shadows with a splash. They heard him thrashing and he shouted once. Then he went under. His body was washed up three days later. No one saw them. They went home and they said nothing.

'A week later a man was arrested and charged with the murder. He was brought to trial. But the only evidence the police had was that he was the friend and workmate of Neil McLaughlin, who had been murdered by a policeman a month before. The story was that, before McLaughlin died on the street where he had been shot, coming out of the newspaper office where he worked, he had whispered the name of his killer to this man who had been arrested. And this man had been heard to swear revenge, to get the policeman—let's call him Mahon—in revenge for his friend's death. There was no point in going to the law, of course. Justice would never be done; everyone knew that, especially in those years. So maybe the police thought they could beat an admission out of him, but he did not flinch from his story. That night he was not even in the city. He had been sent by his newspaper to Letterkenny twenty miles away, and he had several witnesses to prove it. The case was thrown out. People were surprised, even though they believed the man to be innocent. Innocence was no guarantee for a Catholic then. Nor is it now.

'Well, I wasn't even in the city in those days. But I met this man several times and we became friendly. I was then a young curate and this man was prominent in local sporting circles and he helped in various ways to raise money for the parish building fund. One night, in the sacristy of the Long Tower Church, just down the road from here, he told me that he had not been to confession in twenty years. He had something on his conscience that no penance could relieve. I told him to trust in God's infinite mercy; I offered to hear his confession. I offered to find someone else, a monk I knew down in Portglenone, to whom he could go in case he did not want to confess to me. But no, he wouldn't go. No penance, he said, would be any use, because, in his heart, he could not feel sorrow for what he had done. But he wanted to tell someone, not as a confession, but in confidence.

'So he told me about being arrested. He told me about the beatings he had been given—rubber truncheons, punches, kicks, threats to put him over the bridge. He told me how he had resisted these assaults and never wavered.

'"Oh," said I, "that's just a testimony to the strength you get from knowing you are in the right."

'He looked at me in amazement. "D'ye think that's what I wanted to tell you? The story of my innocence? For God's sake, Father, can't you see? I wasn't innocent. I was guilty. I killed Mahon and I'd kill him again if he came through that door this minute. That's why I can't confess. I have no sorrow, no resolve not to do it again. No pity. Mahon shot my best friend dead in the street, for nothing. He was a drunken policeman with a gun, looking for a Teague to kill, and he left that man's wife with two young children and would have got off scot-free for the rest of his days, probably got promoted for sterling service. And Neil told me as he lay there, with the blood draining from him, that Mahon did it. 'Billy Mahon, Billy Mahon, the policeman,' that's what he said. And even then, I had to run back into the doorway and leave his body there in the street because they started shooting down the street from the city walls. And I'm not sorry I got Mahon and I told him what it was for before I threw him over that bridge and he knew, just too late, who I was when I said goodnight to him. It was goodnight all right. One murdering bastard less.'"

'Boys, that man went to the grave without confessing that sin. And think of all the wrongs that were done in that incident. Two men were murdered. Two men—three, for there was another man whose name was never mentioned—were murderers. Indeed maybe there was another murderer, for it's possible that Mahon was not the policeman involved. And there were perjurers who swore that the accused was elsewhere that night. And there were policemen who assaulted a man in custody. And there were judges who would certainly have acquitted any policeman, no matter how guilty, and would have found guilty any Catholic, no matter how innocent, on the slightest shred of evidence. The whole situation makes men evil. Evil men make the whole situation. And these days, similar things occur. Some of you boys may feel like getting involved when you leave school, because you sincerely believe that you would be on the side of justice, fighting for the truth. But, boys, let me tell you, there is a judge who sees all, knows all and is never unjust; there is a judge whose punishments and rewards are beyond the range of human imagining; there is a Law greater than the laws of human justice, far greater than the law of revenge, more enduring than the laws of any state whatsoever. That Judge is God, that Law is God's Law and the issue at stake is your immortal soul.

'We live, boys, in a world that will pass away. The shadows that candle throws upon the walls of this room are as substantial as we. Injustice, tyranny, freedom, national independence are realities that will fade too, for they are not ultimate realities and the only life worth living is a life lived in the light of the ultimate. I know there are some who believe that the poor man who committed that murder was justified, and that he will be forgiven by an all-merciful God for what he did. That may be. I fervently hope that it is so, for who would judge God's mercy? But it is true too of the policeman; he may have been as plagued by guilt as his own murderer; he may have justified himself too; he may have refused sorrow and known no peace of mind; he may have forgiven himself or he may have been forgiven by God. It is not for us to judge. But it is for us to distinguish, to see the difference between wrong done to us and equal wrong done by us; to know that our transient life, no matter how scarred, how broken, how miserable it may be, is also God's miracle and gift; that we may try to improve it, but we may not destroy it. If we destroy it in another, we destroy it in ourselves.

'Boys, as you enter upon your last year with us, you are on the brink of entering a world of wrong, insult, injury, unemployment, a world where the unjust hold power and the ignorant rule. But there is an inner peace nothing can reach, no insult can violate, no corruption can deprave. Hold to that; it is what your childish innocence once was and what your adult maturity must become. Hold to that. I bless you all.'

And he raised his hand and made the sign of the Cross above our heads and crossed the room, blew out the candle as the bell rang wildly in the chapel tower, and asked that the lights be switched on. He left in silence with the candle smoking heavily behind him at the foot of the statue, stubby in its thick drapery of wax.

'That was your grandfather,' said McShane to me. 'I know that story too.'

I derided him. I had heard the story too, but I wasn't going to take it on before everyone else. Anyway, it was just folklore. I had heard it when I was much younger and lay on the landing at night listening to the grown-ups talking in the kitchen below and had leaned over the banisters and imagined it was the edge of the parapet and that I was falling, falling down to the river of the hallway, as deaf and shining as a log.

GRANTA

BACK ISSUES

GRANTA **5: Don Bloch, THE MODERN COMMON WIND:** Russell Hoban, 'Mnemosyne, Teen Taals and Tottenham Court Road'; Susan Sontag, 'Elias Canetti'; Jonathan Schell, 'Nuclear Arms and the Fate of the Earth'; T. C. Boyle, 'Mungo among the Moors'; Jorge Ibarguengoitia, 'The Dead Girls'; and others. 320 pages. Limited stocks; please list alternative choice.

GRANTA **6: A LITERATURE FOR POLITICS:** 'Interviews with Argentine Soldiers from the Falklands'; Jeremy Seabrook and Trevor Blackwell, 'Mrs Thatcher's Religious Pilgrimage'; Boaz Evron, 'An Indictment of Israel'; Milan Kundera, 'The Story of a Variation'; Ariel Dorfman, 'How to Read the Comics'; Nadine Gordimer, 'A City of the Dead, A City of the Living'; Peter Weiss, 'The Aesthetics of Resistance'; and others. 336 pages. Limited stocks; please list alternative choice.

GRANTA **7: BEST OF YOUNG BRITISH NOVELISTS:** Martin Amis, 'Money'; William Boyd, 'Extracts from the Journal of Flying Officer J.'; Maggie Gee, 'Rose on the broken'; Kazuo Ishiguro, 'Summer after the War'; Adam Mars-Jones, 'Trout Day by Pumpkin Light'; Salman Rushdie, 'The Golden Bough'; Graham Swift, 'About the Eel'; and thirteen others. 320 pages.

GRANTA **8: DIRTY REALISM—NEW WRITING FROM AMERICA:** Jayne Anne Phillips, 'Rayme—a Memoir of the Seventies'; Elizabeth Tallent, 'Why I Love Country Music'; Richard Ford, 'Rock Springs'; Raymond Carver, 'The Compartment'; Tobias Wolff, 'The Barracks Thief'. Plus Michael Herr, 'The State of the State of Things'; Angela Carter, 'Sugar Daddy'; Carolyn Forché, 'El Salvador: an Aide-Mémoire'. 256 pages.

GRANTA **10: TRAVEL WRITING:** Jonathan Raban, 'Sea-Room'; James Fenton, 'Road to Cambodia'; Bruce Chatwin, 'A Coup'; Martha Gellhorn, 'White into Black'; Colin Thubron, 'Night in Vietnam'; Redmond O'Hanlon, 'Into the Heart of Borneo'; Paul Theroux, 'Subterranean Gothic'; Jan Morris, 'Interstate 281'; Patrick Marnham, 'Holy Week'; Saul Bellow, 'Old Paris'; Gabriel García Márquez, 'Watching the Rain in Galicia'. 256 pages.

GRANTA **11: MILAN KUNDERA:** Ian McEwan, 'An Interview with Milan Kundera'; Milan Kundera, 'Soul and Body', 'A Kidnapped West or Culture Bows Out'. Plus Salman Rushdie, 'Outside the Whale'; Martha Gellhorn, 'Testimonial'; Redmond O'Hanlon, 'Deeper into the Heart of Borneo'; Gabriel García Márquez, 'Mystery without End'; Mario Vargas Llosa, 'Cheap Intellectuals'; and others. 256 pages.

GRANTA **12: Stanley Booth, THE TRUE ADVENTURES OF THE ROLLING STONES:** Plus Fiction from America: Jayne Anne Phillips, 'Danner, 1965'; Raymond Carver, 'The Cabin'; Richard Ford, 'Winterkill'. And David Caute, 'The *Guardian* and Sarah Tisdall'; Günter Grass, 'Resistance'; Breyten Breytenbach, 'Prison-Scribe'; Gabriel García Márquez, 'Julio Cortazar'. 256 pages.

GRANTA **13: AFTER THE REVOLUTION:** Milan Kundera, 'Paris or Prague?'; Josef Škvorecký, 'Miracles'; Edward Said, 'Reflections on Exile'; Timothy Garton Ash, 'East Germany'. Plus Fiction in Britain: Doris Lessing, 'Writing under another Name'; Anita Brookner, 'A Wedding'; Martin Amis, 'The Time Sickness'; Russell Hoban, 'A Conversation with the Head of Orpheus'. 272 pages.

GRANTA **14: AUTOBIOGRAPHY:** Norman Lewis, 'Jackdaw Cake'; Beryl Bainbridge, 'Funny Noises with our Mouths'; Breyten Breytenbach, 'Punishable Innocence'; William Boyd, 'Alpes Maritimes'; Josef Skvorecky, 'Failed Saxophonist'; Don McCullin, 'A Life in Photographs'; Jaroslav Seifert, 'Skating with Lenin'; Adam Mars-Jones, 'Weaning'; Bernard Crick, 'On the Orwell Trail'; and others. 256 pages.

GRANTA **15: James Fenton, THE FALL OF SAIGON:** Nadine Gordimer, 'The Essential Gesture: Writers and Responsibility'; George Steiner, 'A Conversation Piece'; Salman Rushdie, 'On Günter Grass'; Günter Grass, 'The Tin Drum in Retrospect'; John Berger, 'Go Ask the Time'; Ryszard Kapuściński, 'Warsaw Diary'; Marilynne Robinson, 'The Waste Land'; Richard Ford, 'On Harley-Davidson'; and others. 288 pages.

GRANTA **16: SCIENCE:** Oliver Sacks, 'Excesses'; Italo Calvino, 'The Loves of the Tortoises'; Primo Levi, 'Chromium'; Stephen Jay Gould, 'Adam's Navel'; Lewis Thomas, 'Co-operation for the Birds'; Plus Germaine Greer, 'Women and Power in Cuba'; David Hare, 'Nicaragua: An Appeal'; Tim O'Brien, 'Quantum Jumps'; David Mamet, 'The Bridge'; Mary Gordon, 'The Imagination of Disaster'; and others. 256 pages.

GRANTA **17: Graham Greene, WHILE WAITING FOR A WAR:** Milan Kundera, 'Prague: A Disappearing Poem'; Patrick Marnham, 'In Search of Amin'; Heinrich Böll, 'A Letter to My Sons'; Joseph Lelyveld, 'Forced Busing in South Africa'; Kazuo Ishiguro, 'October, 1948'; Alice Munro, 'A Queer Streak'; Doris Lessing, 'My Mother's Life'; John Updike, 'Italo Calvino'; Amos Oz, 'Notes from Israel'; Hanif Kureishi, 'Erotic Politicians and Mullahs'; and others. 256 pages.

Back issues at $7.50 each (or $6.50 on orders of four or more) are available from Granta, 13 White Street, New York, NY 10013. Please enclose a check made payable to Granta. *Allow 6-8 weeks for delivery.*

GRANTA

ADAM NICHOLSON
WETNESS

Wetness is not a substance but a quality, that seeps and leaks into everything like a stain. Wetness blurs and softens any margins, making distinctions indistinct. When the novelist Richard Jefferies lay on Liddington Hill in Wiltshire, he felt himself pushed up and out of the earth by the solid chalk under his back. The low wet moors of the Somerset Levels, thick with their waters, are the negative of that, the most female of landscapes, and if you lie and sleep there on a summer afternoon you will dream of absorption, of the half-liquid jelly beneath you, shifting in all its ambiguities, curling its flesh around you in the soft kiss of an insect-eating fungus.

If a tractor drives past, the peat will shiver and ripple under you like a belly, wobbling the earth in a slow-motion swell. In the days before tractors, horses that went out on the moor needed sacks around their hooves if they were not to sink into the fields. Others, too sharp-footed—the best Levels horses had feet like frying pans—would quite slowly subside where they stood, their four legs slipping into the peat like the pins of a plug into a socket.

It is as though the grass were no more than a tightened membrane over the body of water. If you sit on the banks of one of the ditches, the high water in the field soaks up into the cloth of your trousers, so that the only thing to do is swim and move over from the watery peat to the peaty water, a half-noticed change from one half-element to another. Simply stand in the shallow margin of the water and let your feet slide down over the warm skin of the peat below you. Slowly the body lowers into the cider-soup, crusty with frog-bit and duckweed, with seeds and reed-shells. The slimed light bodies of the secret eels release a bubble each as they shift away from the strange disturbance. The still water is slick on the skin. Everything hangs there in suspension. Time stops. Your body seen through the whisky water is a golden unnatural brown. You are embedded in the place as though in a tomb, with some strange osmosis of the water sliding into the heart through the skin. It is a soggy, ambivalent fringe world, a world hinged to *both* and *and*. A thousand million years ago all life was water-life, and to float in the semi-substance of a summer rhyne is to return to that antiquity.

It is an eely place. These one-fin fish, the eels—the fin swept along from neck to tail and back along the belly—are secret and discreet, the real water-spirits of the Somerset Levels. They seep into all

Photo: Patrick Sutherland

the tiny capillaries of the moors, with none of the terminal drive of the salmon or the lamprey, which boringly insist on pushing on up the main current towards the source to breed. Instead, the eel infiltrates its living quarters at any point, slip-seeking any hidden overhang, any dark obsessive pool, any ditch or sunken rhyne, where in weed or under stones it can feel the touch of solid, moory substance around its skin. Eels are *thigmotic:* that is, they love to touch—not to roam in any pike-like abstraction, but to slide down into the bottom-stuff of ditches and rivers.

So hungry are they for cover, for this touch, that one can catch an eel simply by putting a sack full of straw on the river-bed, with a length of drain embedded in it. Leave the sack overnight, which is when eels move, and, with no bait and no entrapment, one of them will be laid up there in the morning. Fishermen who catch eels (usually in a fyke net, where entry but no exit is possible) store them in tanks before sending them to market. If a length of drainpipe is left in the tank the eels will crowd into it, slipped in there as tightly as the coils of gut inside the body wall, slid up easily—one wants to say *affectionately*—against the others, so that if you pick the cylinder up and tip it a sliding clotted mass of them, folded together as though of one piece, will flop out as a sort of solid liquid into the water. They are embodiments of touch, *addicts* of touch; each eel is a map of a river shifting over time.

Put them in a bucket and they do not slither noiselessly over each other as you would expect. They are too mundane for that; there is nothing abstract about the eel. Out of the bucket instead comes a soft tactile gossip from their bodies, the rasp of liquid kissing. Or, according to Michael Brown, the eel man from Thorney, the noise of sex on a hot afternoon.

The eel is at one extreme, the heron at the other, with the Levels strung between them. Zoologists call eels *benthic,* meaning they are not free-floaters but live down in the depths of their chosen water. The eel is perfect, in its sheen of efficiency, its introversion, scarcely distinct from the place it makes its own, like a cancer, spread into every cell of the moors. And the heron is public, bedraggled (nothing could ever bedraggle an eel), alert on the edge of a rhyne with all the electric, neurotic poise of a man waiting to bid and careless of his appearance, then clumsying away from one water to the next, its legs straggled out backwards, its head zigzagged back into an awkward body. Nothing is more incongruous, more unlikely, than a heron—it is no more than the mechanical sketch of a fish-catching bird with the parts somehow bolted together. And nothing more congruous than the eel. It is animal made chic, made similar. The eel and the heron, the effortless and the vigilant, the actual and the imposed, the langorous and the taut, the heart and mind of a wetland.

I have seen a heron catch an eel only once. I had imagined that it would be a deep draught of solid Guinness to gorge the impertinent bird. But it ended up nothing of the kind. There was no climax in the act. The heron stood on the bank of the Langacre Rhyne on King's Sedgemoor looking spare. Some distance away, a man was swinging at the bankside growth with a ditch-hook. Two motorbikes went off down the Beer Wall, slewing on the thirteenth-century bends as the heron struck. It was no more than a licked finger flicking over the last note in a bundle of fives and the eel was out on the bank, an ignominious wriggle, all grace gone, that liquid pouring of the one curve travelling the muscles of its black back forgotten in the horrible ignobility of being eaten. The heron jumped sideways as if away from a fire, jerked the eel around in its mouth and, in glutinous stages, swallowed it. The bird looked shocked, stared sideways and then bounced into flight with a spring at its elbow-knees to flap off back to some tree-top nest. That was that. The bikes came back down the Beer Wall and the man cleaning the ditch moved over to the other side.

The eel which the heron picked out of the Langacre Rhyne had begun life 4,000 miles away in the Sargasso Sea, 300 miles south-west of Bermuda, maybe eight years before, in March, a hundred fathoms below the surface of the ocean. For three years the willow-leaf larva had floated towards England, until it arrived over the continental shelf and, somehow recognizing the change in the seabed in a process still not understood, had metamorphosed into a tiny transparent eel called an elver in England, and in Holland and Germany a glass-eel. From willow-leaf drifter, distributed by the currents anywhere between Norway and the Sea of Azov, the eel turns deliberate, able to swim against the current and equipped with the most extraordinary sense of smell in nature. Experiments on adult eels have shown that they can smell one part in three million million million, or one millilitre of rosewater (it was a German experiment) in a lake fifty-eight times the size of Lake Constance.

You must imagine this in the springtime all over Europe, at the mouths of rivers from the Dnieper to the Jakobselv and, in Somerset, England, in Bridgwater Bay at the mouth of the Parrett, as the indescribable mass of glass-eels gathers at the estuaries to move inland. The numbers are incalculable, but it is known that each female eel in the Sargasso Sea lays between five and ten million eggs. The elver hordes smell the fresh water from out at sea and begin to swim in towards it. They sink away from light at ebb tide as the water drops and only come up into the high water at flood. When high water coincides with the hours of darkness, it is then that the thick harvest of them comes in. This is the great springtime impregnation of the moors as the sperm mass of eel life pushes into the wetland, and this is where the people are waiting for them.

The elvers ride the night tide. All along the banks of the Parrett, from Bridgwater up to Oath Lock, and on the Tone from Burrow Bridge up into Curry Moor, fishermen wait with their elver nets, giant scoops like the shovels in sweet shops with which the humbugs are dug out of jars. The frame is willow or aluminium, the net itself a fine nylon cheesecloth. There is competition for places on the bank and the fishermen are there hours before the flood. The elver brokers set up receiving stations on the bank, with scales hanging from a floodlit tripod beside the van carrying tanks into which the elvers will be poured. Each station has its own team of catchers spread out along the river; these have been recruited in a long courtship of men who are naturally independent and mildly suspicious. The air is thick with conspiracy and expectation—heightened by the darkness, the storm lanterns reflected in the river, the urge to defend your own spot, the muttering of catchers pulled at by the breeze and the faint tinge of illegality.

While the tide is running, the elvers stay with it in midstream. The first sign of dead water is a stillness at the bankside which gradually spreads in towards the middle of the river until there is no movement at all. Then the deep lick of the tide, like a lolling tongue into Somerset, starts to slide away and the elvers move into the banks where the outward flow is least. This is the moment. The electric pumping station is turned on and the artificial fresh upswelling sends warts of silver water out into the dropping river. The nets go in, held against the bank just downstream of the pump's own concrete outflow. You might find nothing. The elver is capricious. If the day has been cold and there is no warmth in the mud, it might never move.

But it might be the night in which the little glass-eels do come streaming into the nets, and then out of them ('We've got one or two here') in twisting filaments of spun glass, as ('We've got a breakfast here') clinging wraiths which drool, like the dripping juices from a cow's lips, into the tin bath, accompanied by the simple hurried excitement of hauling in a gift from the river. The elvers weave a constant slimed rope in the torchlight, generating from their slime a sort of froth, called vump. The sliding of each individual body matches the shape of the others', so that it is no confused mass of elvers but an organized wreath of them, scores thick, twisting up here and there into candle-flame points which peak and collapse to restore the continuity of the animated wave.

There are hundreds of elver stories invoking not lengths but numbers. Hogsheads and bathfuls caught in one night; enough to feed one fisherman's ducks for ten weeks; so many that another once spread them over his garden as manure. Their traditional fate is in an omelette with a duck's egg—the sensation is of faintly marine spaghetti—but the quantities of elvers now caught in the Parrett and Tone have a different destination. As long ago as 1965, aeroplanes were flying English elvers from Gloucester to Poland. There are annual deliveries to Lake Balaton in Hungary. Until recently, they have been air-freighted live in ice-packed polystyrene boxes to Japanese fish-farms. One Somerset eel farm at Hinkley Point takes several hundred kilos a year. Dutch and German merchants buy Somerset elvers to make up the shortfall from their own over-fished and polluted rivers. But the most extraordinary trade in these extraordinary animals began in 1985.

Several tons of elvers, a mixture of those caught on the Parrett and the Severn, were transported live in cooled aerated tanks across the width of Europe to Minsk in Byelorussia. The Russians had demanded a veterinary certificate of health for the animals. A

Taunton vet who had spent forty years looking up cows duly came out to the tanks, peered in at the infinite transparent threads, pronounced them in peak condition and signed some flamboyant, stamped-on document. This was produced at the receiving station in Minsk. The vodka came out. Reflections were exchanged on Nato and the Warsaw Pact and then bucket after bucket of Somerset elvers was poured from the English lorry into a fleet of Russian trucks standing about in the Byelorussian frost. At length the trucks set off for the east, to deliver the elvers to the Volga and the Ob', to the Jenisej and the Lena where, of course, the life in ditches or under the roots of a willow would be indistinguishable from Curry Moor or the Langacre Rhyne.

If the eel has survived elvering, trapping, netting and spearing by man or heron, it might live six or seven years in the rhyne before the last great metamorphosis. The back darkens, the belly silvers, the eyes grow larger and acquire a golden shimmer. The snout sharpens and, as the eel stops feeding, the gut shrinks away: the eel is now mature. These are preparations for the sea, for the 4,000-mile return journey to the birth-ground. The time of migration begins in October, as the water starts to cool, and continues throughout the winter.

But it is no dribble of fish out from the land to the sea. Many conditions have to be satisfied before the silver eel will run, and there may only be three or four nights in the whole winter on which those conditions hold. The eels are great romantics: the night must be dark, at some time between sunset and midnight, between the last and first quarters of the moon; it must be wild and stormy, best if there is a deep low over the Channel and a fierce easterly blowing the land water out to sea; the river must be brimful with dirty thick flood water, impenetrable with the silt in it, and the tide must have been a good deep one, pushing the smell of salt far into the moors. Then and only then will the eels go. It is the autumn equivalent of the elver nights in the spring, and if the elvers are the moment of conception, the seeding of the Somerset Levels, then the thundery wildness of the night of the silver run is a sort of birth. Now the moors deliver up their fruit that has been gestating seven, ten or even fifteen years, as secretly as in a womb, never seen except when caught or when, in exceptionally dry summers like 1976, up in the headwaters of the Parrett, the drying sticky bodies of eels were found in the last crusting bits of mud.

But on the silver night the eels emerge, make one great display and go. A fisherman from Stretcholt, Bob Thorne, was out walking one night a year or so ago at the beginning of November. 'It must have been near midnight. It was blowing a good gale and pouring. I could hear this rustling all around me. I shone my torch about and the ground was alive with eels. They were making for the main watercourse, travelling at about walking pace, I suppose. They were everywhere. They were all going about the grass, like when you want to herd a lot of sheep, and away they went off into the river and then out past Stert Island and God knows where they got to. They always do pick a wild night.'

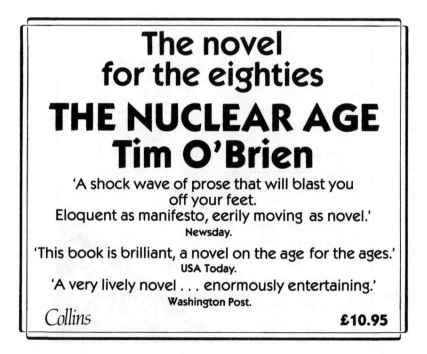

The novel for the eighties

THE NUCLEAR AGE
Tim O'Brien

'A shock wave of prose that will blast you off your feet.
Eloquent as manifesto, eerily moving as novel.'
Newsday.

'This book is brilliant, a novel on the age for the ages.'
USA Today.

'A very lively novel . . . enormously entertaining.'
Washington Post.

Collins   **£10.95**

'One of England's best selling and most influential literary magazines.'
Time Magazine

'A barometer for the current heady climate of the British publishing world.'
International Herald Tribune

'An exciting index of the freshest international writing of this decade.'
Newsweek

Most of our readers are subscribers. They enjoy savings, special offers and postage-free delivery to their homes.

Subscriptions to Granta:
- ☐ $22 for one year (4 issues).
- ☐ $40 for two years (8 issues).
- ☐ $55 for three years (12 issues).

Write to Dept H1, Granta,
13 White Street, New York, NY 10013,
enclosing a check made payable to Granta.
Or if you wish to pay later,
ask us to invoice you.

SUBSCRIBE NOW

DAVID HARE

JOINT STOCK: A MEMOIR

David Hare

I've been involved in founding two theatre companies in my life. The first, Portable Theatre, ended for me in the Marylebone Magistrates Court some time, I believe, in 1973. I kept no diary in those days—I was young, and events moved so slowly—so I have no way of remembering. I do know I shook and sweated a great deal, since I'd only learned on the morning of my appearance that Tony Bicat and I would have to appear in court. The charge was non-payment of actors' National Insurance Stamps. Since we had relinquished the running of the company some time previously, we were both surprised to find ourselves still legally responsible for its present state—although, to be fair, I had recently seen its administrator at Schiphol Airport in Amsterdam drinking gin at seven thirty in the morning, and might have guessed that the books were not in too solid a shape. The magistrate fined us—was it £35? I misremember—and ordered us to pay all our debts. When the company later went bankrupt, we learned that your debt to the state is the one debt that can never be absolved.

Things have changed a great deal in theatre in the last fifteen years. In those easier days you needed less money to start a new company, and everyone accepted that theatres might naturally flower and die. The fringe had not been institutionalized to the point where companies fear to relinquish grants from the Arts Council long after their artistic life has been exhausted.

Max Stafford-Clark, David Aukin and I met among the ruins of Portable Theatre and decided that since we were all freelance members of the awkward squad, we were likely to need our own facility for putting on plays. All our experience had been with presentation of new work, usually of a modestly controversial kind, and we were all well aware of how producers' expectations then rarely fitted either with our personalities or our tastes. I went away, to be honest, with little intention of using that facility—struck much more by the way Max, unknowable then as now, was going through a phase of insisting that there was too much snobbery in the world about what people ate and drank. To prove his point, he created Joint Stock in conversation while drinking large schooners of viscous sweet sherry.

For a while we seemed to choose plays which we rehearsed and presented in the regular way, although our bent was for the pornographic. (One of our shows was later to be debated in the House of Lords, where its artistic merit was vigorously contested.) But unknown to me, Max had begun talking to Bill Gaskill about doing a period of work on Heathcote Williams's book *The Speakers,* with no specific intention of showing the result to the public. I was therefore surprised when I met Bill in the street one day and he remarked ironically on the fact that, as a member of the three-man Joint Stock board, I was now his employer. Only five years previously I had been the greenest recruit to his celebrated regime at the Royal Court.

When in 1974 Max and Bill finally decided to show their work to friends at the Floral Hall in Covent Garden—after it was a fruit market, but before it became a roller disco—I was taken aback. The directors had re-created Hyde Park Corner by simply upturning a few boxes and asking the audience to wander freely from speaker to speaker. The evening appeared to be casual, and yet turned out to be highly structured. There was a great density of characterization. (In fact, I believe when the 'real' speakers came to see themselves impersonated, they were perfectly satisfied.) Since the play appeared on the surface to be plotless, there was none of the usual wrenching and shifting of gears to which a playwright's ears are especially attuned. There was nothing flashy or insincere. The evening was dry, in the best sense, like good wine. I had long known it to be Bill's aim as a director to achieve work in which the content of the play was in perfect relief—there was to be no impression of artifice—and yet often in the past I had felt the very austerity of his approach to be mannered. Now, perhaps because his talents allied exquisitely with Max's gift for detail, the audience was actually presented with the illusion of meeting and getting to know the speakers at Hyde Park Corner. No more, no less. The speakers were in the round, unforced, *themselves.*

All three of us suspected that the main reason for the evening's success had been the absence of a writer. The directors had cut the pages from Heathcote Williams's book, which had provided the dialogue for the play, into slivers on the floor with a big pair of scissors. There was a general feeling, perhaps brought on by Max and Bill's recent directorships of writers' theatres, that writers always spoil things. Both the greatest English directors of the post-war theatre, Peter Brook and Joan Littlewood, had ended up without writers in their rehearsal rooms. Pauline Melville had lent Bill a copy of William Hinton's massive book *Fanshen* and the very impossibility of adapting it appealed to him. Yet he passed it on to me with a poorly disguised heavy heart.

A particular tension in Joint Stock has never been very satisfactorily resolved. Writers have a reputation for being tied to one view of the world—their own—but in experimental work actors and directors must feel free. The actor wants to own his character. The director wants to control the evening. The company has been at its most successful either when using writers with very strong personalities—Caryl Churchill, say, or Barrie Keefe—or when working on shows in which the writer appears to stand out of the way of the raw material altogether. In *Yesterday's News* a group of actors sat facing the audience, using transcripts of interviews which they had secured themselves with British mercenaries who had been in Angola. The same technique served in *Falkland Sound,* half of which is made up from letters sent by David Tinker to his father from a ship in the expeditionary force, and half of which dramatizes, in their own words, the lives of people caught up in the Falklands War. Both plays, although apparently documentary, were more artful than they at first appeared. The company's touch was less sure when playwrights were compromised somewhere in the middle, not quite knowing whether to set down the actors' research, or to try and create a play of their own. With *Fanshen* Bill had little choice, for the book is nearly 700 pages long and playwrights, for all their faults, are good men with pickaxes.

Hinton is a Pennsylvania farmer who was in China for six years as a tractor technician. *Fanshen* records the life and struggles of the people in the village of Long Bow during the great land reform programmes which Mao's revolution instituted in the late 1940s. I worked on trying to digest and master the extraordinary complexity of the book, while, in workshop, the actors flung themselves at whatever bit they fancied, more or less in whatever style they fancied. The writer represented reason, the actors imagination. There were certainly masks in the rehearsal room, and there was talk of puppet shows. Stylization was much discussed. At one point, I was asked to play a bird. It was important to the directors that the method of workshop reflect the subject and that it therefore be genuinely democratic. For that reason Bill once insisted as we returned from lunch to our basement rehearsal room in Pimlico that neither he, Max nor I should be the ones to suggest resuming work that afternoon. We would simply wait until an actor suggested it. I think we waited about an hour and a half.

After the workshop I went off by myself and spent four months mining a text out of the book. I threw away a great deal of the more obviously dramatic material, because I was not interested in portraying the scenes of violence and brutality which marked the landlords' regime and its overthrow. In shaping the play, I was very little influenced by any particular discovery in the workshop, but I was crucially affected by its spirit. Although Bill had thrashed about seeking to find a suitable style for the work, often lapsing into long and sullen silences, he never relaxed his basic intention: that we should do justice to the sufferings of the Chinese peasants. This was a matter of the utmost gravity to him. His criterion for examining any scene was to ask whether it was adequate to the experience the peasant had originally undergone. Although the subject-matter of the play was political, the instincts of the company were in essence moral. We were not revolutionaries. I think that is why, especially in later seasons when it sought to apply the lessons of *Fanshen* to English material, Joint Stock became confused about whether it was a political group or not. In making *Fanshen,* none of us believed we could duplicate the over-turning we described. We knew any form of change here was bound to be different. But we all admired the revolution, and shared an obligation to describe it in a way of which its people would approve. The adoption of a rehearsal process based on the Chinese political method of 'Self-Report, Public Appraisal' might, in other hands and with other material, have degenerated into a gimmick. But here it had weight and was surprisingly quick and effective. The self-criticism was real.

At Christmas I finished, and a few days later was sitting beside my wife's hospital bed when Bill breezed in from two weeks with the aborigines in Australia. He took one uninterested look at our two-day-old son and said, 'Yes. Very nice. Where's the play?' Soon after he arranged a reading with the whole company. It was very long and lugubrious, and at the end people said almost nothing, though one actor shook his head at me and said 'Sorry'. Given the general gloom, I had no idea why I was not asked to re-write much more. Only the beginning was rearranged and that somewhat peremptorily. If I had been more experienced, of course, I would have recognized that moment at which a group of people, expecting everything, are delivered something.

The play opened in Sheffield in April 1975 to a refreshingly intelligent and multi-racial audience, then came to London. I was on a beach in Greece when word came that I was needed at once to work on a television version. Hinton had hitherto ignored the whole production assuming that, like the two previous dramatic versions, ours would disappear without trace. But when he read the reviews, he appeared in England almost at once. He consulted with his daughter, who had been a Red Guard, and then with officials from the Chinese Embassy, before insisting that the play must be altered if its life was to be prolonged. The BBC flew me back to his farm to argue with him, and I found him waiting with a list of 110 changes, most of which sought to rid the play of what he called—I am using shorthand here—my 'liberal' slant and to give it more of what I would call his 'Marxist' emphasis. An exceptionally generous and decent man, he proved a wonderful host, even as we set out on two days of attritional argument, which resulted in my once or twice giving the play a slightly more optimistic tilt. A line about justice which I had hitherto believed to be the fulcrum was removed. The play still stood. If I ever felt resentful about this, I only had to remind myself that his notes had twice been seized, once by the US Customs and then again by the Senate. The writing of the book had taken him fifteen years. I had given barely six months.

The television version was, in my view at least, something of a fiasco. I had an early bet with Bill that I would give him a shilling for every time the BBC director said 'no' to anything which was suggested to him. After all the pain and profound argument we had had about how best to represent a revolution on stage, we were now in the hands of a man who believed that all you had to do to televise a play was to point a camera at it. Bill told me not to be ridiculous, but at the end I didn't have to pay him a penny.

Subsequently *Fanshen* was revived whenever Joint Stock was in trouble. It became our *Mousetrap*. Once, humiliatingly, I attempted to do a couple of days' directing one of its many revivals and found it to be a lot less easy than it seemed. Although I thought I understood the process whereby Max and Bill had done their work, in practice I was hopeless at imitating even their most casual effects. The spirit of the show was best guarded by actors like Paul Freeman and David Rintoul.

The two directors and I sought many times to work together again as a team. I asked Bill to direct a couple of my plays, but he always turned me down. We all found it hard to imagine material which would suit us as well. In part this was because *Fanshen* describes a period of history in which people's lives were unarguably improved: when someone suggested we do a similar show about the Russian revolution I pointed out that it was quite hard, in view of what we all knew happened later, to bring the same relish to describing the heady days of 1918. It would have been dishonest. We tried to acquire the rights to Studs Terkel's *Working.* When it subsequently flopped as a musical on Broadway, Studs asked us to reconsider, but the moment had gone. I worked listlessly on Tolstoy's *Resurrection,* only to be told by Bill that I was getting nowhere. I headed instead to run my own workshop with Tony Bicat as my writer. I tried, for once, to work on less political material. But I lacked Bill and Max's flair for letting things run away of their own accord. Later, however, a friend was driving from Stratford to London with Trevor Nunn, who was about to do a workshop of *Nicholas Nickleby.* 'I have no idea what a workshop is,' Nunn was saying, 'I've never done one. Can you give me any idea what David does?'

Joint Stock, inspired by *Fanshen,* then chose to go co-operative, and all decisions were taken by group discussion. The actors were brought in to help run the company. Some fine work followed, and for two years they managed both to maintain a high standard of performance and to attract a large and dedicated audience. Usually the characterization had much more quirkiness and vitality than we had managed in *Fanshen.* Both Howard Brenton's *Epsom Downs* and Barrie Keefe's *A Mad World My Masters* had much more gaiety. And yet you sensed that the principles of the work were the same as those we had forged when trying to do a play about China. Although the subject-matter changed, the ideology became a little stuck. I suppose

I reluctantly concluded that an openly political way of working only pays off with dialectical material.

I stopped going to company meetings after a group discussion in which I called someone a cunt. Although I was referring to somebody who wasn't present, I was told by one of the group that she objected to my using a piece of her anatomy as a term of abuse. I replied fatuously that it had hardly been *her* anatomy in particular which I had had in mind. Of course she was right, and I have never again used the word as an insult, although it remains the one English swear-word with a genuine power to shock. Yet somehow the incident oppressed me disproportionately. An actor made a long speech about how the only purpose of theatre now must be to work for the overthrow of the Thatcher government, then left as soon as his best friend arrived to have a separate conversation in the garden. He had actually cried during the speech. The politics of gesture seemed to have replaced the politics of need. Now we were all to have silly arguments about words.

Of all art forms the theatre is most susceptible to fashion. There is good and bad in this. There are times at which audiences seem to respond to an idea, almost irrespective of how well or badly it is expressed, as if it is already in the air, and nothing will now stop them getting to it. All of us sensed that happening with *Fanshen,* and the actors and directors worked to some common imperative. Nobody was frightened. This is not the only kind of theatre I wish to work in, but the feeling has come upon me only twice, and the first time was with Joint Stock.

KEEP IN TOUCH WITH

EVERYWOMAN

Every month we present news, current affairs, ideas, issues, interviews, debates — by women, for women.

Not to mention our regular features on new books, arts and media, style...and our regular short story, sport page, financial advice and a review of women's organisations of all shapes and sizes...all served with a dash of humour.

75p from your newsagent — or subscribe: £9.60 basic/£12 institutions/£15 Europe/ £22 airmail.

EVERYWOMAN

**34a Islington Green,
London N1 8DU.**

EN VENTE DANS LES KIOSQUES
n° 8 printemps 86

*C'est une grande chose
Quel exemple !
Là est l'avenir.*

Régis Debray

*Parie sur la curiosité
du public hexagonal,
s'entête et gagne.*

L'Express

*Un forum unique
des voix les plus importantes
de notre temps.*

Radio Stockholm

*Ses articles
ne vous laisseront
jamais indifférents.*

Bernard Frank,

Le Monde

LETTRE INTERNATIONALE

QUI NE TRAVAILLE PAS
MANGERA
J.DARWIN A.GORZ L.SMITH

FRIEDRICH DURRENMATT
ACHTERLOO

NOTRE TELE
QUOTIDIENNE
B.GHEUDE R.IGNATIEFF R.KLOPFER

VIENNE
C.SCARPETTA R.JANJON

T.GARTON ASH S.CSHRKA
A.FINKIELKRAUT J.GRISA D.KIS
G.KONRAD A.OZ L.VACULIK P.VASTBERG
MONOLOGUES A BUDAPEST

A.BARNETT D.HALIVARSEN J.BRUGUERZA
B.SPINELLI T.TODOROV.

DISCOURS A STOCKHOLM
CLAUDE SIMON

Le numéro 30 F. Abonnement 100 F, étranger 140 F.

NOM ....

ADRESSE ....

CHEQUE A L'ORDRE DE « AUJOURD'HUI INTERNATIONAL »
14-16, rue des Petits-Hôtels, 75010 Paris Tél. (1) 42 77 12 53 – FRANCE

Notes on Contributors

James Fenton is the author of 'The Fall of Saigon' (*Granta* 15). His 'Road to Cambodia', a memoir of his travels in Indochina, appeared in *Granta* 10: Travel Writing. **Mark Malloch Brown** is a journalist and a member of a political consultancy, D.H. Sawyer. **John Berger's** previous work of fiction, 'Boris', was published in *Granta* 9. His most recent book is an anthology of essays, *The White Bird.* The first part of **Alice Munro's** 'A Queer Streak' appeared in *Granta* 17. The whole novella will be included in a new collection of fiction, *Progress of Love,* to be published by Chatto and Windus in January 1987. **Seamus Deane** is Professor of Modern English and American Literature at University College, Dublin. He is also the author of *A Short History of Irish Literature,* to be published by Hutchinson in May. 'Wetness' is taken from **Adam Nicolson** and Patrick Sutherland's *Wetland,* to be published by Michael Joseph on 30 June. **David Hare's** 'Joint Stock: A Memoir' will be included in *The Joint Stock Book,* to be published by Methuen in January 1987. His 'Nicaragua: An Appeal' appeared in *Granta* 16. **George Steiner's** 'A Conversation Piece' was published in *Granta* 15. His most recent book is *Antigones.* **Primo Levi's** most recent publication in English is a novel, *If Not Now, When?* He contributed to *Granta* 16: Science. **Gianni Celati** teaches Anglo-American Literature at the University of Bologna. 'Thoughts of a Storyteller on a Happy Ending' is taken from *Narratori delle Pianure* (Storytellers of the Plains), published by Feltrinelli in 1985.

Note: Italo Calvino's 'The Loves of the Tortoises' and 'The Blackbird's Whistle' (*Granta* 16: Science) were translated from the Italian by William Weaver.